THE LYRICAL AND THE EPIC

Studies of Modern Chinese Literature

Studies in Chinese Literature and Society

Editors
Irving Yucheng Lo
Joseph S. M. Lau
Leo Ou-fan Lee

THE
LYRICAL
AND THE
EPIC

Studies of
Modern Chinese Literature

by Jaroslav Průšek
Edited by Leo Ou-fan Lee

INDIANA UNIVERSITY PRESS

Bloomington

Library of Congress Cataloging in Publication Data

Průšek, Jaroslav.

The lyrical and the epic.

(Studies in Chinese literature and society)

Bibliography: p.

1.Chinese literature—20th century—History and
criticism—Addresses, essays, lectures. I.Lee, Leo
Ou-fan. II.Title III.Series.

PL2302.P7 895.1'5'09 80-7491

ISBN 0-253-10283-9 1 2 3 4 5 84 83 82 81 80

Contents

FOREWORD   vii

ACKNOWLEDGMENTS   xiii

1. Subjectivism and Individualism in Modern Chinese Literature   I

2. Introduction to *Studies in Modern Chinese Literature*   29

3. A Confrontation of Traditional Oriental Literature with Modern European Literature in the Context of the Chinese Literary Revolution   74

4. Reality and Art in Chinese Literature   86

5. Lu Hsün's "Huai Chiu": A Precursor of Modern Chinese Literature   102

6. The Changing Role of the Narrator in Chinese Novels at the Beginning of the Twentieth Century   110

7. Mao Tun and Yü Ta-fu (from *Three Sketches of Chinese Literature*)   121

8. Yeh Shao-chün and Anton Chekhov   178

9. Basic Problems of the History of Modern Chinese Literature and C. T. Hsia, *A History of Modern Chinese Fiction*   195

APPENDIX 1   On the "Scientific" Study of Modern Chinese Literature: A Reply to Professor Průšek C. T. Hsia   231

APPENDIX 2   A Selected Bibliography of Průšek's Papers on Modern Chinese Literature   267

Foreword

In the field of Chinese literature, the pioneering scholarship of Professor Jaroslav Průšek has received wide recognition. His painstaking research into the origins, genres, and social and historical milieu of Chinese vernacular literature has long been taken by students of traditional Chinese literature as a point of departure in their own work. Some years ago, a fairly comprehensive volume, which includes most of Průšek's important scholarly papers on literature of the traditional periods, appeared under the title of *Chinese History and Literature* (Dordrecht, Holland: D. Reidel, 1970). However, his contributions in the field of modern Chinese literature, published mostly in European journals and in book-length monographs, were never collected. This volume of selected papers by Professor Průšek, spanning more than a decade (1957–1969), is designed to fill in such an obvious gap and to provide students (especially in the United States and other non-European countries) who may not otherwise have easy access to European scholarly journals with a representative sampling of his seminal works. Professor Průšek has been kind enough to leave the choice of these papers entirely in my hands, and I alone bear the responsibility for any deficiencies in the final selection and format. The innumerable merits in the content of these papers belong, of course, to Professor Průšek.

The selection of these papers has been determined by three kinds of concerns: their scholarly quality and originality, their representativeness of Průšek's general approach to modern Chinese literature, and their suitability as basic reading and teaching material in the classroom. While my assessment of the individual merits of Průšek's papers may not be entirely sound due to my own limitations, I have chosen those papers which have exerted significant impact on myself and on my students. I would have liked to include more had I not been pressed by a practical concern to make this volume widely available to scholars and students at a cost they can afford. I have also left out, with great reluctance, some important papers written in other European languages. Whatever its faults of omission, I am nevertheless convinced that the present collection provides sufficient evidence for the kind of broad sweep combined with detailed analysis which is so characteristic of Průšek's work. In these papers we can also find a number of recurring themes which, in my judgment, are central to an understanding of Průšek's thinking on modern Chinese literature.

One of the paramount themes in Průšek's treatment of modern Chinese literature is the close connection between the New Literature and China's classical tradition. As one of the very few European sinologists who feel equally at home in traditional and modern Chinese culture, Professor Průšek perceives with great insight the complex reverberations from a long history of China's literary past on the formation of modern literature. He is most impressed by the variety, spontaneity, artistic inventiveness, and increasing dynamism of traditional Chinese popular and folk literature (hence his extensive research in the subject). But at the same time he has not neglected to take note of the so-called literati culture—its moral weight, its precision of language, its finesse and sophistication of expression. This bifurcation of traditions seems to recall Hu Shih's verdict concerning the gradual ossification of the latter and the increasing vitality of the former, thus affirming the vernacular strains since Sung times as the main living tradition of Chinese literature. Unlike most May Fourth leaders, including Hu Shih, Průšek emphatically points out that the lyrical side of literati culture, as manifested in particular in classical poetry, has also left an enduring legacy in shaping the literary sensibilities of May Fourth writers.

This "lyrical" tradition, which tends to focus on the subjective feelings of the writer and on an artistic evocation—of mood, color, or imagery—has persisted in the works of many modern Chinese writers—Lu Hsün and Yü Ta-fu are but two prime examples. This lyrical sensibility is by no means the exclusive prerogative of the literati. Though Průšek has not gone deeply into the Ming phenomenon of the literati novel—that is, the vernacular novel as used by highly educated scholar-intellectuals who for one reason or another had chosen this "popular" form as medium to convey their artistic vision—it can be inferred that this elitist "appropriation" of a popular genre may have been one of the factors contributing to what Průšek considers to be the gradual blending of genres, which in turn signifies the merger of literati and popular strains in the past three or four millennia. The growing popularity of the diary, the personal note (pi-chi) or essay (hsiao-p'in wen), as well as the novel (hsiao-shuo) from the late Ming to the late Ch'ing, in Průšek's view, indicates that the earlier barriers between poetry and prose, and between the moralistic, elitist "great tradition" on the one hand and the more carefree, fanciful popular tradition on the other, were breaking down. By late Ch'ing times, there was, according to Průšek, a noticeable tendency toward subjectivism and individualism, as evidenced in such works as Shen Fu's *Fu-sheng liu chi* (Six chapters from a floating world), Liu O's *Lao Ts'an yu-chi* (The travels of Lao Ts'an), Wu Wo-yao's *Erh-shih nien mu-tu chih kuai hsien-chuang* (Strange things witnessed during the past twenty years) and others. Thus the late Ch'ing period can be singled out, as Průšek did some twenty years ago, as the crucial transitional era between traditional and modern literature in China.

While Průšek devotes considerable attention to analyzing late Ch'ing fiction (treated in several papers of this collection), he has not given this literature undue praise in terms of artistic significance. With the possible exception of *Lao Ts'an yu-chi*, he finds most of the late Ch'ing novels lacking in the sophisticated technique needed to represent reality. In this regard, he considers modern Chinese fiction from 1917 to 1937 to be far superior. The example he cites again and again is the fictional *oeuvre* of Mao Tun, who aspires to and in some degree achieves what Průšek calls the "epic" quality in his works.

The term "epic," used by Průšek more often as adjective than noun to cover a broader spectrum of literary genres than poetry, is posed in contrast to the term "lyrical" as ,the other central artistic approach to reality. If the stories of Yü Ta-fu and Lu Hsün are in some ways reminiscent of poetry in their lyricism, Mao Tun's novels are "epic" in the sense that they are conceived as massive, objective panoramas of life and society. Průšek traces this "epic" orientation to the tradition of nineteenth-century European realistic fiction, but he also goes into great detail in qualifying Mao Tun's indebtedness to European theories of realism and naturalism. While Mao Tun professes to be a naturalistic writer, he does not, in Průšek's analysis, concern himself, as Zola did, with "a slice of life" by concentrating on the *individual* fate of his characters. Thus in a curious way Mao Tun may be said to have inherited—or revitalized—the Chinese "epic" tradition of fictional writing which invariably presents a broad social canvas in which no individual protagonist stands out. Mao Tun's fictional world is one in which social, economic, political as well as personal forces are inextricably intertwined. As a Marxist, however, he is assuredly more preoccupied with the socioeconomic forces and their attendant class configurations as the overarching themes in most of his fiction. But even in this most "epic" of all modern Chinese writers, we can also find, as Průšek has

pointed out, certain subjective concerns: the characters' personal emotions are not deemphasized; rather, they become vivid, often tortured,
expressions of the interplay with larger historical forces. It is this
dialectical combination of the objective and the subjective, the "epic" and
the "lyrical," that gives the mainstream of modern Chinese literature its
major hallmark. While Průšek might have been temperamentally attracted to the lyrical strain, he is intellectually committed to both.

In delineating these two "subtraditions" in modern Chinese literature, Průšek also seeks to establish their possible "correspondences" with
European literature. As mentioned earlier, he finds in the epic works of
Mao Tun certain implications of nineteenth-century European realism.
In the realm of the lyrical, however, Průšek presents the daring thesis
that May Fourth literature exhibited some tendencies which are very
akin to modern lyrical strains in European literature produced between
the two World Wars. He further argues that, given the lyrical heritage of
classical Chinese poetry, it is by no means accidental that the prose
poetry of Lu Hsün, for instance, shows amazing similarities to the
symbolist poetry of Baudelaire (though Lu Hsün may not have read
Baudelaire extensively). In his analysis of the stories of Lu Hsün and Yü
Ta-fu, he asserts in a similar vein that the two writers' preoccupation
with constructing evocative, lyrical tableaux at the expense of plot and
the narrative line are likewise characteristic of European fiction of
roughly the same period.

This intriguing thesis, though argued with analytical brilliance (see
the article "A Confrontation of Traditional Oriental Literature with
Modern European Literature"), seems nevertheless unconvincing. The
avant-gardist ethos which infused European art and literature since
Baudelaire stems, in my judgment, from an entirely different set of
artistic presuppositions and is therefore qualitatively at variance with the
May Fourth ethos, despite many formal similarities in their literary
products. From the perspective of literary history, a more significant
phenomenon which awaits detailed exploration is the "modernistic"
experimentation in modern Chinese poetry of the 1930s and 1940s—the
works of Li Chin-fa, Tai Wang-shu, and Pien Chih-lin and the statements printed in the influential journal *Hsien-tai (Les contemporaines)*, for
example—and the subsequent blossoming of modernistic writing in
Taiwan poetry and fiction of the 1960s. Here the European influence is
more direct and relevant, and the correspondences (as well as differences)
may yield more fruitful "leads" for comparative studies. Despite these

minor reservations, it is revealing that Průšek should have deemed it necessary to make a strong case for modern Chinese literature in the light of Western literary developments. May we take this to be a testimony to Průšek's own modern sensibilities, nourished as he was by the likes of Joyce, Mann, Eliot, Hesse, and Picasso? Or could we surmise that, perhaps unconsciously, he feels the need to defend the artistic merits of this new and fledgling literature out of a deep sense of love for Chinese culture and the Chinese people? (Průšek is in a position to count Mao Tun, Cheng Chen-to, and Ch'ien Hsing-ts'un as his former personal friends.)

In a sense all scholars of modern Chinese literature outside of China are faced with the same problem: how to make this very "Chinese" body of literature comprehensible to non-Chinese readers? Against typical Western standards of literary criticism, this literature can be found deficient in many aspects. It is, therefore, fascinating to follow the scholarly exchange of views between Professor Průšek and Professor C. T. Hsia, the leading authority of modern Chinese literature in the United States. Průšek's critical review of Hsia's book, *A History of Modern Chinese Fiction*, and Hsia's lengthy reply have demonstrated not only differences of methodology and approach but also varying standards of literary judgment. It is also intriguing to note that Hsia, a Chinese scholar with an impressive grasp of Western critical canons, is more harsh in his judgment of the general quality of modern Chinese literature, whereas Průšek, a European scholar, is more sympathetic to Chinese writers and more positive about their achievements. Their differences in the "scientific" approach are derived, to some extent, also from their divergent conceptions of the proper functions of the literary historian. Following the great tradition of F. R. Leavis, Professor Hsia considers it an inherent duty of any literary historian to discover and *evaluate* the major literary works of any period. Professor Průšek, on the other hand, tends to seek a broader understanding by placing the literary texts in the social and historical contexts of the period in which they were written. Their respective analyses of Lu Hsün's stories provide a most instructive case in point. And it is from the scintillating insights emerging from these two opposing approaches that a student of modern Chinese literature gets his first rewarding lesson on how to analyze a literary text.

The debate between these two eminent scholars took place in the pages of *T'oung Pao* between 1961 and 1963. Since that time, the study of modern Chinese literature in the West has made considerable strides as a result of several academic conferences and publications. The volume which emerged from the Dedham Conference of 1974, *Modern Chinese Literature in the May Fourth Era* (Cambridge: Harvard University Press, 1977), bears in its front matter a brief but fitting dedication: "To Jaroslav Průšek, whose work made this book possible." I am tempted to add that Průšek's work has, together with Hsia's, performed a task of more monumental consequence: he has not only pioneered in the establishment of the scholarly discipline of modern Chinese literature studies but also, in several decades of dedicated service to the cause of modern Chinese literature through teaching and writing, has inspired an increasing number of young scholars to follow in his footsteps and discover new exciting terrains in this not yet fully developed field. It is hoped that Průšek's followers and friendly opponents will find in these papers a wealth of insight and information which may provide a source of renewed faith in their own chosen profession.

Indiana University   Leo Ou-fan Lee
Bloomington, Indiana
July 26, 1979

Just as this book was going to press, I was deeply grieved to learn of the death of Professor Průšek, in Prague, in April 1980. It is my hope that this volume will serve as a commemoration of his decades of teaching and scholarship.

June 1980

Acknowledgments

I would like to thank Professor Průšek for his encouragement and also the publishers of the following journals and books for permission to reprint the articles contained in this volume:

Archiv Orientální
Harvard Journal of Asiatic Studies
T'oung Pao (E. J. Brill, Leiden)
Studies in Modern Chinese Literature (Akademie-Verlag, Berlin)
Three Sketches of Chinese Literature (The Oriental Institute in Academia, Prague)

I am very grateful to Professor C. T. Hsia for kindly permitting us to reprint his 1963 "reply" to Professor Průšek, "On the 'Scientific' Study of Modern Chinese Literature," as Appendix One of this book.

My special gratitude is to Mr. John D. Coleman, Ph.D. candidate in the Department of East Asian Languages and Cultures, Indiana University, for compiling the selected bibliography and for editorial assistance. Sincere thanks are also due Professor Milena Doleželová of the University of Toronto who was kind enough to go over the bibliography and suggest several important titles for inclusion. Mr. Jason Wang of the University of Wisconsin has provided the elegant Chinese calligraphy.

Leo Ou-fan Lee

THE LYRICAL AND THE EPIC

Studies of Modern Chinese Literature

I

Subjectivism and Individualism in Modern Chinese Literature

In this paper dealing with modern Chinese literature, that is, more especially, with literature of the period following the first World War and of the Manchu period, I wish to follow a single complex of features which may be summed up under "subjectivism and individualism." I understand these terms to cover an emphasis on the creator's personality in art and a concentration of attention on the artist's own life. The artist sees in artistic production above all the opportunity to express his views, feelings, sympathy or maybe hate; in extreme cases a work of art may provide the means for expressing, developing and finding scope for those aspects of his personality which in real life are somehow suppressed or not given full play. The work of art then, as a rule, does not document objective reality but rather reflects the author's inner life and comprises descriptions or analysis of his own feelings, moods, visions and even dreams; the artist's work approaches more and more closely to a confession in which the author reveals the different sides of his character and of his life—and especially the gloomier and more hidden sides. In my view, the growth of these features in the literature of a given period may serve as an important indication of certain changes in the social structure in which it arises and is not seldom the sign of the individual's emancipation from traditional views in the spheres of philosophy, religion or ethics, or even of actual revolt against the inherited social order. In the case of Chinese literature of the period referred to above, I should say that the measure of these features is one of the symptoms of the

Paper read at the IX Conference of Junior Sinologues in Paris. Published in *Archiv Orientální* 25 (1957), 261–283.

emancipation of the individual from feudal traditions, the breaking of all those fetters restricting the freedom of the individual in the old society, whether in family or in public life. There is no doubt that only when the individual realizes his own entity and singularity can he begin to claim his right to order his life in his own way and determine his own fate. In tradition-bound societies, this feeling for individual self-determination is weak or even completely stifled by the demands and claims of religion and traditional morality. Thus, for instance, Buddhism, in the teaching of Karma, of the chain of cause and effect, conceived this life as only an episode in an endless series of similar episodes which man must pass through in ever new incarnations. If his fate happens to be hard, the causes must be sought in a previous life, and if man bears his burden without complaint, he will be rewarded in a future life. Thus the importance of this life and of the lot of the individual was very much diminished. Man was not responsible for his own life, did not direct it or determine it, for everything was pre-determined by fate. The belief in the pre-determination of the personal lot was also shared by Confucianism, which in addition placed duty to the family and to society altogether above the interests of the individual. The belief, too, that human nature was naturally good and only deformed by the world's temptations, merely obscured the real problems both of individual psychology as well as of the motivation of the actions of others. No more did Taoism with its yearning for complete merging with the universe, for a state in which the individual ceased to exist, do anything to strengthen the consciousness of the significance of the individual life and lot. It is natural that the birth of a modern, free and self-determining individual was possible only at the price of shattering and discarding these traditional views and customs and the whole social structure on which they were based. The modern revolution in China is thus, first and foremost, in the sphere of ideas, a revolution of the individual and of individualism in opposition to traditional dogmas. In this context, we can then realize the immense importance of subjectivistic and individualistic tendencies in modern Chinese thought and art. It is equally natural, however, that this consciousness of self, this investigation of one's own personality, must go hand in hand with realism, with the ability to look at oneself and at the facts of existence without the spectacles of tradition. This is an aspect of literature, however, which would require special study. An accompanying feature of this consciousness of self, of one's own entity and significance is a feeling for the tragedy of life. If we are confined to this life alone, and if it is full of hardship and suffering, then nothing can recompense us for this tragedy, it is a misfortune that cannot be repaired. We shall see later on how this feeling for the tragedy of existence—very weakly developed or not at all in older literature—is in fact a characteristic feature of modern art. In the same way, along with this new feeling of the singularity of existence, goes hand in hand the revolutionary character of the new man and his art. In this life alone is all the content and purpose of existence, and so it is necessary to remove everything that would stand in the way of its full development and full enjoyment—and by force if necessary. The other side of this mentality, however, is a tendency to self-destruction. If only this life exists—and it is not worth living—then it is better to make an end of it. These are, in rough outline, the different aspects of this new, modern mental complex which we call subjectivism and individualism, and to which we wish to devote our attention in this paper.

It is evident that we cannot here give by any means an exhaustive or complete picture of these tendencies in recent Chinese literature of the Manchu and revolutionary periods. Besides, the present state of our knowledge is far from sufficient for such a task, for we should need to have a good knowledge of the character of this period not only in literature, but also in all other sectors of Chinese life. In literature, too, we are faced with a complete insufficiency of monographs providing systematic studies of the various personalities, trends, problems and so on, on the basis of which we could then attempt to build up a synthetic picture of the successive stages of development, in which all the facets of social life could be evaluated and taken into account for the epoch in question. As it is, all we can do is to call attention to certain symptoms and indications rather than present a systematic account of the whole development in all its aspects. So, too, it will be possible only in a later study to classify the individual writers according to the different social groups to which they belong and to establish the relations between their ideology and their class origin.

There can be no question that subjectivism and individualism, joined with pessimism and a feeling for the tragedy of life, along with an inclination to revolt and even the tendency to self-destruction, are the most characteristic qualities of Chinese literature from the May Fourth Movement of 1919 to the outbreak of war with Japan.[1] Typical, too, for the mood of the time was undoubtedly the fact that the Bible of the new

---

[1] For the literature of this period see my study: "Die neue chinesische Literatur," *Das Neue China* VI (1940) 39, pp. 456–465; 40, pp. 523–536; 41, pp. 588–600.

youth was *Die Leiden des jungen Werther*. In proof of this, it is sufficient, perhaps, to quote at least one passage from the novel *Tzu yeh* 子夜 , by Mao Tun 茅盾 .[2] Captain Lei 雷, one of those who took part in the May Fourth Movement, a former student and later a cadet of the Huang-p'u Academy, is speaking to Mrs. Wu吳, his one-time student love, now the wife of a Shanghai industrialist:

"Captain Lei lifted his head and drew out a book from his pocket. Opening it quickly, he extended it toward Mrs. Wu with both hands. It was an old, well-worn copy of *Die Leiden des jungen Werther*. The place at which it was open was marked with a pressed white rose. Like a flash this book and this white rose recalled to Mrs. Wu the stormy times of student meetings during the Movement of the 30th of May, and so vividly that she found herself trembling . . .

"Captain Lei smiled a little bitterly and sighed as it seemed, but then he went on: '. . . This book and this white rose are dearer to me than all else . . . I took part in the campaign against Hu-nan, I rose from a lieutenant to the rank of captain, I was present at the taking of Ch'ang-sha, Wu-han, Chêng-chou and of Peiping. I made my way over thousands, indeed tens of thousands of corpses. Innumerable times I escaped death by a hair's-breadth, I lost everything, only from this rose and book I never parted . . .'"

The passage is extremely interesting for the way it shows how the greatest product of European Romanticism found a kindred spirit and mood among Chinese revolutionary youth. It testifies to how the moods in China were reminiscent in many aspects of the moods of European Romanticism and its exaggerated individualism, tragic coloring and feeling of "Weltschmerz." It is well known that *Die Leiden des jungen Werther* was translated into Chinese by Kuo Mo-jo郭沫若,[3] who in this period was the principal representative of Chinese romanticism, individualism and even titanism, and also the chief propagator of revolt and revolution. In the early works of Kuo Mo-jo, we also find strong echoes of the great German model as, for example, in the highly romantic and lyrical tale of love and suicide entitled "The Grave of Yeh Lo-t'i 葉羅提 之墓."

Characteristic, too, of the subjectivistic-individualistic tendency of that time is the fact that Kuo Mo-jo wrote an account of his life,

---

[2] See Mao Tun, *Šerosvit*, translated by J. Průšek, Praha, 1950, p. 109 et seq.
[3] Under the Chinese title of *Shao-nien Wei-t'e ti fan-nao*.

especially his early youth and literary beginnings, up to the Great
Revolution, in seven autobiographical novels of which the best is perhaps
"Childhood" [*Shao-nien shih-tai* 少年時代], published in 1929. His other
work is also strongly autobiographical in character, in fact not seldom his
works are the raw material rather than the finished product of literary
art, records and notes of personal experiences rather than stories and
novels in the accepted sense, examples of which are to be found, for
instance, in the collection "Olive" [*Kan-lan* 橄欖].

There can be no doubt that their own lives, their own experiences
and feelings are the main source of writers' inspiration in the inter-war
period, and these sources are always gloomy and tragic in coloring. This
melancholy subjectivism also pervades to a large extent the work of the
greatest of modern writers—Lu Hsün 鲁迅. Here we shall quote no
more than the beginning of his introduction to the collection "Call to
Arms" [*Na-han* 吶喊], where Lu Hsün alludes to his own sad experiences in childhood and early youth as the source of his inspiration: "I,
too, in my young days dreamt many a dream, but later I forgot the
greater part of them. But this I by no means regret. People say that such
so-called reminiscences can give one pleasure, but equally often they
cause us grief, for the silken threads of our thoughts may renew long past
stabs of pain. What delight is in that? Besides, all our proneness to grief
is in the impossibility of complete forgetfulness. And so that part of my
recollections which I am unable to forget gave birth to 'Call to Arms'."
Here we have a subjectivistic explanation of the author's creative work.
If we go through the collection *Na-han*[4] or *P'ang-huang* 徬徨,[5] we shall
have little difficulty in persuading ourselves of the subjectivistic character
of Lu Hsün's work—even though we must bear in mind that this man of
genius also created some of the most convincing and most penetrating
pictures of Chinese society. This subjectivity is particularly clear in his
collection of poetry and prose, "Wild Grass" [*Yeh-ts'ao* 野草], while its
autobiographical character is indicated in the title of the collection,
"Dawn Flowers Plucked at Dusk" [*Ch'ao-hua hsi-she* 朝華夕拾].[6] It is, of
course, necessary to note that even the vision and dreams recorded in

---

[4]See Lu Sün, *Vráva—Polní tráva*, translated by J. Průšek and B. Krebsová, Praha,
1951.

[5]See Lu Sün: *Tápání*, translated by B. Krebsová, Praha 1954.

[6]See Lu Sün: *Ranní květy sebrané v podvečer—Staré příběhy v novém rouše*, translated by
B. Krebsová, Praha 1956.

"Wild Grass" do not express Lu Hsün's personal desires and experiences, but that their only theme, as is clearly shown by B. Krebsová in her book *Lu Sün, sa vie et son œuvre* (Praha 1953), is revolt, the revolution of the Chinese people and the liberation of the whole of Chinese society.

The pessimistic, tragic mood of Chinese youth in the period of the Great Revolution is most effectively expressed by the greatest contemporary writer of epic, Mao Tun [Shen Yen-ping 沈雁冰], in his excellent trilogy "Eclipse" [*Shih* 蝕]. The first part of this trilogy, characteristically called "Frustrated Hopes" [*Huan-mieh* 幻滅], is the story of a disillusioned and defeated generation, which set out with great hopes and ended in complete despair. Similarly, the second part of the trilogy "Agitation" [*Tung-yao* 動搖], shows how futile were all attempts of young intellectuals, endowed with good will but too weak to ride the storm which was sweeping the whole of society. Finally the rebel peasants murder the girls with short hair who come to help them, but who have become for them the symbol of the hated town. Most tragic of all is the conclusion of the third part, called "Pursuit" [*Chui-ch'iu* 追求], describing three young couples whose lives are a complete failure, because the partners are never equally matched. Every good is immediately opposed by an equally great evil which in the end gains the victory. It is an account of poor, broken lives which end, after short-lived attempts at escape, in death or suicide. This first major work by Mao Tun gives us the impression that the author sees around him nothing but dissolution and death. There can be no more convincing document of the feeling for the tragedy of life with which the youth of that time was filled.

Equally subjective and emotionally highly-keyed is another writer of this time, Yü Ta-fu 郁達夫, whose Romanticism brings him close to Kuo Mo-jo. His best-known work actually bears the title "Nine Diaries" [*Jih-chi chiu-chung* 日記九種], which in itself points to the subjective character of the work. In this book Yü Ta-fu retells with unusual candor the history of his love. Similar subjective and pessimistic elements are to be found in the writings of Pa Chin 巴金, whose first work, which also immediately won him fame, bears the suggestive title "Destruction" [*Mieh-wang* 滅亡]. The same subjectivisim permeates his other well-known work, "The Family" [*Chia* 家]. We could thus enumerate the works of one author after another and everywhere, in greater or lesser measure, we should find the same traits of subjectivism, individualism and pessimism. They are present, too, for instance, in the work of the authoress Ting Ling丁玲, who, however, was the first, along with Lu Hsün, to realize that this *Weltschmerz*, these despairing and unhappy moods, do not lead anywhere, and that it is necessary first to change the world, if we are to change ourselves and our destiny. As she rightly puts into the mouth of Jo-ch'üan若泉 in her novel, "Shanghai in the Spring of 1930"一九三〇年春上海 :[7] "I sometimes have the feeling that if we stopped this writing it would not be a pity. We write something, a handful of people read it, but in a short time it vanishes from their minds. What sense has it all except perhaps that you get some kind of a fee for it? Maybe there are readers who are moved by some passage or by the style, but what kind of readers are they? Petty bourgeois students—adolescents who are extremely easily affected. They feel that it is very close to their own spiritual mood and read into it the spleen which is in them but which they cannot express. It is possible, too, that what they read is the embodiment of their own desires, with some of the characters in the novels they actually fall in love, while with others they identify themselves. They also believe that the writer describes himself, and for that reason adore him and write him naïve and admiring letters. And we cannot help feeling touched that perhaps our work has had an effect and reply with still greater care to these young lads . . . And the result? I know now that we have only harmed them with it. We are drawing these young people on to our old path. A painful sensibility, egotism, futile self-torment, grief! . . . Where are they to find a solution, a way out? Finally they give way, day by day, increasingly to their melancholy, and fail to grasp the connection between society and their suffering. When they themselves try their hand at writing, they turn out some essay or poem and win the praise of older writers. Tell me, what good is it to them? And what gain is it for humanity? And so I myself now intend to give up writing. I expect, too, that our writers will think all this over a little and that they will take a different path. And small though the hope may be that they will create something outstanding in the near future, perhaps what they write will find its place in a future history of literature." Here we have summed up the basic character of the literature of this period and of those moods of youth of which we have spoken above.

Even Ting Ling, it must be noted, wrote at the beginning of her

---

[7]See D. Kalvodová: *Ting Ling*, Praha, 1955, p. 82.

career the deeply subjective "Diary of Miss Sophia" [*Suo-fei nü-shih jih-chi* 莎菲女士日記] and other works of a like kind.

This orientation toward the writer's own fate and own life, which we call subjectivism, is testified to by numerous autobiographies and memoirs, works which, as we shall see, were up to that time extremely rare. We have already alluded above to the autobiographical works of Kuo Mo-jo. Besides these, we may mention, for example, the "Autobiography of a Forty-Year-Old" [*Ssu-shih tzu-shu* 四十自述], by one of the leaders of the literary revolution, Hu Shih 胡適, or the well-known autobiography of the notable historian Ku Chie-kang 顧頡剛 with which he prefaced his work *Ku-shih-pien* 古史辨 and with which the West became familiar in Hummel's translation,[8] further, the autobiography of the writer Shen Ts'ung-wen 沈從文, entitled *Ts'ung-wen tzu chuan* 從文自傳, and others. At the same time, a whole series of books of memoirs appeared, which is all the more interesting as all the literature in the period between the wars was written by young people who, at the end of this period, in very few cases were over forty. As a rule, however, memoirs are written by persons in the evening of their lives. This again points to the authors' quite extraordinary interest in their own lives and possibly also in the lives of their friends. As an example of such memoirs, we may cite the two volumes by Shen Ts'ung-wen 沈從文, dedicated respectively to the writer Hu Yeh-p'in, shot by Chiang Kai-shek's henchmen [*Chi Hu Yeh-p'in* 記胡也頻], and to his wife, the above-mentioned writer, Ting Ling [*Chi Ting Ling* 記丁玲].

If we compare this literature that arose in China after the War, as the product of the tremendous ferment evoked everywhere by the Great October Revolution, with the literature of the preceding period, it seems to us that it is hardly possible that the same nation can have produced both. Let us consider only the differences in language: the creation of a new national language—*kuo-yü* 國語, differing sharply not only from the old written language—*wen-yen* 文言 , but also from the old *pai-hua* 白話. Further, the differences in literary form and subject-matter; the disappearance of the old essay, whose place was taken by modern newspaper and magazine articles; the passing-away of the old poetry and the creation of quite a new prosody with new poetic themes; the replacing of the old novel with its chain of episodes by the complex

---

[8] A. W. Hummel, *The Autobiography of a Chinese Historian*, Leyden, 1931.

modern novel; the introduction of the modern short-story with a skilfully
built up psychological situation; the rise of a new, realistic drama, or
even tragedy, in place of the old *Singspiele;* the new accent on psychology
instead of description or dialogue; the change of setting—instead of the
old country towns and villages—the city, and mainly, as we pointed out
above, the gloomy pessimism permeating all this literature and taking the
place of the former affirmation of this world or at least reconciliation
with the existing state of things. The sum of all these differences is so
great that it seems to us that whole centuries and thousands of miles
must needs separate the two epochs and not a mere decade and a shift of
scene of a few dozen or score miles from some provincial town to
Shanghai. Only on looking somewhat closer into the texture of the works
in question, do we discover in them a greater connection with the
literature of the preceding period than might be expected after such a
revolutionary upheaval.

We can, indeed, affirm that it is just this subjectivism which we
have found to be the characteristic feature of the revolutionary epoch
that is the main link between the literature of the inter-war period and
the literature of the preceding period. In short, we may say that modern
literature, in a certain sense and on a new formal and thematic platform,
as well as in a different environment, inherits and carries on the old
literary tradition of the Manchu literati, of the educated, ruling class of
the Chinese people. We need not be misled by the fact that certain
conservative men of letters waged a stubborn fight against the new
literature, which they condemned and rejected along with its creators.
Were we to seek the main characteristic whereby we could distinguish
most clearly the production of the literati for their own consumption
from what was created for the people in the older period (such a dividing
line is necessarily rough, but actually it is provided by the criteria which
the literati themselves applied to what they included in their catalogues
of literature such as the *Ssu-k'u ch'üan-shu tsung-mu t'i-yao* 四庫全書總
目提要, we should most certainly find it in the greater emphasis on the
lyrical and subjective aspects of literary production as compared with the
predominantly epic and objective character of folk literature. The lyric
occupies the foremost place in the literary output of the old Chinese man
of letters, whether in the form of a poem *(shih)*, or of a song *(tz'u)*, or of
the long compositions in rhymed prose *(fu)*, or in the lyrical mood and
approach permeating and coloring all the other domains of literary art.
To a certain extent, the essay, too, has a lyrical quality in its descriptions

of natural scenery and of personal experiences and feelings which, apart
from works of a political character or deriving from the author's official
activities, comprise the greater part of its subject-matter. Besides, the
formal features of the *ku-wen* style, with its emphasis on balanced
phrases, on rhythm, on the regular alternation of shorter and longer
paragraphs, its love of parallelism in the word-arrangement and the
thought-structure, its frequent use of antithesis and similar stylistic
devices, comprise qualities which we are wont to associate with poetry
rather than with prose. The same is true of the strict layout of the essay,
of the rules about how to begin, how to make a transition, how to
present the main idea, how to work up to the point and what particles
are to be used and in what positions. These lyrical and subjective traits,
however, are also to be found in letters, which form an important part of
the literati's prose work, as well as in other forms of artistic expression,
such as pictures, and so on. Epic in the form of narrative poems, tales
and novels scarcely appears in the works of the literati at all, or if it does,
remains on the margin of their production in the form of those *pi-chi*
which document in artificial and impartial style, and with the utmost
brevity, all the noteworthy events of which the man of letters hears or
which he sees or reads about. This form of literature becomes increasingly intimate and subjective. For whereas formerly all experiences had
to pass the censorship of beauty, only what was *wen* or "beautiful" being
allowed to pass into the temple of literature, also designated *wen*, while
all evil and ugly emotions were excluded, literature in later periods began
to embrace an ever wider range of human experience. This tendency to
greater intimacy, to the introduction of broader and new spheres of
personal life into higher literature, is also noted by G. Margouliès in his
introduction to *Le Kou-wen Chinois* (Paris 1926, p. XXXIII): "Pour ce qui
est du style, il est impossible de ne pas remarquer de grandes mod-
ifications: L'auteur semble s'épancher plus ouvertement et plus libre-
ment, il paraît plus intime et plus personnel. . . ." A little further on, he
writes (p. XXXIV): "Enfin, parurent Han Yu et ses continuateurs; . . . Il
n'appartenait qu'à eux d'imprimer à la littérature un caractère bien
personnel et bien intime, de faire passer dans les notices et les préfaces
offertes en cadeau, genres autant dire inexistants avant cette époque,
élément de sincérité et de franc épanchement qui auparavant ne pouvait
être observé et encore sous réserves, que dans le genre épistolaire.
Cependant ce caractère une fois imprimé à la littérature, les époques
postérieures le conserveront avec les genres créés et servant à son

expression . . . les auteurs des Song et des Ming auront de plus en plus nettement cet accent personnel et intime; ils s'ouvriront, ils se donneront de plus en plus entièrement au lecteur. C'est là le grand changement et la grande importance littéraire de l'époque dès T'ang. C'est peut-être pour cette raison que, l'accent personnel de l'auteur devenant trop fort et trop perceptible, la haute littérature, ainsi que nous l'avons dit plus haut, se popularise, perd ses traits distinctifs et se fond avec les autres genres littéraires du Kou-wen."

Margouliès here formulates very exactly those tendencies which, however, in an unusually high degree, characterize modern literature, as we pointed out above. We shall show from a number of examples that such tendencies were particularly strong in the Manchu period and thereby provide the proof that modern literature, at first glance so very different from that of preceding epochs, is in fact the culmination of tendencies which had, for a very long time, been at work and slowly maturing in Chinese literature. Naturally, we shall not seek these trends pre-eminently in essays and poetry, which no longer occupy the foreground of interest in Manchu literature, but are becoming the domain of mere imitators. We must turn our attention to the new genres which constitute the main and characteristic expressive means of this epoch. First and foremost it is the novel which is probably the high-point of artistic expression of the Manchu period. Strongly subjective, intimate and individualistic traits characterized the novel in this period. I myself had the occasion some time ago to point out how intimate and personal was the approach of the author of the novel *Hung-lou meng* and of his circle to this work.[9] Even though it is not a purely autobiographical work, yet individual characters in the novel were conceived by the author, or at least by his circle, as personifications, doubles or representations of themselves. Certainly it is in the light of such an intimate link with this work that we must grasp the marginal notes appearing in the manuscript of this novel entitled "*Shih t'ou chi,* with a new commentary from the study Chïh-yen-chai 脂硯齋, from the year 1760."

For example: "How deserted today is he who knows the story of how Chïh-yen held the brush for Fêng-chïeh (one of the female characters in the novel) when she was to choose the play (to be sung by the actors). How then should he not be downcast?" And further on: "He

─────────

[9]J. Průšek, Neues Material zum Hung-lou-mêng-Problem, *ArOr* XIII (1942), pp. 270–277.

who once wrote this: 'How deserted today is he who knows this story,' is now in the year 1767 only a mouldering corpse. Is it not sad?" These short quotations are enough to show that this novel is not only a story for entertainment, as it used to be with the novels of the Ming Period, but a work expressing the most intimate experiences and feelings of the author and his friends who regarded the characters in the novel as personifications of themselves.

A no less definitely personal relation between the authors and their work, though in a somewhat different sense, is observable in the novel *Yeh-sou p'u-yen* 野叟曝言, by Hsia Ching-ch'ü 夏敬渠, c. 1750, and in *Chin-hua-lu* 鏡花緣, by Li Ju-chen 李汝珍 (1763–1830). In these cases, the authors looked upon their novels as a kind of compensation for their lack of success in life, as a means of satisfying their longing for fame and immortality. Into them they put all their learning, all their knowledge, all they wanted to achieve, all they had dreamed and meditated upon. What we see then is a quite new, individualistic conception of literature and, at the same time, a complete re-evaluation of literary genres and traditions. Even for traditional learning, as comes out especially clearly in the second case, the best medium for its display is now the novel which, in the same way as the novel in Europe, became the platform from which everything could be discussed from politics to metaphysics. This, too, is an entirely new feature in Chinese literature, especially as the novel was a medium formerly despised by Chinese men of learning.

Similarly, I once drew attention[10] to the fact that Lao Ts'an, in the novel *Lao Ts'an yu-chi* 老殘遊記, is, on the one hand, the embodiment of the traditional ideal of Chinese culture, a "hidden scholar," and, on the other hand, a personification of the author of the novel, Liu O 劉鶚, just as other characters are representations of his friends, patrons and even of his opponents and enemies. Still more marked is this strongly personal tendency in other novels toward the end of the Manchu Period. Thus Wu Wo-yao 吳沃堯, already in his novel bearing the title "Strange Things Seen During Twenty Years" [*Ehr-shih nien mu-tu chih kuai hsien-chuang* 二十年目覩之怪現狀], sets his own person and character in opposition to the whole of society and, in the opening chapter, formulates his dismal view of the world: "But now, when I take stock and look back over these twenty years in which I have stood face to face with life, I see that I have met with only three kinds of beings: insects, beasts of

---

[10]J. Průšek: Liu O et son roman, Le Pèlerinage du Vieux Boiteux, *ArOr* XV (1946), pp. 352–385.

prey and vampires." Personal, autobiographical elements of an equally pronounced kind are present in another novel of this type, in "A Picture of the Present-day Class of Officials" [*Kuan ch'ang hsien-hsing chi* 官場現形記], by Li Pao-chia 李寶嘉, better known under the name Li Po-yüan 李伯元 (1867–1906).

This thoroughly subjective and intimate note is to be found not only in the novel, but in the whole domain of literature in so far as it seeks to say something new and original and does not merely reproduce old patterns and ideas, as did the literati of the T'ung school 桐城, or was customary among the writers of traditional novels of adventure (usually of Manchu origin), such as Wen K'ang 文康, author of "Tales about Heroes and Heroines" [*Erh-nü ying-hsiung chuan* 兒女英雄傳], c. 1868.

In order to demonstrate these tendencies, let us take at least a cursory glance at the work of one of the most outstanding authors of the Manchu Period—P'u Sung-ling 蒲松齡 (1640–1715), who in many respects anticipated all these trends which have reached their full development at the present time. P'u Sung-ling created, as did Lu Hsün some two hundred and forty years later, the perfect short-story. Just as did the authors of the May Fourth Movement he composed the social novel, and, like the authors in the liberated regions during the Patriotic War, he composed for the people long songs and narrative ballads. And finally, like all progressive educated persons in the revolutionary epoch, he was interested in raising the educational and cultural standards of the masses and wrote a whole series of handbooks dealing with their principal spheres of interest: folk characters, calendars, agriculture, medicinal herbs, wedding and other family ceremonies, etc. As is to be expected in the work of an author who in so many ways was ahead of his time, those trends come out most clearly which became the distinguishing traits of the following epoch. No doubt, in the mind of every reader of his collection of curious tales, *Liao chai chih-i* 聊齋誌異, repeatedly translated into European languages, there remains fixed in his memory the intense lyricism and pathos of the passionate introduction to this collection. Let us recall only the words "My life is like a flower tossed by the wind and falling at last into the manure-heap beyond the fence." And he describes his book as "the fruit of his desolation and bitterness," adding: "The fact that I must give outlet to my feelings in this way is sad enough."[11]

---

[11]See: Pchu Sung-ling, *Zkazky o šesteru cest osudu*, translated and with an epilogue by J. Průšek, Praha 1955.

Here we have a cogent formulation of the new, modern attitude to a work of art: A work of art is not the product of leisure and good spirits designed for the entertainment of friends, which was the purpose for which earlier writers published their books, but it is the manifestation of the innermost feelings, the expression not only of love, but of bitterness and even hate. It required great courage and a quite unprecedented self-confidence, the consciousness of the significance of one's own personality, for the author of the feudal epoch so openly to formulate his program and stress the claim that his feelings, his point of view, are the most important factor in art. "Mea res agitur" is the credo of the modern writer. It would be unnecessary here to allude once more to the biting ridicule and the active hate with which P'u Sung-ling attacks different social evils, such as the corruption of the officials, the arrogance and rapacity of the powerful, and so on, which Chinese and European scholars have repeatedly underlined. Much more important will be to investigate the intimate connection of P'u Sung-ling's stories with his personal life and show how he paints into the pictures of the gentle, unresisting young man of letters, part of himself. And how the various, colorful adventures which he invented lit up the grey monotony of his life as a private tutor in the houses of rich and overbearing patrons. Yet another typical expression of the personal key in which P'u Sung-ling's work is pitched is his output in traditional forms, his essays, notes and especially his poems. Here I shall give at least one or two examples in illustration. When he was seventy-three, he wrote a biography of his deceased wife, which speaks with surprising frankness of himself, of his family and even of his parents. Thus, for instance, of the scholarly predilections of his father, a businessman who gave up his business and devoted himself to study, P'u Sung-ling speaks as follows: "The book was never out of his hands and, in consequence, not even old scholars could compare with him as regards the depth and extent of his learning. Only it was like when the Chou became impoverished and wanted to build a temple—he ceased to care about his property." That is, considering Chinese traditions, an uncommonly candid verdict on his own father. With no less daring and candor, P'u Sung-ling speaks of the dissension that arose between his wife and the wives of his brothers, so that in the long run he had to move out of the family house: "But the silliest pretext was good enough for them (his sisters-in-law) to find fault with her (P'u Sung-ling's mother); they made a great din and (their) long tongues never stopped wagging. The private scholar (P'u's father) said: Things cannot go on like this; divided up our property and gave Sung-ling twenty *mou* of land. It was a bad year and Sung-ling got barely five *tou* of buckwheat and three *tou* of millet, besides some implements. They were all discarded things, rotten and broken, but when Sung-ling protested and tried to get something that was still in good condition, Mrs Liu (P'u Sung-ling's wife) remained dumb as if she had not a tongue in her head. The older and the younger brother got the main house where the kitchen and the sitting room were in perfect order. Sung-ling alone had to move out. He got an old peasant's cottage where not one wall was whole; a thicket of small trees flourished there and everything was covered with a tangle of thorns and weeds."

We could quote other passages from this short autobiography, which would support what was said above—that the literature of that time already embraces the whole of life, in all its breadth, and that it does not exclude even the shadier and uglier facts of existence. We see, too, that a system of ethics emphasizing the solidarity of the family unit failed to assert its hold where material interests were at stake, and there can be no doubt that the breaking-up of large families is the first step towards freeing the individual and, at the same time, the prelude to a general social revolution. We could quote from P'u Sung-ling's work a great number of things testifying to this new, unsentimental, realistic view of his own life and of society around him. Equally unassailable, too, is the contention that the individualistic, revolutionary attitude of modern man is determined by the individual seeing through the haze of philosophical and religious conceptions in which tradition has wrapped everything and seeing life as it really is. Here I shall quote only one poem to show how P'u Sung-ling's art grew out of this ability "to see life steadily and to see it whole." (I have, of course, to confine myself to a more or less literal prose translation.)

Song about the Drivers-out of the Demons of Drought[12]

In the sixth month there was a terrible heat and dampness so
    that everything was in decay,
Nor would it have been a wonder if the stones on the hills had
    crumbled and the hills of copper turned molten,

---

[12]*Chi pa hsing* 驅魃行, *Liao chai ch'üan chi* 聊齋全集, *Shih-chi* 詩集, *shang*, p. 16 et seq.

Benches and stools burned as if you were to sit on the bottom
    of a red-hot pan,
Grain withered, the leaves curled and rustled rustily in the
    wind.
The people suffering from the drought feared it and began to
    spread rumors;
The rumor sprang up that the demons of drought wish to
    destroy the peasants.
The corpses in the graves—those that have been mouldering
    three years already—
Their bones, they say, have power to cause this catastrophe.
The people from twelve villages came rushing in a single
    stream,
Wildly waving spears and bows, and their noise was like the
    roaring of a flood.
They overran the country like excited ants or swarming bees.
The owners of graves pressed back their tears and clasped their
    hands to their hearts,
They dared not, however, even peep, not to speak of showing
    their anger!
They sat and listened as hundreds of spades struck each other
    in a circle,
The dust from the dwellings of the dead flew on all sides,
    coverings roads and paths.
In the dug-up grave they came upon the remains of the dead,
Smashed up the coffin, crushed the bones and hung up the
    skull,
Even in the grave misfortune may overtake you.
Thus they drove out the demons of drought and the drought
    persisted all the more;
What harm have these mouldering bones done, why are you so
    cruel?
The families made complaint and immediately a strict order
    came:
To catch the runaways, bind them and bring them in, as you
    would roll a mat.
Those caught were beaten till their innards were in ribbons and
    their bones broken.
Those who got off with their lives had to bribe agents, and
    fields and gardens were gone with the wind.

In the Chou-liang 鄒 梁 [13] district, during such a disturbance, a
　still stranger thing happened.

When they opened the coffin, a yellow rat sprang out and made
　off into the corn.

The crowd vainly chased after it till they met an old villager;

His eyes were glaring, he mouthed and gasped for breath,

He stumbled and measured his full length on the ground and,
　at that moment, hundreds of halberds struck him.

In Ch'i and Lu,[14] up to eighty places were affected by this
　calamity,

Is it possible that a hundred different devils have gathered to fill
　Shan-tung?

If the demons can regulate rain and mist,

Then the Emperor in Heaven sits serenely, unseeing and
　unhearing.

If heaven does not intervene, we shall find ourselves on the
　verge of destruction.

Sad indeed are all these stories, stupid and idiotic!

This poem is a valuable testimony to how clearly P'u Sung-ling saw
the world about him, the foolishness and superstition of the masses, the
cruelty of the ruling class and, not least, how sceptical and mistrustful
was also his attitude to traditional religion. From this poem there speaks
to us a modern spirit, rejecting all illusion, no matter how cruel the
truth. Proof that P'u Sung-ling regarded his personal entity as a biological fact is forthcoming in a whole series of poems dating from his old age.
Nowhere do we find a trace of any attempt to console himself for his
approaching end with some hope of an existence after death. Here we
shall quote again a single poem in corroboration:

Old Age — A Complaint. Dedicated to Pi Wei-chung[15]

Four hundred and forty-five *chia-tzu*[16] days,
Have flown like the wind.

---

[13]Present-day Chou-p'ing hsien 鄒平縣 in Shan-tung. Belongs to Chi-nan-fu 濟南
府 .

[14]Two old States in the Shan-tung territory, Shan-tung Province.

[15]*Liao-chai ch'üan-chi, shih-chi, hsia*, p. 53 et seq. Pi Wei-chung 畢偉仲 was the son
of P'u Sung-ling's friend and patron, Pi Chi-yu 畢際有 .

[16]First day of the sixty-days-cycle. Accordingly P'u Sung-ling was 73 years old when
he wrote this poem.

I remember how long since, in my youth, when I saw a
     decrepit old man,
I used to ask myself whether this life was short or long.
Who would have thought that the number of white hairs would
     be ever greater,
That bones would grow tired and senses lose their acuteness,
And alone my forgetfulness shows how I am growing old and
     going downhill.
From the aches in my bones I can tell whether it will be fine
     weather or foul.
What teeth remain are loose and ready to fall out,
They are hollow and decayed, loath to do their work, and the
     stomach complains of hunger.
When the left gum begins to hurt me, I chew with the right,
And still every mouthful that I swallow is hard.
If your ears turn deaf, you can get on without hearing,
If your eyes grow dim, you must not see,
Only teeth serve the digestion,
And when they begin to ache, you cannot give up your two
     meals a day.
This I wish to tell my friends,
So that you, my old friend, may pity me and not mock me.

This poem illustrates as convincingly as one could wish that basic
tendency in the literature of the time, namely, the directing of attention
to one's personal lot, one's own life, of which we spoke above.

The most important documents for this continually growing tendency toward subjectivity and intimacy are, naturally, those works directly recording the individual's experiences and thoughts, such as notes,
diaries and autobiographies. In them, we see most clearly how gradually
and in increasingly large measure the focus of interest shifts from
external things and actions to inward experiences. The same view is
reached by Yüan Wu-ming 阮無名 in his preface to "A Selection from
the Diaries" [*Jih-chi wen-hsüeh ts'ung-hsüan* 日記文學叢選], where he
cites Lu Hsün, who twice makes mention of the diary of his country-
man, Li Tz'u-ming, 李慈銘 of which he says that "his heart is not to be
seen in it." Yüan, commenting on this, says that it was true of the
majority of people in older times that it was not possible to see their
inner life. He attributes the cause to the feudal order of society. We shall

find (he says) in them only very faint flashes of what the representatives of the old philosophy call *hsin-fou* 心浮 , "movements of the heart." The present-day diaries (he affirms) are quite different; in them events are related in detail and descriptions of feelings become day by day more profuse, so that (in his opinion) today diary literature is at its height. Further, he considers that the majority of older diaries had another defect: Most of them described journeys, while very few described everyday life. According to Yüan Wu-ming, the reason was that private life had no connection with the administration of the State and so the authors had no wish to write about it. In other words, Yüan Wu-ming comes to the conclusion we already reached above, that the feudal order checked and suppressed the individual and discouraged the free expression of personality. And, in fact, the first of the diaries that have been preserved, the "Notes from a Journey to the South" (*Lai-nan lu* 來南錄) by Li Ao 李翱 , dating from the T'ang Period, is nothing more than a bare retailing of facts. Here follows a short excerpt:[17]

"An order having come in the tenth month of the third year of the Yuan Ho (808) Period from the Miniser in Ling-nan (today the two provinces of Kuang and Vietnam), I set out on my journey in the first month of the fourth year. Along with my family, I left our family house—*Ching-shan-ti* 旌善第 , and took ship at the Canal. On *i-wei* I departed from the Eastern capital (Lo-yang). Han T'ui-chih 韓退之 and Shih Chün-ch'uan 石濬川 hired a boat and accompanied me. The following day I reached old Lo-tung 洛東 , where I paid a visit of condolence to Mêng Tung-yieh 孟東野 , whereupon I continued my journey."

This is the style of the whole diary, one fact after another, while traces of an inner life are extremely rare. Similarly, diaries from the Sung Period usually describe travel experiences. They devote their main attention to the beauties of the scenery, are altogether lyrical in tone and regularly written in a rhythmed, prosodic style. They are all very concise in form, each item being described in a few strokes of the brush. As an example, here is a short excerpt from the diary of Fan Ch'êng-ta 范成大 (about 1200 A.D.), describing a journey to Canton: "At night we disembarked at The Falling Rainbow (place-name). The hazy moon filled the river; I could not bring myself to give the command to set sail.

---

[17]Yüan Wu-ming 阮無名 , ed., *Jih-chi wen-hsüeh ts'ung-hsüan* 日記文學叢選 , 1936, p. 3.

My guests, too, had no thought of returning. So we anchored beneath the bridge."

Let us now, for the sake of comparison, take two diaries from the end of the Ming Period. The first can serve to document the refined, sensitive art of lyrical description, the other the remarkable powers of introspection and analysis of one's own spiritual states, without which every attempt at recording the individual's spiritual life would be vain. The first diary, which is anonymous, describes how the author fled to the hills before the victorious Manchus and lived there in seclusion as a monk.[18]

"On the fourth day of the ninth month, on *jen-tzu* at dawn, just as the sun was rising, I 'struck oar' (as the poet Ch'ü Yüan says) and set out on my journey. It was raining again. I passed the Stone Gate (place-name), walls falling to decay, the enclosure in ruins; everything destroyed and devastated. You could count on the fingers of both hands the people who still remained (fewer) than the stars at daybreak. The spectacle of a countryside scorched by war evoked a heavy sigh from my breast. I got as far as T'ang-hsi 塘西, where I again met in with the boats of barbarians. Fortunately it was pouring and a strong wind was blowing so that the barbarians could not see as far as the bridge. I was dead tired. I lost my way and my head was splitting. In the evening mist the ravens returned and the flowering reeds were silent. It seemed to me as if I was in the jungles of the South on a rainy day, the raindrops beat down on me unceasingly. I had already lost my head when the bank appeared before me, on which rose like a peak the monastery of Yang-yung 漾永. So I tied up the boat and stepped out on to the bank. The head of the monastery, Ssu-ming 嗣明, allowed me to stay the night in the waterside pavilion. Green weeds covered the little lake, rusty willows were planted along the bank, mist enveloped the countryside and exuded rain; the round moon was cold and cheerless."

This extract is sufficient to illustrate the lyrical mood characteristic of this kind of literature. Nor does such a man of letters forget even amid his troubles and tribulations to note the beauties of nature and the poetical impressions evoked by the changing moods of the day. The second extract is chosen to illustrate the path on which Chinese literature had already set out toward a deeper and wider knowledge of human psychology, that careful and painstaking introspection to which Chinese

---

[18]Ibid., p. 77.

literati were brought up by Confucian ethics fertilized by Buddhism. Essentially it serves the same function as the Catholic confessional, only it is more rational. The passages are from the diary of Huang Ch'un-yüeh 黃淳耀, *tzu:* Yün-shêng 蘊生 and date from the first three months of 1644:[19]

3rd day of the 1st month. "I got up late—that is my first transgression. Kuan Jou-an 管幼安 puffs himself up when he says: 'I was always lazy in the morning; when, however, I lay abed three mornings running, it was necessary to look upon it as a transgression.' How could I accept that as a rule under my present regimen?

"Even the saint Confucius was human, but when he was forty he had no longer any doubts. Today I have not yet reached the stage at which I have 'become firm.' That is my first reason for concern. Master Yen affirms that he never committed the same offence twice. But when I transgress, I commit the same trespass repeatedly. That is a second reason for misgiving. [The Master] says: 'If I hear about the Journey in the morning, in the evening I am ready to die.' Could I die today? That is my third reason for misgiving. Men in olden times were well brought up in their youth and so were capable of directing the world and administering the State. Myself, however, always commit some mistake and only then do I learn from it, and so I have a fourth ground for doubt, and namely this: that I have wasted all the previous years and months and that they will be of no use to me.

"If we say no more than a few words to someone, there should be something in it that strengthens the character and serves some purpose; broad jokes and uncurbed laughter, just as giving the first answer that occurs to us, is not proper and is without substance.

"I have long felt that the years and months pass easily, but nowhere, unfortunately, do the results of work pile up.

"In the evening I went to have a glass of wine with Hsi-mêng 熙孟. My heart was half pure and half troubled. Men of olden times burned incense every night and gave an account of their acts to heaven. If in their hearts there was the least foulness or dregs, they had not the presumption to converse with heaven.

"Human life, that is directness, sincerity. Directness means following one's natural disposition.

"Empty chatter is a great fault. Often something slips out that we do not intend.

---

[19]Ibid., p. 111.

"(In the evening) by the light of the lamp, I read twenty-eight pages of 'History in a Pragmatic Presentation' [*Chi-shih pen-mo* 記事本末]."

7th day (op. cit., p. 114 et seq.). "The main reason why we eat and drink is alone in that we may nourish our spirit. Rich foods and strong wine, like soft cushions and a heap of pillows, can only, on the contrary, darken our spirit. No sooner is our spirit darkened, however, than our desires become active.

"Let us train our hearts so that we may fulfil our duties. But, should our hearts be thus prepared, we must test it on our duties. My pupils, Wang Ch'ang-shih 汪長士, called Sui 遂, and Wang Chin-chih 汪進之, called Li 立, came together to visit me.

"K'ai-yin 開尹 and Tzu-i 子翼 were here to see me. In the afternoon I went to I-fu 義扶, and we met Chieh-an 伫庵. When we were chatting and laughing, I all at once became aware of a certain shortcoming—namely, that I am obstinate in defending my views. I probably carry my persistency too far and so go to extremes."

18th day (op. cit., p. 116). "Patriarch Fu [Fu Hsi 傅翕] (a patriarch of Buddhism in the 6th cent. A.D.), worked during the day as a laborer, and at night devoted himself to his religious duties, but we must realize that when he was working as a laborer, he was actually doing nothing else (than when he was devoting himself to his religious duties).

"In his sermons, Patriarch Fu says: 'Our body is what we must most abhor and for which we must have the greatest contempt, for it is the source of all our suffering. Thus it is necessary for us to keep a close guard on our three organs (namely, the mouth, the body and the mind) and strenuously cultivate the Sixfold Path to the attainment of Nirvana (good deeds, right behavior, patience, energy, calm meditation and wisdom). If we descend into hell, we shall find it difficult ever to get out, and we shall eternally regret it.'

"On this day I expended much energy on matters connected with festivals. Besides, together with Wei-kung 偉恭, we took stock of the past and made plans for the future, and so awakened in ourselves many impulses still germinating; it is clear that we ourselves have walked into a trap. In the afternoon a letter came from Shêng-chü 聖舉 asking me for a manuscript copy of commentaries on the two Ch'êngs [Ch'êng Hao 程顥, (1032–1085), and his brother Ch'eng I 程頤, 1033–1107, famous Sung philosophers]. A letter arrived, too, from Master Yung-ssu 永思, enclosed with which was the book, *Tieh-shan pi chi* 疊山筆記) for me to look through. Tzu-i 子翼 came to see me and left again after dinner. I continued my reading of 'History in a Pragmatic Presentation' and finished the eleventh chapter. At night I had very confused dreams. I dreamt that I was in some kind of garden surrounded by walls. Such dreams, according to Ch'i-lin 啟霖, are usually called forth by what the heart is attached to. Then in my dream I saw Ling-yung 令融 rowing towards me in a boat. He had a red kerchief bound round his head and trousers tied at the bottom. I also dreamt that Shêng-chü 聖舉 was the incarnation of the teacher Chia-t'an 家覃. He sat with crossed legs like Buddha and expounded the Law."

Unlike the preceding diary, that of Huang is written very simply; the author nowhere lingers over descriptions of scenery and poetical experiences—his main aim is evidently self-improvement in the sense of Sung Confucian philosophy. The diary shows very clearly how this philosophy, with its emphasis on unceasing self-improvement, led to the study of self, awakened an interest in the refinements of psychology, encouraged the analysis and evaluation of all feelings and emotions, and even sought to interpret dreams. Here then are the roots of those dream-motifs which appear in modern times in China, in Lu Hsün's collection *Yeh-ts'ao*, and in Japan in the work of Natsume Sōseki.

The other source of this trend toward psychological analysis is clearly Buddhism with its shunning of sin and probing of conscience in which it resembles Christianity. These philosophical and religious tendencies brought out the contradictions in the human soul, the conflict and strife of antagonistic desires and feelings, the ceaseless struggle of man between his nature and his ideals, thus enabling future literature to find in man's inner being the spring of conflicts much more effective than were mere outward conflicts such as we find described in earlier literature. Here, then, is to be found the literary origin of what we call subjectivism, the interest in one's own inner life and, at the same time, the beginnings of that psychologically oriented literature so characteristic of the period between the two wars. In former times, Confucian philosophy greatly simplified the problem by asserting that man is naturally good and so ignoring the complexity and contradictions of human nature. No more could it be realized by the Taoist philosophy, the aim of which was the merging of the personal ego with the Cosmos in which the individual gradually ceased to exist as a separate entity. Only then did China discover the intensely interesting, bizarre, complex and stormy world of man's inner being, and this fundamental fact cannot fail to be reflected in the whole of Chinese literature.

We could document the penetration of subjective elements into literature in various descriptions of nature, where at a later stage the *tableau* or lyrical "picture," striving to evoke the impression of pure and perfect beauty, was always set off by some intimate experience, reminiscence or anecdote. In this way, the too impersonal and cold impression evoked by description assumes a warmer coloring and is brought within the sphere of human life and interest. Similar traits are observable in Chinese prefaces which regularly serve to bring the impersonal, unemotional material of the book closer to the reader, to form a bridge to his sympathies and in doing so make use of the same means: they introduce a personal note, talk of various intimate experiences and, in short, give the author the opportunity to open his heart to his readers.

The most striking manifestation of this general tendency to subjectivity, intimacy, to the description of personal experiences, but also to a realistic view of life stripped of all illusions, and even to a comprehension of all its tragedy, is the Chinese autobiography. How entirely new was this literary genre, which first arose under the Manchu dynasty and which, as we showed above, is very typical for the period between the first and second World War, is to be seen best of all in the fact that the greatest Chinese literary historian, Chêng Chen-to, in an article published already in 1934,[20] in which he treats of the various literary forms, affirms that "in China there existed only very short autobiographies, such as 'The Life of the Master of the Five Willows' (*Wu-liu hsien-sheng chuan* 五柳先生傳), the well-known poetical auto-portrait of T'ao Yuan-ming 陶淵明, and that there never arose a work which would form an independent volume." Similarly, he also asserts that memoirs and reminiscences did not exist in China. Today we know that the first Chinese autobiography of any length arose about 1809, at the beginning of that long period of storms, revolt and revolutions out of which the New China was born. It is a work well known in Europe today — Shen Fu's *Fou-shêng liu chi* 沈復．浮生六記, translated by Lin Yutang in his book, *The Wisdom of China and India*, New York, 1942, pp. 968–1050. At the same time, and independently of Lin Yutang, I translated this book into Czech, it being published in Prague, in 1944, under the title, *Šest historií prchavého života* (Six Stories of Fleeting Life). It is therefore unnecessary to give here any quotations, as these translations are easily accessible.

---

[20]Chêng Chen-to, *Yen-chiu Chung-kuo wen hsüeh-ti hsin t'u-ching* 研究中國文學的新途徑, *Chung kuo wen-hsüeh lun-chi* 中國文學論集 pp. 1ff.

Chêng Chen-to's assertion confirms that this first work of its kind was undoubtedly very original, which is also stressed by Baccalaureate P'an Lin-shêng 潘麐生 in the foreword to the book, in which he says: "the discovery of this book is the equivalent of raising a new banner." It is natural that such an author, creator though he was of a new literary genre, remained in many ways in the shackles of tradition. Thus, for instance, his narrative does not yet form a single, epic stream, as in the case of biographies or autobiographies of modern type; the author, on the contrary, divides the events of his life into six "histories" or six categories of records, according to the subject-matter. The constructive principle on which his work is based does not, therefore, differ from that of other works of the preceding period, as, for instance, historical works, different kinds of notes, and so on. He vacillates, too, in the aim of his work: obviously the real character of the genre he is creating is not yet quite clear to him. The author is not certain whether he should confine himself entirely to the description of his life, for such material is not yet "canonized" in literature, especially as regards the everyday, sorrowful, gloomy aspects of life, which are just those aspects which give his work its realistic character. And so he often introduces into his book the traditional subject-matter of various old notebooks, speaks of the arrangement of flowers, of architecture, and devotes a large amount of space to the description of rambles and pilgrimages, which, as I have said above, had at that time a long and worthy tradition in polite literature. These traditional elements, however, are quite compensated for and, indeed, are given a new significance, by the altogether new and definitely modern emanation of the author's personality, the expression of his intimate life, the declaration of his loves, passions, feelings, interests, dislikes and hates. Here, in many places, we have the direct avowal of individuality—and of an individualist—almost without reservations, an avowal which links Shen Fu with the authors of that new revolutionary epoch to which we made reference above, and not with the old, strictly regulated spirit and literature of feudal times. It is certain that this desire and courage to put in words all that he felt, the passion and obsession with which he threw himself into life, and with which the pages of his book vibrate, enabled him to shatter the framework of the old, aesthetically highly polished essays and notes and create a work which, in comparison with similar products of the preceding epoch, was forceful and voluminous, though lacking in homogeneity and balance.

Shen Fu has the courage to speak of the most intimate experiences of his life, of his love for his wife, of his family, of the relations between himself and his father, his mother and his younger brother, with a frankness that would be surprising even in a European author. What daring was then needed to write with such openness in an epoch in which every resistance to parents and family was punished with the greatest severity and social ostracism! He says in effect that his father was a man who loved ostentation and liked to show off, but had not the smallest understanding of or compassion with his own son. His father took a concubine and his son had not enough to live on. He is bitter about his younger brother who was the cause of dissension with his parents and cheated him of his inheritance. Unsparingly he pillories the greed and rapacity of relations and friends who were glad of his help, but when he fell on bad times, left him in the lurch; from his book, too, we get a picture of what the members of the "cultured" feudal class were often really like. We may say that, in this respect, the work of Shen Fu offers a parallel to the celebrated novel by Wu Ching-tzu 吳敬梓, from the first half of the eighteenth century, *Ju-lin wai-shih* 儒林外史.

If Shen Fu speaks openly of his family and friends, he also does not try to make himself out to be better than he is. He tells of his adventures with courtesans in Canton and makes no attempt to whitewash his fast mode of life after his father's death, on the island of Ch'ung-ming. He speaks of his misery and humiliation when he was forced to beg at the doors of his unfeeling relatives and friends, and when he had sunk so deep that he was afraid to show his face. He also relates his rather discreditable nightly flight from his creditors and similar escapades.

The fact that the author succeeded in fusing all this dissimilar material—on the one hand, traditional observations on flowers, on architecture, descriptions of rambles and natural scenery, and, on the other hand, new and original descriptions of intimate experiences from his life—in a single whole, that he made of traditional, compositional mosaic a picture whose parts are linked up with a single unifying thought and feeling, that he worked up his episodes into an impressive and truly artistic work of art—the explanation for this success is that he conceived (though no doubt intuitively rather than consciously) his whole work as a uniform, one-piece tragedy of human life. His work culminates in a description of deep and unaffected pathos of how he and his wife became impoverished, broke with their parents, how his wife sickened and eventually died—a few pages which in their overpowering truthfulness and depth of feeling are probably without parallel in Chinese literature. These pages are the core and focal point of the whole book and in relation to them all the other episodes of the work assume a new significance and a new context, so that they form a unity. Certain episodes show the development of the author's personal tragedy culminating in the death of his wife and of his only son. Other episodes, with their beauty and poetry, color and heighten the final tragedy, giving to the author's life story, as also to his work, a remarkable breadth and pathos and multiplying the scale of emotions which the book evokes in the reader. For, in reading every lovely and touching episode, he has at the back of his consciousness the feeling that it is only for a short time, that it is only a tiny fragment of happiness, that lying in wait is misfortune, destruction and death. The consciousness grows that every little bit of human happiness is paid for many times over with misery, hardship, pain, the loss of those dear to us and, finally, with death. In this way the author succeeds in connecting up all the parts in perfect artistic unity and in creating, on a different plane, an analogy to the modern autobiography composed as a single stream of action in chronological development. This unity of conception is yet another aspect of the work of Shen Fu which links it up with modern rather than with older literature.

Besides, the tragic pathos of Shen Fu's work shows greater affinities with modern literature, those works mentioned above from the period between the two Wars, than with the old traditional literature that preceded it. A truly religious man in feudal society became reconciled to his fate and to the losses he suffered thanks to the belief or illusion that he would meet with his loved ones in the next world or in the next incarnation. Shen Fu, too, plays in moments of happiness with these illusions, but in times of despair they altogether fail him. The death of his beloved wife is for him a cruel, frightening tragedy and his grief cannot be mitigated by any idea of a life beyond the grave. We may, indeed, say that the consciousness of tragedy is the price which the individual pays for his freedom, for his having emancipated himself from the old order and way of thought and feeling—it is the penalty for the assertion of the human individuality. In Shen Fu's work we already find all those qualities which are so characteristic of the literature between the two wars: subjectivism, individualism, the disregard for traditional bars and considerations, the awareness of the tragedy of life. It is, without doubt, the most interesting document of the close connection between revolutionary literature and the literature of the Manchu Period.

I have tried in the course of my paper to formulate and illustrate certain tendencies which, in my opinion, link up the literature of the revolutionary period with the literature produced under the Manchus. Naturally I could not, within the limits of a paper of this kind, as I remarked at the beginning, do more than indicate some of the signs and symptoms of a general trend. The presentation of a truly exhaustive picture of this period will require an immense amount of labor, for it involves the investigation of all the notable works of this epoch and their monographic treatment. Here my aim was to show from a few selected examples what seems to us to be a preparation and leading-up to the literature of the revolutionary epoch. If then the literature of the revolutionary period reflects the revolt of the Chinese people against the old feudal order, we must presume that the similar tendencies which we come across in Manchu literature are the first intimations of impending crisis in the feudal order. The subjectivism and individualism which we find in it testify to a certain emancipation of the individual from traditional ways of thought, are an indication of the loosening of the bonds which the feudal order imposed on the individual and an intimation that the individual is beginning to free himself—at least mentally—from all these limitations of the past.

Our view that the Manchu Period marks the preparation for and beginnings of a change in the structure of Chinese society is further confirmed by the complete re-evaluation of traditional literary criteria. The traditional literature represented by the essays and different forms of poetry lose their importance and the main literary medium of the time becomes the novel and the short story, as in the following revolutionary epoch. In this epoch the old written language is no longer the main vehicle of literary expression, its place being taken by *pai-hua* which is essentially the spoken language. All this points to the fact that, in literature, the lower, folk stream now takes over the dominating rôle. The literature of the gentry was thus forced out of its positions in the same way as the landed gentry were swept away by the people's revolution.

These traits which we have singled out testify in their sum to the correctness of our assumption that the present great change in Chinese society has its beginnings in the Ming Period and is initiated in the main by internal, Chinese forces and has its purely Chinese origins. The European invasion only accelerated a process that would have achieved its goal without any such external factor.

II

Introduction to *Studies*
in Modern Chinese Literature

1. General Aspects: The Political and Cultural Revolution

The purpose of the collection of studies we are presenting to the public is to cast some light on the great transformation the Chinese nation has been going through, a transformation which undoubtedly is one of the greatest ever witnessed in history.

The volume contains a collection of analytical studies, with a single exception, devoted to Chinese literature of the period from 1917 to 1937. We chose the method of analytical studies for two reasons: First of all the work was done by beginners—mostly my students, a majority of whom are now working in the Oriental Institute of the Czechoslovak Academy of Sciences, and one German colleague who is a very close co-worker of ours. The initial attempts of beginners to cope with the obscure tangle of problems and facts, as new Chinese literature appears to be today, can aim at no more than a survey of single problems, or figuratively speaking, the laying of the first beams on which further structures would rest. This method, motivated by our facilities, would not justify the publication of the material, rather, it would be sufficient to collect it for our archives. The second, and decisive, reason for publishing our collection is the complete lack of European analytical studies on the individual personalities, problems and works of new Chinese literature; consequently no attempt at synthetic work on the material can be successful. The need for such analytical studies in the sphere of modern Chinese literature is evident even after a first glance at the contemporary situation of this branch of sinology. I give here at least a brief survey of the present state of literary studies.[1]

Chinese scholars have written several synthetic works on new Chinese literature, such as the two-volume book by Wang Yao 王 瑤 *Chung-kuo hsin wen-hsüeh shih kao* 中 國 新 文 學 史 稿"Draft of History of Modern Chinese Literature,"[2] the book by Liu Shou-sung 劉 綬 松 *Chung-kuo hsin wen-hsüeh shih ch'u kao* 中國新文學史初稿, "First Draft of a History of New Chinese Literature,"[3] the book by Ting Yi 丁 易 *Chung-kuo hsien-tai wen-hsüeh shih lüeh* 中國現代文學史略 "*A Short History of Modern Chinese Literature*" translated into English[4] and a number of others. In addition there are a great number of studies devoted to various problems and aspects of new literature, especially to Lu Hsün's works. In contrast, it is very difficult to find a thorough study of important writers such as Mao Tun, Kuo Mo-jo, Yü Ta-fu and others. On some writers we find only single articles, mainly of pre-war origin; there exists no modern evaluation.

Soviet literature on the subject is relatively rich and most of the important works of modern literature have been translated into Russian. Of the synthetic works I would mention at least H. T. Fedorenko, *Kitajskaja literatura*, "Chinese Literature," Moskva, 1956; L. Ejdlin, *O Kitajskoj literature naśich dnej*, 'Chinese Literature of Our Time," Moskva 1955, the important collection of articles published under Fedorenko's supervision, *Voprosy Kul'turnoj revolucii o KNR*, "Problems of Cultural Revolution in the Chinese People's Republic," Moskva 1960, and a large number of monographs mainly on Lu Hsün and his works, such as L. D. Pozdnejeva: *Lu Sih, žizň i tvorčestvo*, "Lu Hsün, His Life and Work," Moskva 1959; V. F. Sorokin, *Formirovanije mirovozzrenije Lu Sinja*, "The Development of Lu Hsün's World Outlook," Moskva 1958; V. Petrov, *Lu sih, Očerk žizni i tvorčestva*, "Lu Hsün, A Survey of His Life and Work," Moskva 1960 and others.

Many new Chinese works have been translated into German by the young sinologists in the German Democratic Republic.

On the other hand, the interest in new Chinese Literature in the

---

[1]My Introduction was finished in 1961. Other studies are still older.

From *Studies in Moaern Chinese Literature*, ed. Jaroslav Průšek (Berlin: Akademie Verlag, 1964), pp. 1–43.

[2]Shanghai, Hsin wen-i ch'u-pan-she 1953.

[3]Peking, Tso-chia ch'u-pan-she 1957.

[4]Peking 1959.

West is very limited. The largest work on new literature in the West is H. van Boven's *Histoire de la Littérature Chinoise Moderne*, Peiping 1946. This book was written from a strictly Catholic point of view and this itself distorts the entire development of new literature and the portraits of the individual authors. It is sufficient to read van Boven's judgments of Lu Hsün, for example, to see what a distorted, not to say even false, picture he gives: "Après 1930 il est communiste, mais communiste mencheviste, adoptant les théories de Plekhanov et Lunacharsky, et non bolcheviste . . . Dans la préface de son livre *Erh hsin chi* il dit clairement qu'il ne faut pas le considérer comme communiste sans plus" (p. 121). It is unnecessary to point out the incorrect designation of Mensheviks as Communists, and of Lunacharsky and Plekhanov as Mensheviks, but it is particularly necessary to stress that Lu Hsün read and translated Lunacharsky and Plekhanov because he wanted to become acquainted with Bolshevik literary theories and thus serve the revolution. Nor does his introduction say what van Boven reads into it.

I see the second main fault of van Boven's work in the fact that a large part of his information on literary works is not based on authentic sources but it is second-hand information. Other books written in the West contain even more serious mistakes than van Boven's. The book by Jos. Schyns, *1500 Modern Chinese Novels and Plays*, Peking 1948, is full of mistakes and most of the facts he presents are insignificant. Other books, such as Jean Monsterleet, *Sommets de la Littérature Chinoise Contemporaine*, Editions Domat 1953, are of an essayistic nature. In comparison with these works we have to evaluate positively, despite a number of in-adequacies, Dr Huang Sung-k'ang's book, *Lu Hsün and the New Culture Movement of Modern China*, Amsterdam 1957. It deals, however, more with Lu Hsün's ideological development than with his artistic activity.[5]

Under these conditions we hope our studies will be, at least, a small contribution to understanding one of the most important phases in the history of man and in the development of world literature.

The analytical study of not well-known, or entirely unknown material—a large part of the literary sources worked on in these studies were subjected to systematic research for the first time—has the disad-vantage that the research worker is confronted exclusively by separate isolated facts. He does not see their relationships and he can hardly judge

---

[5] See my review of this book, *Lu Hsün, The Revolutionary and the Artist*, OLZ 1960 (LV 5/6) p. 229–236.

their significance. Most of the time he must be satisfied with descriptions and listings and he has to postpone any eventual synthetic conclusions and judgments that may, at the time, seem likely to him until they are verified on the basis of richer material and are checked with conclusions arrived at in other fields. Undoubtedly, at this stage, the results of our work look rather colorless and lacking in depth and pattern. There was no way of avoiding this; thus far our work is no more than a construction site where the foundations are being dug and not a single house has as yet been completed. Now it is only a question of making the foundation sufficiently solid.

In order to offer the reader more than mere chaos and to enable him at the least to see the perspectives of further development and the meaning of what seems to be an agglomeration of unconnected details, this volume of studies will be complemented by a second volume in which I shall try to give a more systematic explanation of what took place in Chinese literature in the period between the May Fourth Movement in 1919 and the beginning of the war against Japan in 1937, on the basis of a substantial analysis of the prose of this period.

I shall limit my introduction therefore to a few remarks that will set this collection of studies in a framework; I shall summarize here some of the results of the book I am preparing.

As I mentioned above, our studies, with the exception of the work of K. Kaden, which deals with the writings of the contemporary author Chao Shu-li, are devoted to the period 1917–1937. We have chosen this period of Chinese literature intentionally. It is the period of the culmination of the revolutionary process taking place in China from the time of the Opium War (1839–1841) and most likely as early as some time in the eighteenth century. I repeat, it is one of the greatest transformations ever witnessed in history. This alone endows it with extraordinary importance for every scholar dealing with the history of mankind. Our studies dedicated to the literature of this period represent part of a broader project having for its aim an understanding of the entire process of the creation of Chinese national literature, an important part of modern Chinese culture. In a number of studies, some of which have been published, while others are in preparation we attempt to give an explanation of the process from the time of the inception of a literature in the colloquial language intended for the broadest masses in the T'ang era, up to the present.

It should be emphasized again that this work is just beginning. As yet it is mainly composed of single studies which are mostly descriptive and only later will it be possible to proceed to work of a more synthetic nature.

We are of the opinion that a detailed study of the history of Chinese literature between the two world wars is also of special importance for literary theory. From the theoretical point of view it is possible to say that here we can follow a tremendous experiment in detail (I use the word experiment purposely because this is practically a unique opportunity in social sciences to follow a specifically limited dynamic process with a very detailed knowledge of all the aspects of its course, as is usual in experiments in natural sciences) of a literary transformation, let us say even a revolution, abolishing medieval literature and creating modern literature, a democratic and later on a socialist literature. We can actually feel the forces that determine the development of literature and thus contribute to the solution of the question of whether the development of literature is immanent or whether it is determined by social forces, and if so by what kind. We are also given the rare opportunity of a sharp confrontation of feudal and modern literature, an encounter which clearly shows up their differences and at the same time the basic qualities of each. Further on it provides us with material for a study of the question of what circumstances led to the origins of modern literature and determined its forms and what was the original meaning of the various artistic processes that appeared in various places of the world, as well as in China, after the Great October Revolution. It is the question of the real meaning of the so-called literary avant-garde and the role it played in this stage of the development. I think that precisely in this aspect the Chinese material can bring out very important arguments, even though these points are not apparent at a first view of the formative process of Chinese literature.

The long revolutionary struggle of the Chinese people, first with anti-feudal aims, and, from the Opium War onwards, with aims of a more and more explicit anti-imperialist character, culminated in the twenty years between the May Fourth Movement and the war against Japan. The May Fourth Movement, for which the Great October Revolution was the main impulse, represents an important turning-point in this process. Until then the main revolutionary force was the small peasantry; then the modern industrial proletariat joined them, and the working class, led by the Communist Party, took the leadership of the revolution out of the hands of the bourgeoisie and the petty bourgeoisie led by the revolutionary democratic Sun Yat-sen Party from 1905. From the May Fourth Movement onwards, the old democratic revolution, which was part of the international bourgeois revolution, grew into a revolution of the new-democratic type and became part of the world proletarian revolution.[6]

There already are a number of works dealing not only with the political, but also with the ideological and general cultural aspects of this revolution[7] so that we can limit ourselves to a few remarks sufficient to let us realize of the depth and size of this transformation in China's social structure and literature for our further discussion. In China the development which in Europe lasted for several centuries or even millennia was packed into the eighty years between the Opium War and the May Fourth Movement, and especially into the following thirty years, ending with the victory of the revolution in 1949.

In most of Europe the anti-feudal struggle was fought out by the bourgeoisie which also created modern European culture. The bourgeoisie, supported by powerful and rich cities with developed crafts and trade, stood up against the aristocracy as an equal political factor, basically shattered the mythological world outlook and spread the rationalistic view of the world. The beginnings of this struggle go back to our Hussism, Reformation and Renaissance. Even before the forces of feudalism were completely defeated modern science and technique were developed, which in turn helped break the established feudal order and its ideology. The germination of modern realistic art and literature took place simultaneously with a rebellion against the forces of religion. From the time of the Renaissance the criterion for artistic creation became reality; the accurate depiction of it, sometimes with almost scientific exactness, is the fundamental postulate of art. It is worthwhile mentioning that in Europe mainly graphic and sculptural art opened the way for

---

[6]Compare the opening chapters of Ho Kan-chih, *A History of Modern Chinese Revolution*, Peking 1959, with particular reference to p. 7.

[7]I refer to the above-mentioned book by Ho Kan-chih, to the extraordinarily thorough Soviet work *Očerki istoriji Kitaja v novejšeje vremja*, Moskva 1959; to both of W. Franke's books, *Chinas kulturelle Revolution*, München 1957 and *Das Jahrhundert der chinesischen Revolution 1851–1949*, München 1958; to the Czech work by Stamberger-Pokora-Slupski, *Na přelomu staré a nové Činy*, "On the Turning Point of Old and New China," Praha 1959; Chow Tse-tsung, *The May Fourth Movement*, Cambridge, Mass., 1960 and a number of others. In these books one can find further references to what by now is a considerable literature.

the realistic orientation in arts. It is in these fields that the first professional artists appear, proud of their mastery, knowledge and techniques.

Although the bourgeois revolution in Europe first brought man complete political liberty and secured his rights as an individual, the cords that bound the individual were in many places loosened earlier. This was due in part to the breaking up of old clan relations during the migration of nations and in part to the fall of the slave system at the end of Antiquity; Christianity, with its stress on the equality of man before God and the moral responsibility of man for his personal life, also had an important influence. In addition the European code of chivalry contained strong ideals of individualism, and on the other hand helped the emancipation of women.

The situation in China was very different. The remnants of primitive communist society, the rural communities, the clan system and the strictly organized patriarchal families were completely wiped out only after the victory of the new-democratic revolution in 1949. It was the revolution that brought freedom to the individual and especially liberated women and children from the yoke of the patriarchal family it had destroyed. Chinese despotism, a tool of the ruling gentry, the official-landlord stratum, relied on these remnants. Whenever the need arose the State could mobilize endless masses of peasants for common labor or military service through the clans and communities. The middle class was helpless against the power of the state and for that reason, too, science, art and almost all culture were in the hands of the gentry. The slow development of literature written in the colloquial language, which originated in the big cities and was at least partially an expression of the Chinese bourgeoisie,[8] is a convincing example. For the entire duration of its existence until the end of the Manchu period, this literature was to a large degree saturated with feudal ideology. Painting never succeeded in emancipating itself from literary dilettantism and establishing itself as an independent profession, with its own tradition of artistic methods and theories. In China, crafts always remained crafts and were never elevated to the level of art appreciated by society. Art was only what the gentry did.

As a conclusion of our reasoning we may say that the main front of

---

[8] I discuss this question in the study *Les Contes Chinois du Moyen Âge comme source de l'histoire économique et sociale sous les dynasties des Sung et des Yuan*, Mélanges publiés par l'Institut des Études Chinoises, T. II, Paris 1960, pp. 113–140.

the class struggle in Europe lies between the cities and the feudal seats. The peasantry appears on the scene only occasionally and, at that, usually together with at least a section of the urban population, as in our country for example, during the Hussite wars. On the other hand, in China, the open and unreconcilable struggle of the poor peasants, tenant peasants and landless peasants against the gentry, the landowners and their state power, practically never ceased. This struggle, even when, for example, it is turned against foreign conquerors—the Mongolians, Manchus—is predominantly of a social and class character. In contrast to the relative political and ideological complexity of the class struggle in Europe, in China even the ideological reflection of this struggle is fundamentally simpler: in opposition to the Confucian emphasis on a social hierarchy with a complex system of relations and connections, which culminate in the person of the ruler, stand the equalitarian desires of the broad masses, who reject all social differences and their external expressions and demand equal division of the land and the establishment of a primitive communist society. That is the slogan *T'ai-p'ing*, "Great Equality," which could be heard in all the major Chinese rebellions from the Yellow Turbans in the second century A.D. up to the great revolution in the middle of the nineteenth century which took its name from this slogan. The class struggle in the Chinese countryside often took the form of an open conflict, grew into an armed uprising of the people, and the landlords regularly had to use force in order to squeeze out their rents and collect their debts. In the south many of them actually lived in fortified residences protected by armed bands. The forms of the conflicts were extraordinarily brutal and this brutality casts a dark shadow over the entire revolutionary epoch and gives literature its dismal and tragic mood.

The anti-feudal struggle of the Chinese peasantry, in which the poor city dwellers and the national minorities often joined, could not succeed. Victory was made impossible by the basic contradiction between the peasants' concept of equality and the individualistic and very backward methods of production; the peasants were not able to formulate a realistic political program, nor to create and maintain more complex political and administrative forms, nor yet to organize an army and protect the economy. Ambitious individuals from the gentry usually seized leadership and used the uprising only to gain power, whereupon they betrayed or liquidated the uprising. The story of the national uprising against the Mongols serves as a good example; its leader Chu Yüan-chang founded the Ming Dynasty, and the same was true of the 1911 Revolution, when all power was seized by various military satraps who leaned upon the old gentry.

The new-democratic revolution that developed in China from the time of the May Fourth Movement had to solve a complete gamut of problems that had been solved in Europe, as we said above, during a thousand years of upheavals, changes, developments and revolutions. This alone points up the great intensity and the unbelievable rapidity of the Chinese revolution in which months and years were equal to tens and hundreds of years in other places. In less than the duration of a human life, the revolution, like a hurricane, swept away all the remnants of primitive communist society, of rural communities, of the clan system and of the patriarchal family. It achieved all the aims of the people's anti-feudal uprisings: it liquidated the landlord class and the rule of the bureaucratic gentry, it divided the land equally among those who toil on it, it wiped out usurers, bond and lease serfdom, and shattered the feudal social hierarchy with its ideology of Confucianism.[9] At the same time this revolution also fulfilled the tasks of a bourgeois revolution, of course, no longer on the basis of a capitalist society but within a people's democratic system. The revolution transformed an agrarian country into an industrial one, it did away with cultural and technical backwardness (illiteracy), it liquidated religious superstitions and strove for a rationalistic, scientific conception of the world, and it advanced scientific materialism. This revolution then grew into a people's democratic revolution taking the road towards socialism. Agricultural production became collective, capitalist business was eliminated from production and distribution, and a new socialist culture was founded.

That is a brief enumeration, in outline, of at least some of the changes brought about by the contemporary revolution in China. In order to understand the specific characteristics of the Chinese cultural development and so also the literary development of this period, for our further discussion, we must be aware of the fact that the role of the Chinese bourgeoisie in the entire process was very small compared with the role of the European bourgeoisie, and that the Chinese bourgeoisie was not able to hold a leading position either in politics or in culture.

---

[9] It is necessary to note that the ideology of the Chinese gentry, in fact called Confucianism, has almost nothing in common with the original theory of Confucius which was of an explicitly progressive nature in its time, as we point out in a special study.

The Chinese bourgeoisie failed to assume a leading role in the 1898 reforms and during the initial phase of the national and democratic 1911 Revolution—in both cases the progressive elements of the gentry were at least of equal importance with the bourgeoisie—and so from the May Fourth Movement on, the dominating role of the Chinese revolutionary movement was taken over by the Chinese proletariat, joined by broad masses of peasants, and the avant-garde of the proletariat, the Communist Party of China. Under the leadership of the Communist Party countless changes were carried out and at the same time the Communist Party preserved the liberty of the Chinese nation in the fight against imperialist aggression. That is the main feature distinguishing the new-democratic revolution from the previous ones. We can comprehend the entire cultural transformation that took place in China, and the founding and forming of a new Chinese literature which followed only in terms of the leading role of the Chinese proletariat and the Communist Party of China.

2. General Questions of the Literary Revolution, Feudal Literature and Modern Democratic Literature

If a revolutionary transformation—the features of which we have tried to outline, at least briefly—brought about a gigantic change in all sections of life for the Chinese nation and a complete separation from the past, the same holds true for literature. A powerful revolution took place here too and when those who originated these events spoke about a revolution in literature,[10] the term was fully justified.

Twenty years ago, when I tried to summarize my impressions after becoming acquainted with the new Chinese literature, I had to say that "the term, new Chinese literature, is not only a conception of time. The differences between the literature of old China and the literature created after World War I are so sharp that it is hard to believe that they were produced by the same nation."[11]

---

[10]The term "literary revolution" has been used overmuch in Europe where any and every literary and artistic movement was called as a "revolution." In comparison to these movements the Chinese literary revolution is probably the only example in history of a real revolution in literature.

[11]*Neue Chinesische Literatur* in: Das Neue China, Berlin 1940, p. 456, 523 and 588, reprinted in the book *O čínském písemnictví a vzdělanosti,* "Chinese Literature and Culture," Prague 1947, pp. 207–256.

I am of the opinion that this first impression rightly grasped the deep cleavage which the storm evoked by the May Fourth Movement brought about, separating the new and old literature.

If we were to define the general character of the revolutionary changes in new Chinese literature we would say that it was a process similar to that which took place in other spheres of Chinese society and culture. The feudal literature of the gentry was defeated and abolished and its place was taken by literature which reflected the life of the people and served their interests.

At the very beginning of the literary revolution the prominent theoretician Ch'en Tu-hsiu, strongly influenced by the ideas of Marxism-Leninism, realized that the primary task of the literary revolution was to break and remove the old feudal literature.[12] In contrast with the overcautious attitude of the leader of the Rightist bourgeois intelligentsia, Hu Shih, who was satisfied with mild reforms of a formal nature which did not differ in the least from the postulates formulated by Liang Ch'i-ch'ao, the leader of the liberal reformists in 1898, Ch'en Tu-hsiu proclaimed the radical program of the Chinese literary revolution in February 1917: "I am willing to brave the enmity of all the pedantic scholars of the country, and hoist the great banner of the Army of the Literary Revolution in support of my friend.[13] On this banner shall be written in big clear characters my three great principles of the Revolutionary Army:

"1. To overthrow the painted, powdered and obsequious literature of the aristocratic few, and to create the plain, simple and expressive literature of the people;

"2. To overthrow the stereotyped and over-ornamental literature of classicism, and to create the fresh and sincere literature of realism;

"3. To overthrow the pedantic, unintelligible and obscurantist literature of the hermit and recluse, and to create the plainspeaking and popular literature of society in general."[14]

What basically differentiates Ch'en Tu-hsiu's principles from the

---

[12]Ch'en Tu-hsiu, however, never overcame the strong influence of bourgeois thinking and finally he was dismissed from the Party for his capitulationist tendencies. See Ho Kan-chih, op. cit., pp. 43, 50 and passim.

[13]Here Ch'en Tu-hsiu refers to Hu Shih. As in other cases, Ch'en was not aware of the basic differences between his own revolutionary demands and the reformist viewpoint of Hu Shih.

[14]I quote Chow Tse-Tsung, *The May Fourth Movement*, pp. 275–276, because he gives an English translation.

former reformist attempts to improve the language and literature—such as Liang Ch'i-ch'ao's above-mentioned attempts and Hu Shih's formulation—and what reveals the influence of the ideas of the new-democratic revolution is his clear awareness that literature has a class character, and that the literary revolution is directed against the literature of one class and aims to help the literature of other classes to victory. Instead of a literature for the aristocracy, i.e., the gentry, literature should now be written for the people, primarily for the workers and the peasants. From Ch'en Tu-hsiu's description of aristocratic literature it is evident that he means mainly literature written in *wen-yen*, because it was exclusively a product of the gentry.

A knowledge of the written language, which required many years of study, separated the gentry from the common people and encouraged its privileged status, because only a scholar could sit for the State examinations and become an official. The main literary genres cultivated by the old scholars of the gentry were essays and poetry. Essays written according to complicated rules and replete with allusions were required for the State examinations and were part of the official routine, because a large majority of these essays were official documents, memorials to the court, various reports, records, etc. Even poetry was often a social matter; it was more of a decoration for official life than a true expression of feelings.

In this respect the literary revolution was a complete success: the old essay disappeared and the old poetry was merely dying out in the few exceptional cases remaining. It is necessary to state, of course, that the literature of the gentry was dead at the very beginning of the literary revolution and that the revolution only removed its decaying corpse. Essays in *wen-yen* died out with the old examinations and old bureaucracy. The old poetry which had been unfruitful for centuries could not be revived by various attempts to breathe new energy into it in the second half of the nineteenth century. Even the stories composed in the written language imitating the artificial and minutely polished novels of P'u Sung-ling of the seventeenth century lost all importance. The opera, the versed parts of which were also written in *wen-yen*, remains merely as a beautiful fossil incapable of further development.

The liquidation of feudal literature goes hand in hand with a complete shift in the hierarchy of genres in literary evaluation. The genres that stood highest according to the old evaluation have now disappeared completely or they have been transformed and their place has been taken by other, new genres or by those that had been on the periphery of literature. It is a perfect parallel to the social struggle going on in the country at the same time. As the gentry was liquidated, so was its literature, and what remained of it became more democratic and turned to serving the people. The essay lives on—written in the colloquial language—as articles and features in newspapers and magazines. And in the hands of the great writer Lu Hsün this symbol of old culture becomes the sharpest weapon against the class that created it and wasted all its talent on it. Even poetry is now composed in the colloquial language and thus its form is changed and, as the revolution advances, its content too. Instead of the old opera a new type of theatrical art begins to take root—the drama. The main means of expression of the new period are the novel and the short story in colloquial language that had existed in China at least from the twelfth century, but which were regarded with disdain by men of letters because they were written in "the language of coachmen and maids." Some time later the new drama achieved a status of similar importance.

We can see that the old feudal hierarchy was at the time replaced by a new hierarchy corresponding to the European literary hierarchy and we can add that the old Chinese hierarchy was not completely without analogy in the ancient and feudal literature of Europe.

If we want to characterize this literary transformation, as far as its internal character and relationship to reality are concerned, we can say that the dominating position which lyrics held in the old literature— essays, inasfar as they served aesthetic aims, also had a specifically lyric nature, the same as the old opera—is now held by epics because even modern drama is closer to the epic form than to lyrics. This in itself indicates the changed attitude toward reality. Instead of observation, feeling for and contemplation of reality which formerly were typical of lyrics, we now find exact rendering of reality, its description and analysis, which are the main aims of modern prose. We can also say that old Chinese literary methods used in old Chinese poetry and prose[15] were synthetical, while the methods of modern prose (and modern poetry as well, of course) are analytical. The basic method of old poetry was to select a few phenomena from reality, which were rich in strong

---

[15]I give a more detailed illustration of these two approaches to reality in the introductory study to the translation of Liu O's novel *Lao Ts'an yu-chi, Putování Starého chromce,* "The Travels of Lao Ts'an," Prague 1960.

emotion and were usually of a general nature, so that we could practically speak of signs or symbols, and through them evoke a certain mood rather than give an exact description of a particular phenomenon or state. These symbols or signs often passed from one work to another; figuratively it could be said that they were somewhat like vouchers worth a certain quantity of emotion. All of this leads to the fact that old poetry was directed more toward general and permanent phenomena and feelings rather than toward concrete details. This trend is intensified by the constant repetition of themes and artificial language, where almost every turn of phrase has a long literary history. We find similar tendencies in Chinese painting, which works with a definite and very permanent repertoire of motifs, and again they are very evident in old opera, in its system of masks, symbolic gestures, etc.

Attempts at an analytical expression of reality, in sharp contrast with literature in *wen-yen*, had already appeared in the old literature written in the colloquial language, mainly in the novel and the short story; nor are they missing in the narrative songs, as well. This also is proof that old literature written in the colloquial language was the real predecessor of modern Chinese literature.

An attempt to depict reality truthfully, to understand and describe the relationships and connections between individual phenomena, as manifested in modern literature, is an expression of an effort to make literature an instrument of knowledge, but of a special kind. The aim of literature is no longer the contemplation of reality, the enjoyment of observing it and relishing it, but to become acquainted with it, comprehend it, and understand its laws. That is the basis of realism in new literature and art. That is why we can characterize the revolutionary process that took place in Chinese literature as a victory of realistic literature over feudal literature with purely aesthetic and ornamental— eventually moral—purposes. And this is an exact expression of Ch'en Tu-hsiu's program, which characterizes old literature with a long list of epithets, expressing its aesthetic and ornamental nature: painted, powdered, obsequious, stereotyped, over-ornamental, etc. To counteract this literature his program calls for the founding of a "fresh and sincere literature of realism."

But it was no easy task to translate these demands into reality and create a really modern, realistic literature which would, moreover, serve the people. In the first place there was a need for new writers who had lived through the spiritual revolution of the time in their own thinking and simultaneously mastered all the possibilities and range of European literature, where feudal literature had long since been surpassed and a modern realistic literature had been created. Above all, these writers had to be in close contact with the people in order to depict their life and express their desires, in order not to lose their own national orientation and become renegade cosmopolitans in the process of mastering foreign cultures.

3. The Relation to the Old Literature

To evaluate the full immensity of the task that faced the new writers putting into practice the positive part of the revolutionary program, that is, the creation of a new literature, we shall try briefly to characterize the literary genre that the literary revolution did not turn against but which emerged at the head of the hierarchy of literary genres, so that it seemed that this was where the new writers could link up with the old literature and use its achievements while creating a new literature.[16] The fact that this did not happen and could not happen is the best proof of the deep gap by which the revolution separated the new culture from the old. I am thinking of the old Chinese novel which gave Chinese literature some of its greatest works, well known all over the world. Moreover, from the eighteenth century onward the novel became an instrument of social criticism. The famous writer Wu Ching-tzu used the traditional novel form for an attack on the entire class of scholars (in his novel *Ju-lin wai-shih* 儒林外史, "The Scholars"). This form—a chain of independent episodes joined by the main hero or connected by links—was employed by writers at the turn of the twentieth century who attacked the bureaucracy of their day and from the position of the newly risen bourgeoisie[17] turned, at least partially, against the gentry.

---

[16]Hu Shih, who paid attention only to the formal aspects of literature, constantly emphasized that it would be possible to continue the old novels in the colloquial language at least as far as their language is concerned. As he did not understand the fundamental difference between literature created by the new-democratic revolution and the old literature, he did not see that this was not possible even in respect of language—or rather style—as we shall point out later on. See *Hu Shih wen-ts'un* 胡適文存 Shanghai 1940, Vol 1, p. 84.

[17]This very interesting fact was pointed out by W. Bettin in his article. *Die Darstellung der Gentry in Li Po-yüans Roman "Beamten." Wissenschaftliche Zeitschrift der Humboldt-Universität zu Berlin, Gesellschafts- und sprachwissenschaftliche Reihe, Jg. XI (1962), p. 425–429.*

We have here literature that seems to fit Ch'en Tu-hsiu's requirement of "plain-speaking and popular literature of society in general." Yet
between these novels and the new prose written after the May Fourth
Movement there is a wide gap—the new-democratic revolution we spoke
of above.

The authors of these novels, such as Li Po-yüan 李伯元 Wu
Wo-yao 吳沃堯 and Liu O 劉鶚 were still convinced of the general
validity of Confucianism and its final victory. Therefore, even though
they attacked the officials sharply and the gentry in part, and Liu O saw
the necessity of a revolution, they never came to understand the necessity of breaking down the entire old social system. Even the most
revolutionary of these authors, Tseng P'u 曾樸 who firmly supported
the revolutionary movement led by Sun Yat-sen, never surpassed in his
views the limitations set by a bourgeois-democratic revolution of the old
type. Fundamentally all these writers remained rooted in the old way of
thinking and their political viewpoints were somewhere between the
more progressive old gentry and the liberal bourgeoisie that was being
created. They could not see the world rationally and scientifically nor
understand its laws, since they were in the grip of an idealistic Confucian
world outlook, the basis of which was the belief that the social system
and human morals were expressions of the immanent laws of the world
so that evil is merely a temporary violation of this system and cannot
achieve ultimate victory. In their thinking they still did not fully discard
the medieval mythological conception of reality, according to which all
phenomena are determined by some metaphysical law which is not to be
understood by the powers of reason, be it the Confucian fate *t'ien-ming* or
the Buddhist chain of deeds and consequences *yin-yüan*, karman, or the
Taoist circle *tao*. That means that, as far as artistic creation is concerned,
the world appears to the artist as an accidental and basically incomprehensible sequence of events, and he does not feel bound or restricted
by natural and social laws in his creative work. Speaking of the "truth"
of an artistic work—a term repeatedly used in Chinese literary
criticism—two things are understood: first, the subjective truthfulness of
feelings and viewpoints—the artist is not "lying"—thus actually sincerity rather than truth is meant; this is usually employed for the evaluation
of a lyrical subjective work of art. Secondly, it means the exact and
truthful depiction of certain individual facts. This is used for the
evaluation of writing dealing with facts in various records and historical
literature. The idea had not penetrated that the artist should express not

only a single feeling or fact, but common laws and typical phenomena and create general pictures which not only reflect details but are a summary and analysis of a large number of phenomena, so that we can understand and evaluate each of them according to the artist's image.

The faults of the above-mentioned novels pointed out by Lu Hsün,[18] A Ying[19] and other Chinese scholars are a result of this unscientific, nonrationalistic conception of reality. The general weakness of these novels is the exaggeration and description of unlikely matters. Further on, in the works of Liu O, for example, we find medieval wild fantasy and instead of synthetic images these writers present a collection of single, isolated facts, narrations, scenes and anecdotes which have not been worked up into a homogeneous unit. The insufficient knowledge of the laws binding facts in unbreakable connections is apparent in the form of the novels, for they do not overcome the principle of the free linking of one episode with another; you could place a third anecdote between two others and the chain could be prolonged endlessly. A more elaborate structure can be found in Liu O's novel *Lao Ts'an yu-chi* 老殘遊記, "The Travels of Lao Ts'an," but this is result of purely artificial architectonics, dictated by aesthetic principles and not by the needs of the story; and in Wu Wo-yao's novel *Chiu-ming ch'i-yuan* 九命奇寃 "A Strange Revenge for Nine Lives"[20] which was obviously inspired by European models. The novel starts with the committing of a murder and then retrospectively tells how it happened. This indicates a certain tendency to stress the perceptive value of the work, its aim being to explain how such a tragedy comes about.

The new authors, however, could not even continue in the style of the old novels. In China the novel and the short story developed from the oral, vivid narration by folk story-tellers at the bazaars, and until the end of the Manchu period they maintained the form and style of narrations. They were conceived as the tales of one specific story-teller

---

[18]Lu Hsün, *Chung-kuo hsiao-shuo shih-lüeh* 中國小說史略, Shanghai, Pei-hsin shu-chü 1932, p. 362 says of Wu Wo-yao's work: "Unfortunately his narration often loses a just sense of proportion; sometimes he errs by painting everything in extremely dark colours and his story departs from anything that is likely."

[19]A Ying 阿英, *Wan Ch'ing* hsiao-shuo shih 晚清小說史, Peking, Tso-chia ch'u-pan-she 1955, p. 9 says of Li Po-yüan's, *Wen-ming hsiao-shih* 文明小史, "Short History of Civilization": "The descriptions in this book are far from the truth and they are exaggerated."

[20]Shih-chie shu-chü, Shanghai 1926.

and they were divided very unnaturally into sections, stages (*hui* 回) at the point of greatest suspense. Their style was the lengthy, slow style of a folk tale in which the story-teller's thoughts, descriptions, dialogues and monologues were blended into one unit. There is no clear distinction between narrated parts, descriptions and parts spoken by the characters. This made it impossible to achieve a more complicated description either of the environment or the psychology of the characters in the story and, what is more important, the narrator had to tell the story from his own point of view; he could not move freely to the scene of action or into his heroes' minds and describe things through their eyes, perception and experiences. The reproduction of their spoken words was always presented as direct speech and in this way it was impossible to achieve a more complicated story structure. An explicit example of this is the psychological short novel, the narration of nun I-yün 逸 雲 , which tells how she overcame worldly desires, in the supplementary six chapters of "*The Travels of Lao Ts'an.*" Since the whole novel was still presented in the form of the narrative of a traditional story-teller, I-yün's narration is practically in quotes. Her story also gives comments by other people and they in turn quote still others so that an impossible tangle of quotations within quotations comes into existence. It is obvious that this entire method of composition had outlived its day and that it was necessary to reject both the narrative structure and this style as a concept for prose works. Already the attempts at analytic descriptions, which are the virtue of Liu O's work and his personal contribution to the development of Chinese realism, completely shatter the old structure of the novel-narration.

It is evident that the new writers had to seek absolutely new ideological viewpoints, take a look at the world with entirely new eyes, with the eyes of other classes, those of the peasants and the workers, create a new artistic structure and finally create a new style, or rather, a new literary language. From all we have said it is clear that at the given stage of the revolution, when a new professional and democratic literature was being founded, the new Chinese writers could not continue in the footsteps of the old literary heritage even in the field of narrative prose.

I must add that the facts I have just presented are in no way an absolute evaluation of the old Chinese novel and short story; I am only searching for what could be of use at the given stage of evolution. In a number of other works, especially in the book *Die Literatur des befreiten*

China und ihre Volkstraditionen, Prague 1955, I have pointed out the superior values of these literary genres in China and I am convinced that in this field of literature Chinese feudal literature achieved such heights that hardly any other literature in the world of the same historical period could surpass it. As soon as the tasks of the literary revolution were fulfilled the new Chinese literature consciously began to revive these old traditions. That took place during the war against Japan, as I pointed out in the above-mentioned book.

In other fields the situation was even more complicated. In drama, except for vast stage experience, there was nothing that could have been taken over from the properties of the old opera and it was necessary to create both a new dramatic structure and a new stage language. The fact that this was accomplished in so short a period is proof of the true greatness of the creators of the new theatre, Ou-yang Yü-ch'ien 歐陽予倩, T'ien Han 田漢, Hung Shen 洪深, Hsia Yen 夏衍 and the youngest of them Ts'ao Yü 曹禺.

It was most difficult to overcome the past and create new forms and a new language in poetry. In old literature Chinese lyrics held an absolutely dominating position; their images and language became the property not only of the scholars but of the broad masses of people as well. It is generally accepted that Chinese lyrics are among the greatest creations of humanity as a whole. All deviations from the poetic code, worked out to the last detail, were considered as iconoclasm and even barbarism. Therefore, all efforts to bring new themes into poetry and to create a new poetic language on the basis of the colloquial language instead of the old wen-yen, in which most poetry was written until then, were not too successful, and it was only at the end of the period we are dealing with that the first great poet of modern China, Ai Ch'ing 艾青 appears.

In conclusion, we may say that a deep break in the development of Chinese literature took place in this period. New Chinese literature was inspired by foreign examples rather than by the old native literature. This is best seen in the case of the writer Lu Hsün. When he recalls how he began to write he states that he was inspired by some hundred foreign stories which he had read and the remnants of his medical knowledge.[21]

---

[21]"I started writing short stories not because I thought I had any particular talent, but because I was staying in a hostel in Peking and had no reference books for research work and no originals for translation. I had to write something resembling a story to comply with

He does not say a single word about old literature although there hardly was anyone who had a comparable knowledge of classical Chinese literature. Old Chinese literature had little to offer to the revolutionary Chinese writers whose mission was the creation of a literature and culture completely different from that of old China. When we do find links with old literature in the works of new writers, we more often find links with the old literature written in *wen-yen*, the literary language, rather than with literature in the colloquial language. The reason for this is that in most cases literature in the colloquial language had too stong a folk flavor, serving as entertainment for the broad masses rather than as an instrument for serious artistic expression. The new writers were faced with the task of founding a new national literature that would fulfil all the exigent demands placed upon this literature. Therefore, they unconsciously identified themselves with what they considered good literature and not with those genres which they felt were to a large degree folkloristic and which, moreover, were more burdened with the old psychology and way of thinking than literary works were. I do not of course speak here of such great works as *Ju-lin wai-shih* or *Hung-lou-meng*. In addition, the new literature had to grow up from the soil, until then occupied by the old popular literature—narrative prose, drama, epics—and therefore it first had to clear the ground and start anew if it did not want to drag the old manners and clichés along with it.

4. The New Writers

It is natural that only writers whose links with tradition had been severely loosened could make such a break with the old literature. The literature created in China after the May Fourth Movement is the work of entirely new writers, a new generation which suddenly entered the literary scene after 1917, and there is not a single writer from the previous generation among them.[22] Seldom have we witnessed such a

---

a request, that was *A Madman's Diary*. I must have relied entirely on the hundred or more *foreign* [underlined by Průšek] stories I had read and a smattering of medical knowledge. I had no other preparation." *Lu Hsün ch'üan-chi* 魯迅全集 , Peking, Jen-min wen-hsüe ch'u-pan-she 1957, Vol. 4, p. 392, Wo tsem-mo tso ch'i hsiao-shuo lai 我怎麼做起小 說來, "How I came to write short stories," pp. 392–393. Compare *Selected Works of Lu Hsün*, Peking 1959, Vol. 3, p. 229.

[22]In this period the eminent publicist of the reform movement in 1898, Liang

complete change of forces in literature anywhere in the world as in China during this era. The new literature is a creation of a single literary generation born in the last decade of the nineteenth century. The oldest one among them is Lu Hsün, who was born in 1881, but it was from 1918 that he first began to devote himself systematically to literature. Only gradually did the writers born in the first decade of the twentieth century join them.

One can say that this was the most cosmopolitan generation that ever appeared in Chinese literature and that it would be difficult to find a comparable one even in foreign literature. Most of these writers studied abroad for many years and became well acquainted with foreign life and culture and mastered foreign languages. The degree of knowledge of foreign languages, culture and literature of some of the members of this generation is quite unbelievable, such as in the case of Mao Tun 茅盾 and Yü Ta-fu 郁達夫. This is what makes them absolutely different from the writers of the previous periods, for example, the authors of the satirical novels we spoke about above. The latter merely tried to graft some foreign knowledge onto the traditional education they were brought up with. It is especially interesting that even the most intimate feelings of the new writers are saturated with foreign images and symbols. They speak of the cross they have to carry, a beautiful woman for them is a Beatrice or Mona Lisa, and so on.

They have completely departed from the old way of thinking, the old philosophy and conception of the world with their foreign scientific and rationalistic education. For them Confucianism is just the "morality of eaters of human flesh" as Lu Hsün expressed it,[23] every mention of the works of the old philosophers evokes laughter[24] and all allusions to the classics have disappeared from their works except when they are part of the theme or are meant to be ironical. On the other hand, their works are filled with motifs, quotations and echoes of European literature.

Ch'i-ch'ao, still continued to write, but he worked more on scientific and popular science books than on literary works. The original works of the famous and respected translator Lin Shu 林紓, of this period are not worth mentioning.

[23] In his first story *K'uang-jen jih chi* 狂人日記, "A Madman's Diary" in the collection *Na-han* 吶喊, *Ch'üan-chi*, Vol. 1, p. 9 et seq.

[24] When Chüeh-hui 覺慧, one of the main heroes of Pa Chin's 巴金 novel *Chia* 家, "Family" (Shanghai, K'ai-ming shu-chü 1933) mentions that in a certain school they read nothing but the works of saints and sages, Pa Chin accompanies the statement with these words: "Chüeh-hui himself felt a rush of uneasiness and he couldn't control his laughter (p. 281).

Their thinking is thoroughly materialistic[25] and as far as any religious ideas appear in their works it is a reflection of European ideas, of Christianity, and not of the old Chinese religious beliefs.[26]

Conversely, this entire generation received a good traditional education in classical Chinese literature and there is a conspicuous antagonism of sympathies and interests in their thinking. On the one hand they know that only modern science and learning can bring freedom to them and the whole of Chinese society, yet on the other hand from childhood they have more of a feeling for old Chinese literature presented in school than for European sciences, which were often taught by half-educated people. That is why many of them return to the old learning again and again in free moments and some of them create great scientific works in addition to their literary works. That was true especially in the case of Lu Hsün and Kuo Mo-jo; Cheng Chen-To's 鄭振鐸 scientific interests were by far the stronger ones, Mao Tun excels in erudition, though he mainly devotes himself to European literature, theory and criticism and deals with old Chinese literature only occasionally. We must constantly be aware of the attachment of this revolutionary generation to the old literature. Certainly their main task was to break down the old world and its culture and here their new European education helped them to do so. But on the other hand it was also their duty to re-evaluate the old Chinese cultural heritage from a progressive and popular point of view. The phenomenal work this generation did under unbelievably difficult conditions has not yet been fully appreciated. It is sufficient to compare the picture of Chinese literature in older European histories, such as Grube's and Gilles', etc., with the image we now have thanks to the research done by Wang Kuo-wei 王國維, Lu Hsün, Cheng Chen-to, A Ying 阿英 and a whole pleiad of their contemporaries, and we clearly see that scarcely anywhere in the world was literary history the subject of such pioneering passion as in China in the period we are discussing.

---

[25]Especially Lu Hsün's expression of this materialistic world outlook in the story *Pu t'ien* 補天, "Mending Heaven" in the collection *Ku-shih hsin-pien* 故事新編, "Old Tales Retold," *Ch'üan-chi*, Vol. 2 p. 307 and further on, is an artistic masterpiece. In this story he describes the origin of man as an unconscious and even unwanted action of the Goddess Nü-wa, representing the productive forces of nature. In his conception man is not the center of the universe as in old Confucian philosophy, but only one of the products of the development of Nature.

[26]See for example, certain traces of Christianity in the views of the heroine of Kuo Mo-jo's novel *Lao-yeh* 落葉 "Fallen Leaves," in the collection *Ti-hsia-ti hsiao sheng* 地下的笑聲, Shanghai, Hsin wen-i ch'u-pan-she 1951, p. 299 et seq.

And here, as in their literary works, we can see the new-democratic revolutionary viewpoint of this generation, which completely discarded the old dogma of the feudal men of letters who limited the huge flow of old literature to a small trickle of feudal letters in the old literary language.

All these tasks: the breaking of the old ideology, the striving towards a new materialistic conception of the world, the liquidation of feudal literature and the creation of a realistic modern literature simultaneously with the re-evaluation of the entire literary heritage and the disclosing of its folk and progressive elements, could be achieved by this generation only because it parted, in its entire way of life, thinking and feeling, from the old ruling class of gentry scholars and officials and changed over to the viewpoint of the working class, the proletariat and the peasantry.

Most of the new writers came from the class of petty landlords and scholars, as was the case in China for centuries. Of the known writers of this period only the dramatist T'ien Han and the writer Lao She 老舍 came from the lower classes. T'ien Han comes from a peasant background and Lao She from an impoverished Manchu family in Peking. At that time the Chinese proletariat still could not produce its own writers. In most cases, though, their landlord origin was counteracted by the fact that they broke with their own class, ran away from their homes, full of hatred for the environment they came from, and often they did not return home at all or if they did only with disgust. Their stay abroad loosened the relations with their native environments even further and when they returned to China they did not take their place among the old ruling class but became members of the newly developing and still weak strata of the intelligentsia. Most of the intelligentsia departed from the class they came from but could not find their place in any other class. One of the weaknesses of the Chinese bourgeoisie, which we have mentioned many times above, can be seen from the fact that it could not draw this modern intelligentsia to itself, create the adequate working and living conditions for them and impress its thinking and ideas upon them. After returning to China most of the intelligentsia could not find employment in the fields they had studied and these new intellectuals led dreary lives as teachers or they tried to live on their writing. Even at the universities the position of a teacher was completely unstable, teachers were hired and fired like servants and the rewards for writing were very poor. Thus this intelligentsia, and especially those who wanted to make their livelihood from writing, constantly lived on the verge of poverty as outcasts of society. Even the lives of Lu Hsün, Mao Tun, etc., were also very poor and Yü Ta-fu, Kuo Mo-jo, Ting Ling 丁 玲, Hu Yeh-p'in 胡 也 頻 and a number of others found themselves at the very bottom of society. Many of them became familiar with the Chinese proletariat not only theoretically but directly through their own lives in the Shanghai slums, which Yü Ta-fu described so magnificently in his autobiographical stories and sketches. Also their personal experiences strengthened the revolutionary spirit in Chinese writers and awakened the feeling that life in China had become unbearable and that there were only two solutions: either to commit suicide or join the revolution. The poet Wen I-to 聞 一 多 described precisely these feelings in his criticism of Kuo Mo-jo's collection of poems Nü-shen 女 神 "The Goddesses": "The indignation and despair of the Chinese youth after the May Fourth Movement burns like fire, swells like the incoming tide, they feel that this world, 'as cold as iron,' 'as dark as lacquer,' 'as foul smelling as blood,' cannot last for another second. The world disgusts them, they are disgusted by themselves. As a result those with quicker temperaments seek their refuge in suicide and the more patient ones strive for reform with all their strength. Yet even those who seek reform feel that their power is not sufficient for all that stirs them, they begin to shake, and they fall."[27]

The reality that surrounded them was extremely cruel—it is sufficient to read Lu Hsün's essays to gather a large amount of shocking evidence on what life in China was like—and even their personal experiences led this generation of writers to understand the necessity of a revolution and turned them finally to the proletariat when they were convinced that the proletariat was the only force able to carry out the revolution. Uniting with the proletariat was the only way in which they could overcome their desperate isolation in a society which, absolutely misunderstanding these people who, educated abroad, had new feelings and needs, belittled them and regarded them as monstrosities. The circle of eyes watching a tortured victim with apathetic interest which constantly reappears in Lu Hsün's stories is an expression of the feeling that haunted every intellectual.

All this drove the writers and the intelligentsia as a whole to rebel

---

[27] Wen I-to ch'üan-chi 聞 一 多 全 集 Vol. 3, Shih yü p'i-ping 詩 與 批 評 p. 185, Nü-shen-chih shih-tai ching-shen 女 神 之 時 代 精 神 "Spirit of the Epoch of [the collection] The Goddesses. This quotation appears on p. 191.

and brought about their final break with the old society. The ground for this had been laid by their stay abroad and their studies of European culture. The confrontation of their recollections of homes, which they often left full of anger and spite, with a foreign environment gave this generation a feeling of the absolute impossibility of maintaining the prevalent conditions in their country. They saw that in comparison with foreign powers China was weak and backward and on every occasion they felt how foreigners looked down upon the Chinese.[28]

The environment in which these writers grew up and lived also explains why the ideas of Marxism-Leninism prevailed so quickly. With very few exceptions the ideological development of this generation of writers can be characterized as the development of revolutionary-minded petty bourgeois intellectuals into conscious members of the fighting front of the proletariat. All honest, thinking writers took this road even though some of them were not strong enough to follow this road up to the very end while others were stopped by fate or native or foreign assassins. The first peak of this development was the founding of the "China League of Left Wing Writers" on March 2, 1930. Almost all of China's significant writers became members of the League. At the inaugural meeting, when the theorectical program was formulated, the members consciously took the standpoint of the proletariat in its fight against capitalism and imperialism and they accepted the world outlook of Marxism-Leninism. Just as on the eve of the patriotic war against the Japanese imperialists all the patriotic elements in China joined in a united fighting front, in the same way all the progressive writers were organized in the League.

It is typical of the political and cultural situation in China that the reactionary forces could not form any organized opposition to this broad front of progressive writers united by the ideas of Marxism-Leninism. We can almost ignore the feeble attempts to defend feudal letters by the famous translator Lin Shu and other old followers of the old literature adhering to the school of T'ung-ch'eng city 桐城, or the reactionaries concentrated around the magazine *Hsüeh-heng* 學衡 founded in January

---

[28]These feelings were expressed, for example, by Yü Ta-fu in his story *Ch'en-lun* 沈淪, "Drowning" (in the collection *Yü Ta-fu hsüan-chi* 郁達夫全集 , Peking, Jen-min wen-hsüe ch'u-pan-she 1954, pp. 1–40); by Wen I-to in the poem *Hsi-i ko* 洗衣歌, "The Washman's Song" (in the collection *Szu-shui* 死水, "Dead Water," p. 28, *Wen I-to ch'üan-chi*, Vol. 3) and by a number of other writers. The story, *Ch'en-lun* has been translated into Slovakian by A. Vlčková in her collection of Yü Ta-fu's works, *Večer opitý jarním vetrem*, "Intoxicating Spring Nights," Bratislava 1960.

1921, in Nan-king. These attempts to defend the old written language in literature were so absurd that the conservatives, with the exception of a few confused polemical articles, did not creat any literary work of art worth mentioning. The writers influenced by the bourgeoisie were able to organize only one important literary society, namely, the *Hsin-yüeh she* 新月社, "Crescent Moon Society" (a magazine under the same name began to appear in 1928). The main theoretician of the society, Liang Shih-ch'iu 梁實秋, regarded the attack against capitalism as an attack against civilization itself and he even repeated the outworn fable of how a diligent worker could accumulate a handsome fortune in a capitalist society.[29]

The most important ideological spokesman of the bourgeoisie was Hu Shih who had dropped his scholarly activities at the time and was devoting his time more and more to politics, struggling with all his energy to build a dam against the all-embracing flood of socialist ideas. The membership of the "Crescent Moon Society" included only two significant poets who by birth and education belonged to the bourgeoisie. The first was Hsü Chih-mo 徐志摩, who died in an air accident in 1931, when he was only thirty-six years of age, and therefore we cannot say what his further development under Kuomintang oppression and the national struggle against the Japanese would have been. The second was Wen I-to, who during the war repeatedly gave voice to the dissatisfied and radical mood of the patriotic Chinese youth in his poetry and critical works and became a spokesman for the democratic intelligentsia against Kuomintang corruption. As a result he lost his life when the Kuomintang agents assassinated him in July 1946. If we take the ideologically unclear and lifeless attempts by the feudal and bourgeois intelligentsia to create an organization—it is, for example, typical that the followers of the "Crescent Moon Society" could express what they were against, that is to say politics in literature, rather than what they were striving for—and compare them to the intensive, artistically and ideologically unusually fruitful activities of the societies uniting revolutionary attuned writers, we see at first glance that neither the old feudal gentry nor the new bourgeoisie could play an important role in Chinese culture any longer. The most important societies, such as Wen-hsüeh yen-chiu hui

---

[29]See *Lu Hsün ch'üan-chi*, Vol. 4, p. 155 and further, *Ying-i yü wen-hsüeh-ti chieh-chi hsing* 硬譯與文學的階級性 "Hard translation and the class character of Literature"; compare *Selected Works of Lu Hsün*, Vol. 3, p. 65 et seq.

文學研究會, "The Society for the Study of Literature," founded in January 1921, the society Ch'uang-tsao she 創造社, "Creation," founded in the summer of 1921, the society Yü szu-she 語絲社, founded in 1924, of which Lu Hsün was the most significant member, and a number of others were of a progressive nature. The leading personalities in these societies were writers who had worked their way up to the ideas of Marxism-Leninism from the position of revolutionary democrats, and who fought strongly against feudal survivals in culture and felt the necessity for revolutionary changes in Chinese society. Their attitude toward the Kuomintang clique was one of complete rejection. All that we have said proves how correct the evaluation of new literature by Wang Yao, the progressive Chinese scholar, is: "The history of new Chinese literature begins with the literary revolution on May Fourth (1919). It is a struggle and a reflection of the thirty-year new-democratic revolution in the field of literature. The new literature used artistic weapons to commence the fight against imperialism and feudalism and it educated broad masses of people, therefore this new literature is a necessary component of the new-democratic revolution and it is closely bound with the political struggle."[30]

5. A General Characterization of New Literary Creation

In this section I wish to say a few words about those fields of creation that are dealt with in our collection, that is about drama— although only one study is dedicated to this particular field—and especially about prose, which is what all the other studies are concerned with. In Prague we have begun to study Chinese poetry intensively, too. Of course to explain the birth of new poetry requires a thorough and long-term study of old Chinese poetry, its artistic processes and especially its prosody. If we accept the thesis we formulated above on the basic tendency toward realism in new Chinese literature and the attempts to express, by analytical methods, the varied phenomena of reality and their relations and to create typical images, there is no doubt that this task would be most complicated in poetry because the methods used in Chinese old poetry, as mentioned above, were the exact opposite

---

[30]*Chung-kuo hsin wen-hsüeh shih kao* 中國新文學史稿 , Hsin wen-i ch'u-pan she, Shanghai 1953, p. 1.

of these requirements. On the other hand, we cannot overlook the fact that old Chinese poetry brought the art of creating general compositions expressing a great number of details through one image in the most economical way to its highest peak of perfection. Some of Tu Fu's poems, for instance, are inimitable examples of how to immortalize the most typical features of society in a few strokes and, in addition, to give them the greatest emotional strength. I would venture to say that the roots of the exquisite modern Chinese short story, such as the short stories of Lu Hsün, in so far as they have roots in old Chinese literature at all, are not to be found in old Chinese prose but in poetry. Probably that is where we have to search for the ability to render the environment, sketch a figure and, above all, create the atmosphere of the story with a few strokes. But as far as poetry is concerned the old form, the old means of expression and their rigidity created obstacles for new poets and therefore the poets of this period often use free verse because any other more elaborate form seems to confine them and prevent them from expressing what they feel. This is especially true of the most revolution-ary poets, such as Kuo Mo-jo, who wrote his *Nü-shen* "The Goddesses" almost completely in free verse.

The sharp difference between the new themes and the new tasks of poetry, and all the poetic means available to poets in those days was felt strongly. The example of Lu Hsün is especially instructive. Lu Hsün occasionally wrote both traditional and modern verse,[31] but undoubtedly his greatest work of art, which corresponds exactly to the concepts of what modern poetry should be, is the collection of his poems in prose in *Yeh-ts'ao* 野草, "Wild Grass." Here Lu Hsün created a work of art which, in relation to the period and environment it was created in, is almost a miracle. His poems in prose, with their emotional atmosphere, complex images and metaphors, and the extraordinary strength of their feelings, assume their place as an exceptional link in the special chain of modern poetry—poems in prose—which begins with the collection by A. Bertrand, *Gaspard de la Nuit*, continues with Ch. Baudelaire's *Petits poèmes en prose*, Lautréamont's *Les Chants de Maldoror*, A. Rimbaud's *Une saison en enfer* and *Les Illuminations* and ends with the collection *Divagations* by Stephane Mallarmé. The question remains open whether Lu Hsün became acquainted with this specific European type of poetry through

---

[31]These poems were collected *in Chi wai chi* 集外集 and reprinted in the 7th volume of his *Ch'üan-chi.*

some Japanese translation or Japanese imitation, or whether he himself through his own poetic genius created a work of art which brought the highest achievements of European poetry to Chinese letters. Since we find similar examples in Lu Hsün's prose, I am inclined to the opinion that the poems in prose are his independent creation and that he succeeded in producing an original parallel to this remarkable trend in European poetry.

In Lu Hsün's poetry there are two striking features: The first is the independent development of metaphors which detach themselves from the original impulse that evoked them and begin to live their own lives governed only by the aesthetic laws of the pattern of the artistic image. Here lies the basic principle of modern European poetry and of other forms of art as well. The second characteristic then tells us much about the particular nature of contemporary Chinese literature. Although these poems in prose are very close in form to the works of the poets called the "cursed poets," *poètes maudits*, who are spoken of as decadent, the impulse for Lu Hsün to create this poetry did not stem from any morbid moods and feelings, but, on the contrary, as B. Krebsová[32] points out very convincingly, these personal confessions are proof of how Lu Hsün's thinking was dominated by one single thought: anxiety for his nation and the fight for its future. At the same time this example shows us that in Lu Hsün's case the creating of avant-garde poetry cannot be connected with any subjective escape from reality as the creation of avant-garde art is sometimes explained; contrariwise its impulse is in the need for new and exact expressions of the feelings of the revolutionary epoch. Naturally these feelings become more complicated the more difficult the fight is which awaits the modern man and the more conscious he is of the responsibility resting on his shoulders and the size of the task he must measure up to. This example proves that even in poetry the new Chinese writers could cope with the problem of expressing the new reality—in this instancce the new feelings of modern man—and master the achievements of European literature.

New Chinese drama closely follows modern European drama and this fact needs no further comment. It was only the European "spoken drama" *hua-chü* 話劇 that was able to fulfil new tasks, draw attention to social problems and in a realistic way demonstrate various aspects of life

---

[32]B. Krebsová, *Lu Sün, sa vie et son oeuvre*, Prague 1953, p. 89.

on the stage, disseminate new ideas and spur the masses to action. It is interesting to compare the most significant Chinese plays of this period with the general aspects of European drama by which they were inspired. I am of the opinion that this comparision will bring to light the fact that the most important plays of this period, the works of T'ien Han and especially those of Ts'ao Yü,[33] are marked in the first place by exceptional concentration. They try to give expression to one single climax, where all the contradictions culminate and clash in a tragic, sometimes even frightening, conflict. It appears to me that these plays are closer to the ancient tragedy, where all the component parts were a preparation for the final catastrophe and where the basic principle was a unity of time, place and action, than to the psychological plays of the closing nineteenth century, such as those of Chekhov, where the conflicts were not expressed in an open clash but took place inside the characters, the play being meant to convey a certain atmosphere. Notice how often the murderous conflicts between close relatives, brother and sister, parents and children, etc. are repeated in T'ien Han's or in Ts'ao Yü's plays. Obviously the same need to underline the general tragic mood is felt, just as it was felt by the authors of ancient tragedies about whom Aristotle speaks in his "*Poetics*": "If an enemy makes an enemy suffer he arouses no sympathy while he is in action nor while he is preparing for it; perhaps the mere fact of suffering may have an effect; it is the same if two people who mean nothing to each other act this way. But when suffering is caused among friends, if a brother kills his brother, for example, a son his father or a mother kills her son, or if they plan to kill or do anything like that, behold a story the poet should look for."

It is also necessary to note that by concentrating on one final moment new Chinese drama completely separated itself from the old Chinese opera, the pattern of which was formed by a long chain of episodes spread over long periods of time and space. Obviously the brutal struggle that was raging all over China at the time needed to be expressed in an exciting, dynamic way full of fighting pathos and tragedy. These plays are also outcries of indignation and despair like a part of contemporary poetry, as Wen I-to expressed so well in his above-quoted criticism. From this point of view Chinese drama, at the

---

[33] A dissertation on Ts'ao Yü was written in Prague by Z. Slezák. Further see the resume of the thesis by L. A. Nikol'skaja, *Dramaturgia Cao Juja, avtoreferat dissertacii,* Moskva 1961.

time, had features that correspond to the larger section of literary creation of the period and I think it is correct to use the term Chinese literary theoreticians apply to this characteristic: revolutionary realism. The author is not satisfied with mere criticism of conditions, he does not only point out the evil that is destroying society, his work is a clear battle call and, in the case of drama, this fight is shown directly on the stage. This is true of the best plays by T'ien Han and Ts'ao Yü. We shall find the same characteristics in prose.

There is one other conspicuous feature in new Chinese drama which we shall deal with while surveying works of prose. We find two distinct and varied sources for dramatic creation which we shall discover later in prose, too. On the one hand it is an effort to express a certain reality objectively—that is the method used especially by Ts'ao Yü. On the other hand drama became predominantly an expression of the personal feelings and ideas of the author, who speaks to the audience through the lips of his heroes, and the majority of the main characters in his plays are nothing more than various personifications of himself. We usually find this method in Kuo Mo-jo's plays. Yet this dramatic subjectivism—and that must be emphasized here—is not self-centered; it is not meant as an expression of any of the author's private moods and feelings but it voices the author's revolutionary thinking, it is a battle-call mobilizing the audience. It is likely that certain lyrical and, even more, some of the sentimental tones of T'ien Han's plays, pointed out by J. Häringová in her study, are an expression of this strong subjective trend in new literature. Such moods are more than understandable in the given situation. Each person had to solve the difficult problems of his day for himself and the sincerity of his solution was often put to the ultimate test: the sacrifice of his own life. On the other hand, we must note that these subjective moods often took the writers away from really important problems and led to futile analyses of personal feelings and suffering which also deepened the gap between this literature and the interests of the broad masses.

On the whole, we can say of Chinese drama of this time that it is amazing with what virtuosity the Chinese dramatists mastered the principles of the dramatic structure so that its effect was most penetrating and with what speed they created a new stage language.

There is no doubt that Chinese prose was the greatest manifestation of this epoch. It is at this time that the modern lengthy social novel appeared in China; the sketch, the essay, the diary, etc., acquired new forms, but it was the Chinese short story that reached the highest degree of perfection. Compared with previous genres, in all of these branches of belles-lettres we find a marked predilection for rigidly outlined and artistically elaborated formations which is undoubtedly, as we stated above, related to the new understanding of reality as a system of necessary processes determined by inherent laws. It is actually at this moment that the modern short story was created in China, that is, a modern prose form which grasps a single psychological situation, where all the parts are linked by one single feeling and are interwoven in a systematically connected, unbreakable entity.

Prose also discovered, in some instances, new theme fields similar to new drama: the life of the lower strata of Chinese society, especially the most important social classes, the workers and the peasants. Only at that time it was discovering methods to depict realistically the life of the petty bourgeoisie, the small businessman and the craftsman, too. It is, however, necessary to add that, at this time, the writer remained within the bounds of his own group, the intelligentsia, and therefore observed the life of other classes only as an outsider.

In prose, as in drama, we can follow two ways of approaching reality. One method strives at creating an objective image of society by applying the methods of European classical realism to Chinese literature. Its main characteristic, according to the Czech literary theoretician, Mukařovský,[34] is the striving to maintain in an epic work of art the highest degree of objective presentation: either 'material' or psychological facts are presented to the reader so that he believes he sees them directly. At most, the narrator may fulfil—it is, of course, only a deceptive pretense—the role of the lens in a camera or of an exact recording machine. These artistic methods were applied most thoroughly by Mao Tun in his works: the best examples can be found in his masterpiece *Tzu-yeh* 子夜 , "Twilight"[35] from 1931, and in a number of stories from approximately the same period. The methods of classical realism were disseminated particularly by the writers belonging to the Society for the Study of Literature.

Mao Tun's methods, which aim at the most objective expression of reality and carefully cover up every trace of the author-narrator's role in

---

[34]J. Mukařovský, *Vývoj Čapkovy prózy,* "The Development of Čapek's Prose," *Kapitoly z české poetiky,* "Chapters from Czech Poetics," Prague 1948, Vol. 2, p. 329.

[35]Shanghai, K'ai-ming shu-chü 1933.

the description, are unquestionably the greatest departure from the patterns of the old Chinese novel and story, which were always presented as the tale of a certain, concrete narrator. From this point of view the works of another realistic writer of this period, Lao She, as Z. Slupski points out in his study, represent an older stage of European realistic prose and at the same time they are closer to the traditions of the old Chinese novel than Mao Tun's works are. Lao She starts from Dickens' novel in which the author-narrator constantly intervenes in the narration in the same way as the Chinese story-tellers. Even the free pattern of the majority of his early novels reminds us of the old Chinese novel where the entire work is rather a series of independent images than a firmly bound formation. This brings out Lao She's close contact with Chinese folk art, which is further illustrated by his interest in various forms of folk literature and by the entire tone of his dramatic creation.

The origins of the second way of approaching reality are far less clear. It is possible that the first wave of European Romanticism at the turn of the nineteenth century had an influence here, for example, Goethe's *Die Leiden des jungen Werther;* further on it was the influence of Naturalsim which led to the very particular style of *watakushi-shōsetsu* (Ich-Erzählung) in Japan, which had its influence on Chinese writers, too. And finally we must not overlook the fact that the second wave of Romanticism hit European literature in the second half of the nineteenth century and especially after World War I all European prose was saturated with subjectivity and lyricism, which permeated and disintegrated all the traditional forms of epic narration. The presence of these foreign influences is quite undeniable; we can, for example, prove convincingly the influence of European Romanticism on Kuo Mo-jo and find exact parallels between the autobiographical lyrical sketches by Yü Ta-fu and the Japanese *watakushi-shōsetsu.* The reason, however, why these foreign influences found such favorable ground in Chinese literature probably lies in the explicitly lyrical and subjective character of the old higher Chinese writing in *wen-yen.*

As we said above, only the accounts of the real facts or a personal experience seemed "true" to the old Chinese men of letters and worthy of the high mission of *wen* 文 writing. Fiction was overlooked as invention or as something "empty" *hsü* 虛, not belonging to higher literature. These views still had their influence in the new period. The writer Yü Ta-fu, for example, maintained that every work was to a certain extent autobiographical. If a work is related in the third person and the writer gives too exact an account of his hero's mental states, the reader then necessarily asks how does the author know these feelings so well. He loses his illusions and that leads to a loss of literary sincerity. Therefore, Yü Ta-fu considers the diary and letter to be the most appropriate literary forms.[36] Lu Hsün was forced to reject these incorrect theories of artistic truth as some kind of factographies with—in this case— explicitly lyrical coloring.

The most distinct examples of subjective tendencies in new Chinese prose and simultaneously the closest parallel with the Romantic subjective prose of the *Die Leiden des jungen Werther* type or of A. Musset's *Confession d'un enfant du siècle* type are the subjective sketches by the two main members of the Society "Creation" Yü Ta-fu and Kuo Mo-jo. We could also call this kind of prose the author's dramatized experiences because in these sketches the author presents his mental states, dissatisfaction and pain that again and again culminated in explosions of despair, self-accusation and suicidal moods. The feature that connects them with the Japanese *watakushi-shōsetsu* is that the author paid little attention to the outer reality of his life; he concentrated on his own feelings which he described with utmost sincerity.[37] Yet he often wove lyrical descriptions of nature and scenery into his narration.

However, the reality surrounding Chinese writers pressed on them too urgently and would not permit them to concentrate only on observing the palpitations of their souls, as the Japanese writers did, and therefore they sought the road to understanding and expressing the reality around them through their personal experiences. Sometimes it was sufficient to suppress all the relations of a certain personal experience with the surrounding reality in the depiction and thus give it a certain general validity; the phenomenon became a symbol. Yü Ta-fu's story *Li ch'iu chih yeh* 立秋之夜, "A Night in Early Autumn,"[38] is a good example of this; here the aimless walk of two friends in the night becomes a symbol of the aimless crawling of the Chinese intelligentsia and perhaps the aimlessness of life itself. Much more artistic is the

---

[36]See Lu Hsün, *Tsen-mo hsieh* 怎麼寫, *Yeh chi chih yi* 夜記之一, *Ch'üan-chi*, Vol. 4, p. 15 et seq.

[37]This comparison is based on the report on *watakushi-shōsetsu* by my pupil M. Novák, which will appear in *Acta Universitatis Carolinae, Orientalia Pragensis* II, Praha 1962.

[38]A. Vlčková translated this story in the above-mentioned collection of Yü Ta-fu's works *"Intoxicating Spring Nights."* A. Vlčková also wrote a dissertation paper on Yü Ta-fu and a study in English which will soon be published.

method of complex stratification of different temporal and emotional levels in describing a particular experience; in that way an unusually complicated structure is created whereby one detail is posed against another distant in time and emotion, and at the same time an extraordinary internal homogenity of story is achieved by this blending and contrasting of details. This is one of the roads that resulted in the creation of the carefully worked out modern Chinese psychological short story.

Most likely the best example of this method is Yü Ta-fu's story *I-ko jen tsai t'u-shang* 一個人在途上, "A Lonely Man on a Journay."[39] The author Ping-Hsin 冰心 used similar methods in her stories, as M. Boušková points out in her study.

Yü Ta-fu uses the same methods in his most important works in which he describes his encounters with the Chinese proletariat, with a worker in a tobacco factory in the story *Ch'un-feng ch'en-tsui-ti wan-shang* 春風沈醉的晚上, "Intoxicating Spring Nights" and with a rickshaw man in the story *Po-tien* 薄奠, "Humble Sacrifice."[40] The deep sympathy and love with which he depicted the noble characters of these representatives of the proletariat against the background of his own poverty and despair made these stories practically symbols of the general situation in China where only the proletariat could bring salvation to all those who were suffering. This emphasis on a personal event, a personal experience as a necessary premise for the truthfulness of a literary work, which this school claimed, was of special importance for the formation of new Chinese literature; at another level and in other situations it was acclaimed during the last war and also at present. It is a conviction that the writer can give truthful expression only to the reality he has deeply experienced. This is where the demand for the re-education of the writers stems from: if he is to depict the life of the people well he must identify himself with them and above all live and work with them.

When Kuo Mo-jo, like Yü Ta-fu, tried to free himself from the somewhat monotonous chains depicting the states of his mind he chose a rather different process for the literary moulding of his experiences. Kuo Mo-jo was influenced by European Romanticism more strongly than Yü Ta-fu; therefore he gave his experiences romantic settings and tragic

---

[39] *Ta-fu ch'üan-chi* 達夫全集, Shanghai, Ch'uang-tsao-she ch'u-pan-pu 1927. This story, as well as the two following, were translated by A. Vlčková in her collection.

[40] *Ta-fu ch'üan-chi.*

perspectives. Thus, he attempted to give voice to the romantic desire for a great, strong life, which can have only one noble end, that is, a tragic death. On the other hand, Kuo Mo-jo has a strong feeling for reality, much stronger than the oversensitive and obviously sick Yü Ta-fu, and this feeling for reality is inseparably connected with his historical interests. These varied interests and moods, his interest in history, his romantic desires and his feeling for reality led to the creation of a number of works which reflected all these aspects of his personality: in some instances he worked up his personal experiences from the point of view of a historian, thus preparing material for a future historian. Here the historian and realist outweigh the Romantic, which is reflected in this kind of writing by a tendency to an objective description of reality, in a detailed picture of the period and milieu and in the small attempt at fictionalization, as M. Velingerová pointed out in her study. In other instances Kuo Mo-jo used historical material to express his own feelings and opinions; he created a number of strongly subjective historical stories in which, as he frequently does in his plays, the historical personalities became his spokesmen; they expressed his judgments and views. At the same time Kuo Mo-jo maintained the coloring of the period and he gave his descriptions bright romantic colors so that he created perfect historical pictures reminding us of similar works by European Romantics.[41]

Mao Tun's works, on one hand, and the works of Yü Ta-fu and Kuo Mo-jo on the other, represent the two extremes of Chinese prose between which the entire body of prose of the period extends nearing sometimes this pole and at other times that pole. The great popularity of the subjective approach to the story is apparent even in the works of writers striving for an objective expression of reality, in the strong activization of their characters so that all actions are seen through their eyes and perceived through their reactions until, in the end, the work is presented as a confession (for example a diary) of the main character. The activization of the characters is apparent already in the first great work by Mao Tun, in the trilogy *Shih* 蝕 "The Eclipse,"[42] and it culminates in the great novel *Fu-shih* 腐蝕, "Corruption"[43] conceived as

---

[41]These stories have been translated into Czech by B. Krebsová under the title, *Návrat Starého mistra a jiné povídky*," "The Return of the Old Master and other Stories," Praha 1961. See further her study *Lu Hsün and His Collection "Old Tales Retold*," Ar Or 29 (1961), pp. 306ff.

[42]Peking, Jen-min wen-hsüe ch'u-pan she 1954.

[43]Shanghai, Hua-hsia shu-chü 1949.

a diary of the heroine. Ting Ling, who otherwise strove for an objective depiction of reality, also used at the beginning of her career the form of the diary of the heroine.[44] On the other hand her largest novel *Sang-kan ho-shang* 桑乾河上 "On the River Sang-kan,"[45] written shortly after the war against Japan, was one of the first Chinese contributions to socialist realism and is written in a purely objective way.

It is necessary to note that the tendency to actualize the characters is very typical in contemporary European prose and this fact alone proves that the Chinese writers had mastered all the technical achievements of modern literature.

On the other hand even the writers with strong subjective inclinations like Pa Chin, as O. Král pointed out in his study of the novel *Chia*, "Family" by this writer, aimed at eliminating details of a purely individual nature and creating on the basis of autobiographical experiences a work expressing certain features typical for society of those days. The writer Yeh Shao-chün 葉紹鈞 [46] uses similar methods in his largest work, the novel *Ni Huan-chih* 倪煥之.

These various methods which we have tried to characterize here can also be found in the works of Lu Hsün which represent a synthesis and culmination of all the efforts to create new Chinese literature during that period. In Lu Hsün's works we find reflections of his most intimate feelings worked into perfect, polished form; these are the poems in prose we have discussed above. Among his works we find a whole range of different ways of writing up subjective material: from the diary, notebook, letter, sketch, memoir to the strongly subjectivized historical story the base of which is an autobiographical experience.[47] This variety of form alone shows that Lu Hsün's aim never was to express some personal experience in an unaltered form and he rejected this demand for a work of art. He regarded a personal experience as a purely artistic

---

[44] *Suo-fei nü-shih-ti jih-chi* 莎菲女士的日記, *Hsien-tai chung-kuo hsiao-shuo hsüan* 現代中國小說選 , Shanghai, Ya-hsi-ya shu-chü 1929, Vol. 1, pp. 1ff. See the book by D. Kalvodová. *Ting Ling, Deník slečny Suo-fei a jiné prózy,* "The diary of Miss Suo-fei and other prose," Praha 1955.

[45] Hsin-hua shu-tien 1949.

[46] Yeh Shao-chün is also known as Yeh Sheng-t'ao 葉聖陶; E. A. Klien has written a short report about him which has not yet been published. The book was translated into English with the title *Schoolmaster Ni Huan-chih*, Peking 1958.

[47] The connections between Lu Hsün's historical stories and his personal experiences are discussed in the above-mentioned study of B. Krebsová, *Lu Hsün's "Old Tales Retold,"* pp. 252ff.

material like any other and he worked it up freely according to the needs of his artistic aim, and never for the purpose of truthfully describing a single detail. This is convincingly shown by the confrontation of all the recollections of Lu Hsün's contemporaries on his actual life with his work because we see how freely Lu Hsün changed and treated real facts in his works and gave them an entirely new meaning, so that the connections between the individual facts and his literary works are very weak.[48] On the other hand, it is undeniable that Lu Hsün constantly returned to his experiences and memories and that they were his main source of inspiration, as he himself says in the introduction to the collection Na-han 吶喊 "Call to Arms."[49] The personal relationship to what he is telling gave his story strong emotional pathos and strengthened its effect on the reader. That is probably why Lu Hsün enjoyed using the form of personal narration (Ich-Erzählung) so much, even in those cases when it obviously was not the question of a personal story, for example in the story Shang-shih 傷逝 "Regret for the Past,"[50] etc. The use of the form of personal narration enabled him to create exceptional suspense in telling the story because we learn only what the narrator knows and he knows only part of the truth and never the whole truth. Thus a mystery is created; we feel there are other things beyond the facts we know, probably more terrible than the ones we were told. We see that Lu Hsün used a method very popular in modern prose (used by W. Faulkner, for example) and, on the other hand, one that reminds us of the old Chinese painting technique with all its white areas. Naturally this is just one of the examples of the varied methods Lu Hsün used which prove that the modern Chinese artist, by his own efforts, discovered all the artistic means that it took entire generations of European prose to arrive at through joint efforts.

---

[48]Lu Hsün expressed all that we have said here very precisely in the following words: "The happenings I described generally arose from something I had seen or heard but I never relied entirely on facts. I just took one occurrence and modified or expanded it till it expressed what I had in mind. The same was true of the models for characters—I did not pick on specific individuals. My characters were often a mixture of a mouth from Chekiang, a face from Peking and clothes from Shansi." See the above-mentioned article. Wo tsen-mo tso-ch'i hsiao-shuo lai, "How I came to write stories," Ch'üan-chi, Vol. 4, p. 394. Compare Selected Works, Vol. 3., p. 231.

[49]"However, my trouble is that I cannot forget completely, and these stories have resulted from what I have been unable to erase from my memory," Ch'üan-chi, Vol. 1, p. 3. Compare Selected Works, Vol. 1., P. 1.

[50]See collection P'ang-huang 徬徨 "Wandering," Ch'üan-chi, Vol. 2, p. 108.

If we ask for the meaning of all the new artistic methods that the new Chinese writers applied to Chinese literature it becomes clear that it is an attempt at a more exact expression of reality, of course not at an expression of the individual facts but the various laws that bind and determine all the phenomena of reality. Writers became aware of the perceptive value of a literary work—that it supplies us with knowledge of reality, of course of a specific kind—and many of them discussed this problem in their theoretical works. Therefore, e.g., Kuo Mo-jo placed this thesis at the opening of his autobiography *Jou-nien shih-tai* 幼年時 代, "My Youth"[51]: "I wrote only about how a certain society gave birth to a certain person, or you could say, how a certain person lived in a certain period."[52] Thus, he emphasized the perceptive, documentary value of his autobiographies.[53] Mao Tun often returned to this problem in his criticisms and theoretical essays; again and again he accused the young writers of not knowing reality or of being satisfied with superficial impressions. Once he blamed the young writers for sympathizing with the oppressed and poor and wanting to pour this sympathy into creation without having the slightest conception of the conditions in which these people live. He blamed another writer for the fact "that his knowledge of this special social life (the life of the railway workers and the miners) is not bad. Yet he lacks a really penetrating understanding of the facts; he cannot analyze his material and classify it properly to be able to create a broad and complete picture. He collects scattered chips which do not touch the heart of the matter and he describes them as they affect him . . . they are impressionistic fragments . . ."[54]

The basic difference, in contrast to critical and satirical works of the previous period, which we have discussed above, lies in the fact that the writer goes "to the heart of the matter," he tries to express the fundamental social problems. This is also where we see the specific features of Chinese realism of this epoch in comparison to European critical realism of the nineteenth century. If we compare the works of Mao Tun, for example, with the works of the masters of European realism (and

---

[51]Shanghai, Kuang-hua shu-chü 1933.

[52]P. 2.

[53]M. Velingerová in her study also stresses this character of Kuo Mo-jo's autobiographies.

[54]See the study by O. Král, *Mao Tunův zápas o vědecký realismus,* "Mao Tun's Quest for New Scientific Realism," *Acta Universitatis Carolinae,* Philologica Supplementum, *Contributions to the theory of socialist realism,* Praha 1960, pp. 96–97.

naturalism), E. Zola and L. N. Tolstoy[55] whom he considered his teachers, we see the main difference in the fact that Mao Tun turned from the detailed, psychological analysis of his heroes to expressing the general social connections. His above-mentioned novel, *Tzu-yeh*, "Twilight" and a collection of stories accompanying it, certainly portrayed through a carefully chosen and ingeniously constructed system of scenes the social and economic situation in China better and deeper than any scientific book. The price he paid for this was that his characters and their stories rather illustrated the general situation than created it. His heroes evidently could not change the course of events, no matter what they did. On the other hand, Mao Tun clearly showed the reader that the general situation was unbearable, that any attempt at individual escape was quite hopeless: and that only nation-wide effort could lead China out of a misery which had no parallel in history.

This tendency toward the typical and general conclusions that the author expresses through his images is, I think, the most common characteristic of the best products of Chinese literature of this epoch. Lu Hsün's art is a good illustration of this statement. It is probably certain that Lu Hsün studied the art of stirring up a certain social group and forcing various representatives of society to show their true character from the Russian writers, especially from Gogol. We can evidently trace that Lu Hsün's method, used already in his earliest story written in 1911, *Huai chiu* 懷舊, "Past,"[56] is in its conception identical to Gogol's *The Inspector-General*. A false rumor forces the representatives of society to take off their masks of Confucian virtue and loyalty and show themselves to be reckless villains and careerists. There is, however, one important difference: While Gogol laughs at his types and caricatures them Lu Hsün's portraits are full of hatred.

The difference between the two writers is even more apparent in *K'uang jen jih chi* 狂人日記, "Diary of a Madman."[57] It is very likely that Lu Hsün was inspired by Gogol's work with the same name, *Zapisky sumasšedšago*, but of what diverse results![58] Not to speak of the generally

---

[55]He speaks about these relationships in his article *Ts'ung Ku-ling tao Tung-ching* 從牯嶺到東京 *Hsiao-shuo yüeh-pao* 小說月報 XIX, 10, 1928, pp. 1138ff. For our further discussion there is no need to distinguish between classical realism and naturalism because we are not dealing here with the philosophical and scientific views of these authors but merely with their artistic methods.

[56]*Ch'üan-chi*, Vol. 7, pp. 257ff.

[57]*Ch'üan-chi*, Vol. 1, p. 9.

[58]This fact was analyzed in detail by B. Krebsová in her article *Lu Hsün's "Old Tales Retold,"* p. 303, where she lists the previous literature.

gloomier mood of Lu Hsün's story; the difference lies mainly in the fact that, in addition to a certain satirical aim, Gogol's chief interest was in the sick imagination of his hero, whereas Lu Hsün used this motif only to be able to voice a crushing denunciation of the entire old system. It is a society of cannibals which is doomed! Here we see clearly the different viewpoints of the two writers and their artistic results. Gogol was never able to break completely away from the old society although he saw its rottenness and misery well, and for that reason his works could not attain the absolute straightforwardness of Lu Hsün's works.

Undoubtedly this is the result of the entirely different class outlook of the Chinese writers we spoke of above. The European writer remained chained to his semi-feudal or bourgeois society, while the Chinese writer became the outcast of society in that era and sooner or later he had to find his way to the proletariat, if he did not want to betray himself and his mission. The Chinese critics, who say that already at this time, as far as his relationship to the landlord gentry is concerned, Lu Hsün accepted the viewpoint of the revolutionary peasants, are probably right.[59]

This departure from the traditions of the old classes and his passionate fighting spirit enabled Lu Hsün to find new artistic methods to give expression to his hatred and will to fight, methods that have no analogy in the old literature and which were explicitly modernistic even in comparison with European literature of the time. Like the European critical realists, Lu Hsün also wanted, as he himself said, to describe the unfortunate people and the suffering. In one place he says: "So my themes were usually the unfortunates in this abnormal society. My aim was to expose the disease and draw attention to it so that it might be cured."[60]

Among Lu Hsün's works we find a number of stories, especially in the second collection *P'ang-huang*, "Wandering" which depict "the unfortunates in this abnormal society." Yet his most important works have completely different tendencies. Let us look at the story *K'ung I-chi*,[61] for example! It seems to me that all the explanations saying that Lu Hsün

---

[59]This opinion was voiced by Ch'en Yung 陳 涌 in his study *Lun Lu Hsün hsiao-shuo-ti hsien-shih chu-i* 論 魯迅 小 說 的 現 實 主 義 , "The Realism of Lu Hsün's Short-Stories" in the book *Lu Hsün tso-p'in lun-chi* 魯迅 作 品 論 集, "The Collection of Essays on Lu Hsün's Work," Peking, Chung-kuo ch'ing-sien ch'u-pan-she 1956, p. 45.

[60]*Ch'üan-chi*, Vol. 4, p. 393. Compare *Selected Works*, Vol. 3, p. 230.

[61]Collection *Na-han, Ch'üan-chi*, Vol. 1, p. 20ff.

wanted to show the tragic results of the old examinations, etc.[62] are
rather doubtful. Certainly Lu Hsün's genius portrayed an unsuccessful
person with a mastery that has few parallels. Yet obviously the aim of the
story was not predominantly in this direction. It aims at something quite
different, at the licentiate who has a person cruelly crippled for a petty
crime, at the entire dark barbarian atmosphere where the poverty and
the suffering of the next man are a subject for laughter and amusement.
We obviously find the same phenomenon here as in Mao Tun's works, a
departure from the individual history and an attempt to express facts of a
general nature and give a picture of the whole social situation. The
individual history became the background text against which the writer
sharply depicted those social phenomena to which he wanted to draw
our attention. We find a similar method in a number of stories, especially
in the collection Na-han, "Call to Arms," for example in the story Yao 藥,
"Medicine"[63] and even in "The True Story of Ah Q,"[64] the story of Ah
Q himself became only the background on which the author could depict
the behavior and character of the gentry during the revolution in 1911.
This method is demonstrated quite openly in the story Shih-chung 示眾
"On the Pillory"[65] in which the story itself is completely suppressed and
the writer presents merely the description of a mob which considers it
most delightful to stare at a suffering person. Incidentally we can
mention that Lu Hsün applied here the same methods that the experi-
mentalists in form worked with after World War I, for example the
Czech writer K. Čapek.[66] What was, however, mere play for them has
full meaning and is completely justified in the general tendency of Lu
Hsün's works, because it fulfils a significant artistic and social purpose.

We could also illustrate this endeavor to express the general and
typical in Lu Hsün's characters, for example, the character of Ah Q,
where the individual portrait and history are very limited and the stress
is predominantly on general features typical of an entire specified social
group or even an entire national community. In this way Lu Hsün's

---

[62]See f. ex. the book of Dr Huang Sung-k'ang, *Lu Hsün and the New Culture Movement of Modern China*, p. 49.

[63]*Ch'üan-chi*, Vol. 1, pp. 25ff.

[64]*A Q cheng chuan*, 阿Q正傳, *Ch'üan-chi*, Vol. 1, p. 72ff.

[65]See Collection *P'ang-huang*, *Ch'üan-chi*, Vol. 2, p. 67.

[66]I am thinking of the story *Historie beze slov* "History Without Words" in the collection *Boží muka*, "The Stations of the Cross," which contains a number of Čapek's experiments with various forms of the short story.

characters acquire that special common validity which is so typical of them; they become representatives, or even symbols, of entire broad circles of society. Lu Hsün's ability to create figures of so general a character as to become symbols can be seen, for example, in the short sketch called *T'ui-pai-hsien-ti tien-tung* 頹敗線的顫動 "The Last Shiver on the Way to the Abyss"[67] in which with a few strokes Lu Hsün created a monumental figure of a mother whose pain stirs the entire universe. In any case, the ability to endow his creations with a great range of meanings so that their target and meaning keep incessantly changing, like the coloring of a rainbow, is Lu Hsün's special artistic principle.

We find the same striving for perceptive value and general validity even in works seemingly limited to a purely individual experience. Certainly the meaning of the intimate pieces by Yü Ta-fu, Kuo Mo-jo, just like the Japanese *watakushi-shōsetsu*, was not only to record the exceptional and inimitable experiences of their authors. On the contrary, I am of the opinion that the exceptional interest in works of this kind both in China and in Japan definitely did not stem from a desire to understand the emotional world of an extraordinary person, but because the readers found themselves in the pages of such records and the author expressed their own feelings. These records were the outcry of a silenced and crushed individual, similar to the poetry of the time, as Wen I-to so aptly put it in the above quoted statement. In a society in which the main task was the fight against the remnants of feudalism it was necessary to show what a person looks like in reality and what his inner life is, what his desires, needs and feelings are, in order to break the false morality and the untrue stereotyped assertions about man and his feelings that were repeated in feudal works of ethics and literature. The pictures of authors' own souls which were bruised and angry were an important part of critical realism, as were the pictures of sick individuals whom Lu Hsün depicted. Mao Tun stressed this in his discussions when he said: "New literature depicts the dark sides of society, uses analytical methods to solve problems and, in poetry, gives vent to individual feelings with the aim of rousing in the reader, feelings of social pity, sympathy and anger."[68]

---

[67] See collection *Yeh-ts'ao, Ch'üan-chi*, Vol. 2, pp. 193ff.

[68] See Shen Yen-ping 沈雁冰 (Mao Tun), *Shen-mo shih wen-hsüeh* 什麼是文學 *Chung-kuo hsin wen-hsüeh ta-hsi* 中國新文學大系, compiled by Chao Chia-pi 趙家璧, Vol. 2, pp. 153ff. The quotation appears on p. 157.

Again and again we must repeat that the rebellion of the individual against family and social limitations was one of the most important parts of the general revolution taking place in China at the time. Therefore literature disclosing the inner life of an individual played an important social role, it fulfilled a revolutionary task. As far as its importance for the creation of new literature is concerned, it is sufficient to point out that only at that time did Chinese literature try to explore the interior of the human mind and describe it exactly. From this point of view we can consider all these descriptions of mental states as important literary experiments, discovering new areas of reality.

Subjective literature, however, had one other important function. It became a direct weapon in the political and cultural struggle of that time. It was very difficult to express all the anger and indignation the writers felt toward the old society and to portray the fight against the old system in objective images, especially when writers seldom witnessed this struggle. But it was possible to express all of this directly as personal opinions, feelings, views, in the form of records, diaries, letters, personal sketches or in other strongly subjective literary forms. For this reason we find the most revolutionary expressions of Kuo Mo-jo in his notes and the same is true of various letters and articles by Yü Ta-fu. In the same way the subjective and romantic tone of Kuo Mo-jo's stories is, in the first place, an expression of his passionate desire to sacrifice his life in the great national and social fight, and this romantic desire puts the weapon in his hand. In other instances he puts his revolutionary political and philosophical ideas into the mouths of the heroes of his historical plays and stories. We must not overlook the fact that to the revolutionary-minded young individualist Lu Hsün "satanic" poetry, that is, European Romantic poetry, seemed to be the highest expression of the revolutionary spirit. All this reveals the specific social function of this subjective and Romantic literature of this period.

Lu Hsün's essays are the best example of the use of subjective literary forms as a fighting weapon and they undoubtedly have a much more militant character than his stories, so that the Chinese critics speak about Lu Hsün's essays as products of socialist realism.

On the whole we can say that Chinese literature of this epoch fulfils mainly the function of the literature of critical realism. It exposes the dark sides and diseases of the old society so that they may be cured, as it was expressed by Lu Hsün. Through an uncompromising attitude to the originators of these evils the literature indicates that the situation in

China had reached such a peak that no social compromise was possible any more and that the revolution was unavoidable. The great majority of the new writers were on the side of the broad masses of the people and began a passionate fight against their native and foreign enemies. A symptom of the fact that various contradictions in China had reached such a peak that it had come to open conflict, is that literature turned from depicting individual fates and analyzing mental states of single heroes and attempted to render this struggle and explain all its connections. It then focused its attention on the culminations of the social struggle either by depicting it directly, like Mao Tun and a number of dramatists, or the authors tried at least to reflect the general tragedy the Chinese nation lived through by emphasizing the tragic moments of human life in their works. At the same time literature became a direct weapon in this struggle. The writer attacked the enemies of the people, not only in artistic images but personally in sharp articles. In this epoch literature was changing from critical realism to socialist realism, at least in the best works.

I have tried briefly to summarize here the results of our work so far. Our work up till now has convincingly showed us the need for monograph studies on the individual authors and problems without which no attempts at books of a synthetic nature can be made. That will be the next stage of our work. Together with our colleagues in other socialist countries we shall prepare a number of monographs on various personalities and on questions connected with the new literature.

III

A Confrontation of Traditional Oriental Literature with Modern European Literature in the Context of the Chinese Literary Revolution

A particularly important subject of study for general literary history and theory is the birth of the new Asian literatures which have arisen as the result of revolutionary changes in the countries of Asia. Their common distinguishing characteristic is the manner and degree in which they measure up with contemporary European literature and draw upon European literary achievements to help them solve the problems with which these literatures are faced in their own environment. We shall not touch here upon the historical perspectives of the rebirth of Asian cultures, of which the history of the rise of these modern literatures is an essential part and, at the same time, a reflection—and this undoubtedly is one of the most significant historical processes in the history of mankind—but concentrate our thoughts directly on what the study of this process can contribute to literary history and, mainly, to literary theory. I think that the knowledge gained from such a study relates above all to two domains: on the one hand there are the questions connected with literary dynamics, that is, the investigation of what is the driving and determining force in literary development; the speed of this process and its relatively narrow time limits offer an especially favorable opportunity for ascertaining whether the main causes of changes in literature are chiefly to be sought within literature itself, that is, in the interplay of tensions between the various components of the literary structure, or whether they are more frequently attributable to extra-literary impulses, especially the relations to social reality; on the other hand a unique chance is here presented to study the character of

Published in *Archiv Orientální* 32 (1964), 365–375.

different literary complexes. In the conflict which forms the substance of the history of the birth of the new literatures stand opposed the very strongly traditional Oriental literature and the new literature which has drawn upon the experience of European literature. By comparing them we can grasp more precisely the character of each and even evaluate the importance of the individual components in these contrary structures; such an evaluation, based on the study of only a single literary complex, as, for instance, modern European literature, is often inadequate, as it fails to bring out clearly the essential qualities in which it differs from the literature of preceding ages, from the literature of antiquity and from that of medieval times. We may assume with a large degree of probability that Asian writers will select from the European literatures what is of greatest value to them in solving the problems and completing the tasks posed by the new reality, and such selective tendencies will then appear in all or the majority of Asian literatures, whereas elements which have no substantial contribution to make will appear only sporadically, or not at all. Here then certain objective criteria will arise for the evaluation of the different components of modern European literature. It would be possible to generalize and say that all the new Asian literatures will have closer affinities with European literatures—with what we call world literature—than with their own literatures of the preceding period. This fact is so evident that when—years ago—I made my first acquaintance with the new Chinese literature, I wrote that the differences between the literature of Old China and that which arose after the first World War are so deep, that it is difficult for us to realize that they are the product of one and the same nation.[1] The significance of this fact comes out the more clearly when we consider that these so widely differing worlds are separated by the amazingly short time of less than a decade. In this connection, we are fully entitled to speak of a literary revolution, as the Chinese call the period culminating in the May Fourth Movement of 1919.

Let us attempt now to define at least some of the features which characterize the birth of the new literature and differentiate it from that of the preceding period. As regards the process of the birth of a new literature, a study of the Chinese material would lead us to conclude that certain changes which it is possible to explain as the result of contact with European literature are to be found in works preceding the literary

---

[1]*Das Neue China*, 6. Jhg., 39, April 1940, p. 456.

revolution. A closer examination, however, would show that these changes in the traditional literary patterns do not in reality imply any true departure from the general character of the older literature. All such works belong, in character and substance, to the old literary complex. New works do not arise as the end-product of successive changes in the traditional structure, but all at once, as new and complete structures qualitatively different from the works of the preceding period. Here I shall cite at least two examples to clarify my thesis. The novel, *Chiu ming ch'i yüan* 九命奇寃 "A Strange Revenge for Nine Lives," by the writer Wu Wo-yao 吳沃堯, written sometime at the beginning of this century, opens with a very impressive scene describing the attack of a band of ruffians on the abode of their enemies, in the course of which nine persons were burnt to death. It would appear that the author was seeking to substitute for the earlier loosely-linked succession of episodes forming a simple chronological continuity a more complex structure in which the action is conceived as the logical outcome of the workings of the law of cause and effect. We gain the impression that here, perhaps, the example of European literature has basically influenced the whole structure of the work. But the following chapters show that this is not so. The opening episode is nothing else than the traditional prologue and in its further course the novel does not differ in any way from all earlier criminal stories. The author did no more than decorate his work with a certain compositional element borrowed from European literature—the transfer of the high-point of the story to the beginning of the work—but otherwise everything remained as before. A merely formal change left the essential character of the work unaffected. A somewhat different example is furnished in the well-known work *Lao Ts'an yu-chi* 老殘遊記, dating from the same time.[2] In this book the author, Liu O 劉鶚, presents a more or less independent psychological short novel describing the love-story and contemplative casting-off of the world by the nun, I-yün. This is, on the whole, new material for the Chinese novel, but the formal treatment remains traditional. The story is told by the nun in the first person and is inserted into the main stream of narrative presented in the traditional story-telling structure. As the nun introduces the utterances of other persons, there arises a complicated structure of quotations within quotations demonstrating a clear clash between the new tendency

---

[2]Translated into English by H. Shadick under the title, *The Travels of Lao Ts'an*, New York 1952.

and content of the story, on the one hand, and traditional form, on the other.

In contrast to this, another work also originating in the pre-revolutionary period (1911), Lu Hsün's story, *Huai-chiu* 懷舊, "The Past,"[3] has all the characteristics of a work belonging to the new literature, although unlike the two works mentioned above it is still written in the old literary language. These examples, which we could multiply at will, show that the substance of a literary revolution does not lie in some gradual change in individual elements, but in a sudden leap, when a completely new artistic structure springs into being.

This very important observation probably explains, too, the striking fact that in the course of the literary revolution in China a completely new generation of writers entered the stage. None of the authors belonging to the pre-revolutionary generation had any active part in the shaping of the new literature, though some of them were still alive. At the same time it provides an important clue to the character of the literary work. If changes in the individual elements do not necessarily imply any basic change, it is clear that what is decisive for the character of a work is what kneads all these elements into a homogeneous whole, that is, the primary organizing force, the way in which the author masters his material and shapes it to his design and purpose. A work is more than the sum of its component parts, its quality lies in the manner and purpose which these elements serve; the character of a work is, in fact, determined by its fundamental and guiding conception.

Let us try now to indicate wherein lie, in our view, the main differences between this new literature and the traditional literature. Expressed very generally, every work of art is the product of three mutually interdependent factors: the artist's personality, reality in the broadest sense of the term and the artistic tradition. It seems to us that we can best characterize the revolutionary process within which the new literature arose as a revolutionary transformation in the relations between these factors—a change in their relative importance and also, of course, in their essential quality. Thus we suggest that the first two factors have greatly increased in importance, in the new literature, whereas the third has very much diminished, besides which its character has substantially changed.

---

[3]*Lu Hsün ch'üan-chi* (6), Jen-min wen-hsüeh ch'u-pan-she, Peking 1956, Vol. 7, p. 257 et seq.

Let us now consider this last aspect of the revolutionary changes in the literature. It is surely unnecessary to elaborate on the normative character of the Chinese literary tradition. In every history of Chinese literature lengthy descriptions are to be found of the immense catalogue of rules and regulations governing especially the classical literature, of the complex canon ruling the intonation in verse, the arrangement of the rhymes, the number of syllables, as well as the length of the stanza, the distribution of poetic images, etc. Equally strict were the rules to which the structure of the dominant prose genre—the essay—had to conform, the whole being based on a scheme of eight precisely prescribed parts (hence the term "the eight-legged essay"). Finally, the written language itself was a norm, it was an exclusively book language, which had to be acquired in long years of exhausting study. The goal of study in China, which was to pass the State Examinations with credit, was in substance the acquiring of a mastery of literary norms, and for that a lifetime was not too long. It must be borne in mind, too, that not only the literary form was normalized, but also the subject-matter—as an extreme example we may cite the prescribing of themes for poetic contests, but of greater weight for the general character of literary production is the unusually small measure of individuality and originality present in Chinese poetry. Although we are dealing here almost exclusively with the strongly subjective lyric, an altogether stereotyped expression of quite general feelings everywhere predominates. Only seldom do we come across a flash of uniquely personal experience. A very interesting example of this normative tendency is furnished by popular literature, which stood somewhat apart from the interest of the literati and so was subjected to less rigorous codification. And yet, there, too, we find very characteristic proof of the strength of the literary tradition. A certain popular theme is worked up again and again in the literary form in fashion at the time. Thus we have here, on the one hand, a succession of certain literary forms (we might almost say models), and, on the other, a certain number of popular subjects rewritten to fit in with them. In these recastings, the author is not interested, as a rule, in presenting the conflict which forms the substance of the story in a new light, but only in exploiting it for the new form. It is natural that in such cases the link with reality is very weak and the scope for creative originality greatly limited.

The main aim of a literary revolution is thus the abolition of a great part of these norms, eventually their replacement by others. The traditional themes disappear completely or, if they are used, a new approach is made to them, a re-evaluation is attempted or their essential substance is presented in a new light. In addition, a small number of themes have survived offering certain possibilities for realizing the new literary intentions. Such subjects were suited to new literary tendencies and, at the same time, they had a certain emotional potential; they were popular and their new treatment was all the more interesting for the opportunity it offered of comparison with older versions. A good illustration of this is the attempt to paint a broad social fresco, a feature shared by both the old socially critical novel (Wu Ching-tzu, Li Po-yüan) and the new realistic novel (Mao Tun, Ting Ling and others). The situation is similar in the recording of personal experience, which has provided the basis for a wide range of literary forms, in the old literature as also in the new.

Above all, the revolution made a clean sweep of the old stock of literary forms. The more crystallized the form and the more categorical the adherence to it demanded, the more complete was its disappearance. In poetry, practically all the old forms have been done away with, because here norms were enforced most rigidly of all. Indeed, the revulsion against any kind of restrictions is reflected in the abundant use of free verse, where it is often very difficult to say whether any organizing principles are still present, or whether the new verse exists only as an antithesis to the old. In prose, the old essays and other related forms disappear, and similarly the old forms of narrative prose. A quite special significance in this process of the liquidation of old norms attaches not only to their disappearance from the old written language but to the fact that old styles in the vernacular, such as the old narrative style of novels and tales, too, have been pushed into the background. A new literary language is taking shape, stratified according to the different functions—social and literary—it must fulfil, and not on a normative basis.

It is noteworthy that in this general abolition of norms, only those forms survive which are free enough to allow of their being used for new aims and given a new content, such as, for instance, the diary, letter, personal notes—forms enabling authors to give spontaneous expression to their thoughts. Similarly, as far as the novel is concerned, that form has a certain attraction in which relatively free episodes may be linked up, thus allowing of the introduction of a wide range of material. On the other hand, a traditional attitude as regards literary forms may have the opposite affect, for not only a strict adherence to norms may be a retarding element, but equally negative in its influence may be an inadequately developed tradition. For instance, in the new Chinese literature, it is only with the greatest difficulty that the more complex and large-scale epic forms (for instance, the counterpart to the European nineteenth-century novel) are being evolved. Here an inadequate tradition in the artistic mastery of a complicated thematic plan on a large scale is evident.

The jettisoning of a retarding tradition is the main reason why the new literature differs so much in externals from that of the preceding period—the most striking traditional traits of literary production have disappeared and links with the past appear, if at all, more in the internal orientation and structure. It is natural that, under these circumstances, those artistic forms have the greatest attraction for writers which are least bound by norms, so that a re-evaluation of all the traditional genres takes place and a new hierarchy of genres is established. First place is given to forms which appear at least superficially to be fairly free—the short story and the novel, forms which, with certain exceptions, were traditionally excluded from classical literature. On the other hand, poetry which had a dominating position in Old China, not only in literature, but in the whole sphere of creative art, is now demoted to a subordinate place. The literary history of the first twenty years of the new Chinese literature is, above all, the history of narrative prose, and perhaps even drama has greater significance than poesy. Not till almost the end of this period does there appear in China the first great modern poet—Ai Ch'ing. It must, however, be pointed out that the literary revolution only codified a situation which had existed for a very long time, perhaps even from the end of the middle ages, at the turn of the fourteenth and fifteenth centuries. Thus we see that the literary revolution is not merely an impact from outside, but at the same time is the outcome of a tendency to resolve certain tensions existing in the organism of the literature in question. Further, it should be noted that the suppression of certain traditional norms does not mean their eradication, so much as their suspension. Thus, for instance, all the popular epic forms which were excluded from literature by the literary revolution play a strongly normative role in the literature which arose during the War, that is, in the years 1937–45. It then became apparent that these forms were a part of the aesthetic sensibility of the broad masses and that if the writer wished to make his work widely accessible and acceptable, he could not afford to disregard this broadly-based aesthetic codex. I think that it is clear from this example that the influence of the consumer may be regarded as a norm-forming factor and that certain general notions about art can at certain junctures stimulate or, on the contrary, retard, the literary development, the latter especially when there is too marked a difference between the artistic and ideological level of a literary work and the general level of the reading public. We may note, too, that even a foreign literature, serving as a model, can in its turn assume the character of a literary norm; here we shall not elaborate on this thesis as it has been adequately demonstrated by the majority of literary historians.

We shall now seek to evaluate the new significance of the other two factors operative in the sphere of literary creation. As regards reality in the broadest sense of the term, the setting aside of traditional norms greatly widens the domain of potential literary subject-matter. Indeed, the areas which were affected by a literary taboo have practically disappeared or are substantially reduced. Almost every fact of the external world, and likewise of the author's personal life, can become a fit subject for literary treatment. That is more or less self-evident and it would be wholly unnecessary to enumerate the quite new domains it has opened up for Chinese literature. Of greater significance is the fact that writers have acquired a new attitude to reality. They stress the intellectual value of literary works as a means of gaining a deeper understanding of the world and often rate it higher than the aesthetic value. It is natural that such a new attitude to reality must exercise a deep influence on literary production, and not only in respect of content—the author must have a thorough knowledge of his reality and the demand for the scientific and philosophical grasp of the relevant material is actually postulated. The mastery of a wide variety of domains of the external world or the ability to analyze the complexities of one's own psyche require, however, at the same time, a new adaptation of literary means, the search for ever new artistic methods better suited to the authors' aims. Already this unprecedented attitude to reality leads to a growing differentiation and perpetual recasting of all the artistic means and precludes any attempt to create rigid norms. This is the meaning of all modern struggles for freedom of artistic creation and the inevitability of the negation of any uniform style, as the expression of some kind of norm. But reality in the new literature acquires a new significance, too, as a criterion, as a kind of measure and evaluation of a work of art, replacing the earlier evaluation for which the yardstick was a certain traditional aesthetic norm. We do not, however, equate this evaluating relation to reality with the demand for the conformity of the artist's picture to reality. An artist is fully entitled, if he so wishes, to deform reality in his work in accordance with his artistic principles—here I stress in accordance with certain principles, but he may not distort it, falsify it or give inadequate expression to it from a lack of knowledge or artistic ability. As an example, we may cite the work of Salvador Dali, where no difference exists between the "proper," "perfect" and "truthful" rendering of the real or purely imaginative components of the picture. An example of a contrary approach to reality in the earlier art is the closing scene of one of the chapters of the novel *Lao Ts'an yu-chi*, of which we made mention above. In this scene the author describes a tremendous bang, in order to achieve the tension required at the end of the chapter by the old compositional scheme of the novel. Only at the beginning of the next chapter do we learn that somewhere in the hills an avalanche had started to descend. Such an irrelevant intrusion of an unconnected motif would be admissable in the new literature only in a grotesque sense, as the creation of a conscious antithesis to the laws of probability. Here we have a clear illustration of the inherent differences between the old literature and the new in the attitude to reality. This confrontation with reality conceived as a system subject to inherent laws is present in every artistic act, as well as its evaluation, and is the basis of all contemporary aesthetics, even where the work of art wishes consciously to deny reality and put in its place a completely subjective system of elements. The interdependence between reality and art remains, even though it may be a negative one, but any kind of traditional norm has disappeared.

All that we have said so far shows that the new art is characterized by a rich diversity of artistic methods and that, naturally, in it the artist's individuality comes prominently into the foreground, as the sole agent who determines in his own way, in the creative act, the mutual relations between the three factors of which we have spoken above. Nevertheless, the artist is not an altogether free and independent agent. Indeed, Chinese literature after the literary revolution testifies to how the artist can never seal himself off from the reality surrounding him and that this reality determines to a very considerable extent the nature of his art. Instructive for the understanding of this question is the difference between Chinese and Japanese literature. Whereas in Japanese literature various European literary trends were quickly taken up which stressed just this independence of reality and the individuality of artistic expression (actually such foreign influences may create a temporary artistic norm), in Chinese literature all artistic effort is dominated by the attitude to reality, even though the artist chooses a very individual form in which to channel it, for he was always compelled by circumstances to say something about reality and to try somehow to influence it.

And yet the new attitude to reality and the postulate of creative individuality and originality led to a widely differentiated literary production, this being perhaps the basic trait in which the new literature differs from the old.

Should we wish to indicate, at least very briefly, wherein the originality of the new literary output lies, as compared with both the old tradition and European influences, we should undoubtedly have to stress the fact that though the new Chinese production was influenced to a very significant degree by European literature of the nineteenth century—as it could not fail to be considering the natural time-lag in the operation of every literary influence—what then arose in China was certainly in its essence closer to modern European literature after the first World War than to the literature of the nineteenth century.

We can demonstrate this by means of several examples: there can be no doubt that the dominating form in nineteenth-century European literature was the widely ramified psychological novel as created by French, English, Russian and American novelists. In China, though this form was attempted, it did not mature and its place was taken by the social novel-fresco, as we noted above, somewhat reminiscent in structure of the best novels of Dos Passos. Besides certain circumstances limiting literary production (unsettled conditions and a lack of time), we must seek the main reasons for this in social requirements, on the one hand, and in the influence of tradition, on the other. The situation in China required that the writer devote all his attention to social questions and not to the problems of individual being. Here, too, the influence of literary tradition makes itself no less strongly felt. In old Chinese literature, we can observe a marked tendency to present the whole broad area of the social stage rather than give a detailed description of an individual fate.[4]

The most characteristic feature of Chinese literature after the literary revolution was the larger proportion of subjective elements. This

---

[4] I have dealt at some length with this problem in the study, *L'histoire et l'épopée en Chine et dans le monde occidental*, Diogène, No. 42, 1963, pp. 22–47.

would seem to be connected with the growing significance of the writer's personality, liberated from the fetters of tradition, which we have already referred to above; operating in the same direction, however, was the old literary tradition, as well as contemporary European literature. The new consciousness of the significance of the human personality, in sharp opposition to the old social order, which so consistently hampered all expressions of personality and individuality, led the writer to come out into the open in his work and, indeed, to make of his work a personal confession and manifesto. This tendency, moreover, was able to link up, on a new level and in a new context, with the fact that the old literature, as we pointed out above, was predominantly subjective, being often the record of personal experiences and emotions, though subjected to strict censorship and regimentation. The main literary stream in Old China was that of lyric poetry, and this predilection runs through the new literary production as well, so that subjective feeling dominates and often breaks up the epic forms. A similar wave of lyricism flooded European literature, too, after the first World War, and had the same disintegrating influence on traditional objective forms, as was particularly evident in the break-up of the form of the classical nineteenth-century novel. Taking the place of the strict epic structure is a free grouping of purely lyrical or lyrico-epic elements. In this point, there was a convergence of the old Chinese tradition with contemporary European moods. In China, this led to an investigation of the intricacies of the human psyche, not along the lines of an objective study of a wide range of human characters, but predominantly by means of intospective observation and analytical description of the author's inner life. An analogy to the recording of the stream of spontaneously generated emotions, eminently attempted by J. Joyce and his various successors, is to be found in the early works of Yü Ta-fu, Kuo Mo-jo and others. More important still is that this working up of the personal experience led to the most perfect form in the new Chinese literature—that of the psychological and also of the social short story. The psychological short story creates a complex composition by a skilful stratification of various experiences and emotions relating to different times and places; and although it embodies a number of heterogeneous elements it is yet absolutely homogenous in its spiritual atmosphere. Such are the best short stories of Yü Ta-fu. The social short story recasts some personal experience of the author, so that its facets reflect the most fundamental problems of human existence and of the social situation of the time. This is the basic creative principle of the best tales by Lu Hsün. These apparently new forms in Chinese literature have also their roots deep in the literary tradition. Common to both is the typical lyrical attitude—the perception of a certain characteristic phenomenon or situation. In the old times the poet's attention was directed for the most part toward Nature, but when the poet turned his exceptionally sensitive powers of observation to the social scene, he was able to single out a situation in which the whole essence of the conflicts of the time in question is summed up, as, for instance, in the work of the poet Tu Fu. This power of reflecting the whole cosmos in a single detail is a legacy which has been taken over from Chinese poetry by modern literature, especially in its concentrated form of the short story. I think that with this example, showing how both the native tradition and European influences share in the shaping of the new literature, but only to the extent in which they help to solve the new tasks of literature, we may close our reflections on the great historical collision of two different cultural worlds, which we call the Chinese literary revolution.

IV

Reality and Art
in Chinese Literature

A common subject of discussion in the field of Chinese literature is the relation of literature to reality, so that it might seem superfluous to return to this theme. If I nevertheless venture to do so, it is because I should like to discuss the matter from a somewhat different standpoint than has so far been usual.

It may be said that the whole history of Chinese literature from the time of the literary revolution culminating in the May Fourth Movement of 1919 up to the beginning of the war with Japan was essentially a struggle for a completely unimpeded approach to reality and for the conquest of the widest possible area of reality. Under "reality," I do not mean, of course, only "outward" reality, but take it to comprehend equally the whole region of man's spiritual life. The purpose of the revolution in literature was to jettison all the old norms and rules with which tradition bound creative art, whether in the realm of composition or of language; and even choice of theme was subject to strict censorship. A large part of the old literary production had consequently very little relation to reality, being a mere form of intellectual exercise, in contrast with a smaller body of literature, of which we shall speak later on, where the connection was, on the contrary, too close. In the light of the ideas under the banner of which the literary revolution was waged, the impression was created that the sole obstacle to the flourishing development of literary art was traditional regimentation, and that its abolition was the main condition for the thriving of literature and the arts in general.

Published in *Archiv Orientální* 32 (1964), 605–618. No Chinese characters are supplied in the original article, but the reader can easily locate most of them in other articles in this collection. — Ed.

There can be no doubt that, in its relation to reality, the new Chinese literature has made considerable strides, especially—and here, at the very beginning of my paper, I should like to stress the point—in the opening up of whole new regions of literary subject-matter. This is a generally acknowledged fact and one treated of in every work devoted to no matter what aspect of the new Chinese literature.

On the other hand, very little attention has been paid to the question of the means and methods employed by the new authors in expressing and organizing that reality. In this respect there is little to choose between literary historians and scholars—both Chinese and European—whether in dealing with the new literature in its historical development, or with individual authors and their works, on the one hand, and between literary and other theoreticians, whose task it is to set and define the aims of the new literature. In a number of my critiques, I have been obliged to express regret at how little even scholars of repute have to say about the artistic methods and creative processes of the authors who are the subject of their studies and how they sometimes express judgments which are complete misjudgments. Thus many such researches are able to give a careful and on the whole accurate portrayal of the intellectual development of their author, but of his art they have, as a rule, very little to say. Similarly, various appeals addressed to Chinese writers, insofar as they touch on the relation of their creative production to reality, usually call upon authors to make themselves thoroughly familiar with the milieu which they wish to describe. In doing so, they stress the perceptive function of literature; the writer's work is to give as accurate a picture as possible of a specific reality, of a specific social context.

This special function of literature is further emphasized by authors themselves in their views of the subject, in confirmation of which we could cite a wide variety of authors, including Mao Tun, Lu Hsün, Kuo Mo-jo, and others. On the other hand, we learn very little about how this reality should be artistically worked up and presented.

Undoubtedly, these two facts are related. Artists think too little about their work (honorable exceptions in this respect are Lu Hsün and Mao Tun) and so provide literary critics with too few points on which to base their analyses. And, on the other hand, theoreticians, whether literary or political, look upon all studies of artistic form unfavorably, seeing in them a kind of *l'art pour l'artisme*, which they feel obliged continually to warn against. It is the view of many theoreticians that it suffices to work up accurately observed reality and a good literary work will be produced, of course on condition that the author gives it a proper bias.

The fact remains, however, that hitherto sinology has done pitifully little in the way of investigating the aesthetic and theoretical views of Chinese artists. We know something of the aesthetic ideas of Lu Hsün, a little has been written about Mao Tun, there exists a study of Ch'ü Ch'iu-pai, but these are no more than fractions of the immense work performed by Chinese literary critics in supplanting old views in the realm of the theory of art. It would be of the greatest importance to publish in some European language, for instance, in German, a systematic anthology showing the development of literary views and contending trends from the beginnings of the May Fourth Movement.

This is a situation with which even we are not unfamiliar. In Europe, too, many authors decline to discuss their literary methods, regarding such questions with a certain contempt, nor is an unwarranted fear of *l'art pour l'artisme* altogether unknown among us, such as led to a distrust of the study of the artistic aspect of a work. The pre-War epoch, on the other hand, with its strongly experimental character, was marked by a particularly intensive study of the problems of artistic method.

We must not, however, overlook the existence of one basic factor operating negatively in all considerations relating to the artistic forms of modern literature. The jettisoning of traditional norms resulted in each author having, to some extent, to work out his own individual creative method, and then every new reality which the author approaches requires a modification of his method. We are thus faced with what seems to be a complete chaos of widely varying forms, which at first glance would appear to have nothing in common and which do not lend themselves to definition, description and classification. To this, too, must be attributed at least in part the reason why the old normative literary aesthetic, with its codification of literary forms and its prescribed formulas, was replaced in the period of capitalism by individualistic, impressionistic criticism, which gave a subjective interpretation and evaluation of the work under review, and insofar as it passes judgment at all, claims only a present validity, such judgments being based on subjective feeling and not on any generally recognized norms or standard of values.

Nevertheless, the question of artistic form, the question of artistic method, is no less important, and possibly much more important, in the new literature than it was in the old. It is, indeed, just this direct and unimpeded approach to reality which obliges the artist ever and again to face up to the problem of how to express and come to terms, on the artistic level, with this new reality. It was the outstanding Soviet literary theoretician V. Shklovski who, in his analysis of the great classical Russian novels, conclusively demonstrated that the creation of the modern realistic novel was, above all, a matter of the creation of a new and individual artistic structure. Perhaps even more evident is the example of the new poetry which, with its altogether new, original and highly complicated forms, and their ever new variants, has cut itself completely adrift from the old poetry.

We see now, in all our countries, how the scrapping of a dogmatic attitude in literature has called forth exceptionally lively discussion of the question of new literary forms; it is being realized that the question of how to create a work that is completely truthful is, in the first place, a question of how to create a work that is completely artistic, that is artistically adequate to the task of expressing the new reality. This has always been the question and, with this in mind, we must also evaluate the whole body of new Chinese literature. Further, it is necessary to point out that the new literary criticism is seeking to find a method whereby order may be introduced into this seeming chaos and making it possible to describe accurately the individual artistic structures, discover their basic elements and so work out a basis for their comparison and classification. It is already clear that these artistic structures are not mutually so unconnected as they seem, but that certain principles are operative in them which it is possible to define, from which it is only a step toward finding the relation between the various elements of the artistic structure and ascertaining the extent to which these structures are identical or related.

The Chinese experience would seem to prove that the attitude to reality may influence art in two different ways: this attitude is the main driving power in literature in the measure that the artist seeks new forms in which to express that reality. I would even go so far as to say that the more active the artist's approach to reality, the more he tries to make clear and win us for his view of reality, the more original will be the form of his work, on condition, of course, that he is at the same time a true artist. I think that especially the example of Lu Hsün confirms the view that the beginnings of what is called avant-garde art are manifest, above all, in this striving to express a new evaluation of the reality portrayed, to draw attention to those features which seem to the artist to be particularly significant and to pass a certain verdict on that reality. This naturally leads to a stressing of some aspects and the exclusion or minimizing of others, the relations between the constituent elements as compared with those in the traditional and "naively realistic" grasp of reality, undergo a change and may even be actually distorted, giving rise to a picture which is deformed but full of new meaning. This deformation has its artistic justification, for such a picture of reality may tell us much more about the nature of the reality described than a so-called faithful representation, where the sense is buried beneath a mass of insignificant detail. If such a distorted picture becomes a mere end in itself, in which, on the contrary, the unimportant is arbitrarily projected into the foreground at the expense of what is really important and stress is laid on relations playing only a minor role, then such art has no more value than any other intellectual toy. I have spoken of these aspects on other occasions and it would be superfluous to elaborate them now.

A too great dependence on reality, however, may act as a curb on creative activity to as great an extent as tradition. In fact, we see that in the new Chinese literature a close link with reality may be actually a part of tradition, that it is also a kind of literary manner, a cliché. Whereas in the case of Lu Hsün it may be observed to what degree he recasts even autobiographical material, giving prominence to and elaborating certain elements, suppressing others and even introducing fictional material—he himself always stressed the fact that autobiographical subject-matter in his work is subjected to the same creative formative processes as any other material—other authors cling closely to it. We see that a great part of the early prosaic work of Kuo Mo-jo and of Yü Ta-fu, remains on the whole the unworked-up record of personal experiences, and that even Lu Hsün has, alongside highly artistic short stories and other art forms, notes, extracts from a diary, presented as literature, letters, and so on. Such productions do not differ greatly from the general run of the literary output of the old literati, notes in the form of *pi-chi*, diaries, sketches of personal interest, letters and lyrical essays. The basis of all these literary products is the record of some single fact or experience, accurately observed and documented, the literary aesthetic value being as a rule limited to the art style—such works are written exclusively in the literary language—and to a certain lyrical coloring and treatment. Such lyrical treatment of autobiographical records is to be found in the works of the above-named authors: in those of Kuo Mo-jo it is usually the expression of the author's romantic moods, with Yü Ta-fu, more frequently of the author's despair. But the underlying structure is always a kind of factography, as in the whole of the old literature.

It is important to note that it is, in most cases, a mere *recording* and not a real *description* of a given reality. This is an extremely important distinction, to which it would be necessary to devote a special study. In the process of recording, the aesthetic element is, of necessity, limited to style, to linguistic expression in its narrowest sense. In description, the detailed and plastic rendering of various characteristics of the phenomenon described constitutes a new aesthetic quality. Such descriptions may even become an end in themselves, as often in the storyteller's art. In this respect, too, as we may here note, there is a difference between the production of the literati and the storyteller's verbal art.

I have already drawn attention, in my Introduction to the volume of Studies in Modern Chinese Literature, to the fact that the new literature which arose after the May Fourth Movement links up, in spite of the vigorous campaign against the production of the old literati in *wen-yen*, more often with that tradition than with the folk tradition. I think that this clinging to the fact, this unwillingness to get away from the specific, individual reality, is perhaps the most striking, and, at the same time, the most noteworthy feature of the new Chinese literature linking it with the old. Here, undoubtedly, we have confirmation of what was said above, namely, that a certain attitude to reality may itself be part of a literary tradition—and that outside the domain of aeshetics. What was always most highly valued in Chinese literary works was "truthfulness," that is, the accurate recording of facts, for which the term *shih* "fullness," "completeness," was employed, whereas fantasy was rejected, as something "empty," existing only in the imagination *hsü*   . The old literature in *wen-yen* constituted in fact an immense archive of facts, elegantly recorded, but not as a rule worked up into a higher artistic unity. It lacked, for the most part, epic character, what Goethe called *Lust zum fabulieren*, which links up, thanks to its inner dynamism, interesting facts to a higher organic whole, unifies and elaborates them in a new, artistic structure.

On the other hand, I think it would not be right to evaluate this love of fact, of truth, of reality, altogether or predominantly as a negative quality. Undoubtedly it was this respect for reality and truthfulness which prevented Chinese literature from falling into the morass of unbridled fantasy, which instilled in Chinese authors their exceptionally sober, conscientious and responsible attitude to literary production and gave to the majority of their works a high moral ethos. Not even from the moral point of view was the author permitted to deform the truth, to turn a literary work into a prostitute avid for gain and fame, as was the case with a number of other literatures. Nevertheless, it is equally true that this sobriety often kept art literature too earth-bound and prevented its full flowering in the realm of imaginative storytelling.

It seems to me that this attitude of guarded reserve toward the imaginative element in the creative process is manifest in the new literature in the clinging to individual facts, then in the lack of courage which would enable the author to cut himself free from the factual groundwork of the tale and, finally, in a certain distrust of and reserved attitude toward the purely aesthetic aspects of the literary art. I see the main influence of this tradition, however, in the excessive underlining of the perceptive, intellectual function of literature, as compared with the aesthetic function, of which we spoke above.

Yü Ta-fu, for instance, considered it incompatible with the "truth-fulness" of a literary work should the author put his thoughts and feelings into the mouth of a third person, and the undoubted reason for a certain artistic weakness in the autobiographical novel "Ni Huan-chih" (name of the hero), by Yeh Sheng-tao, is the inability of the author to cut himself loose from the chronicle of his life.

We may further add that this clinging to reality, as a sum of individual facts, makes it difficult for new authors to create typical characters and plots, and draw general conclusions from their observation of specific individuals and their behavior. In the work of Mao Tun, this reserved attitude to all purely aesthetic elements is apparent in the way in which he limits his choice of phenomena strictly to those necessary for the buildup and comprehension of the plot, and expunges from his work not only himself, his feelings and judgments, but also all elements whose function it is to evoke merely aesthetic effects such as descriptions of Nature (insofar as they do not underline the mood of certain scenes), or work on the reader's emotions.

This "intellectual" orientation, as we have called it, this liking for facts and rejection of the elements of fantasy, which acts as a check on lesser writers, may nevertheless provide a firm structural basis for a great writer who, thanks to his philosophical conceptions and to his pathos, is able to weld this accumulation of facts into a single whole, without either distorting or violating them. I would stress that for this two things are, above all, necessary: First, a certain moral pathos, which in evaluating these facts gives them a new significance and creates a homogeneous atmosphere in which all have their appropriate place. And then a certain philosophical or philosophico-scientific conception, which, instead of welding these facts through the power of pure poetic imagination, explains them and links them up in their proper sequence of cause and effect. This Mao Tun undoubtedly succeeded in doing. His novel *Tzu-yeh*, "Twilight," with its scientifically worked out system of episodes, mirroring all the essential components of contemporary Chinese society and its basic contradictions and problems, along with a group of tales dating from the same time, is probably the most exact portrayal of the social situation at the time in question, and one that, in this respect, no other writer could measure up to. In this work, Mao Tun created as true a picture of China in the 1930s, but of course with a much greater fund of scientific knowledge, as Balzac's, a century earlier, of France at the time of the July Monarchy. But what this picture gained in scientific accuracy was offset, to a certain extent, by its loss of artistic effectiveness.

As I said above, Mao Tun systematically expunged from his work purely aesthetic elements and directed all his attention to identifying and presenting all the main forces and laws determining social existence. This led to a certain schematization of the characters; his heroes do not actively shape the social situation, but for the most part merely illustrate it; here, besides the difference in artistic method, the social situation itself had a certain influence, too, the individual being a mere straw in what was one of the most terrible storms in the history of humanity.

I also said that to make a complete break with the factographic tradition of the literati and to create a truly great work of art, two things are necessary: deep emotional engagement and a scientifically founded grasp of social processes. In the case of Mao Tun, a rational command of the material and its interpretation is vouchsafed by his Marxism, which enables him to see the world as the logically necessary clash between various social forces. Nor is he lacking the great moral and emotional pathos which equally derives from his philosophical interpretation of the world. The struggle which he describes is not only a clash of blind forces, but a struggle for the highest human justice and humanity, and the works of his pen are his contribution to this struggle.

This basic combination of essential elements for this literary trend is even more clearly evident in the work of genius which stands at the beginning of this stream in Chinese literature, namely, Wu Ching-tzu's *Ju-lin wai shih*, "Unofficial Chronicle of the Literati." The intellectual tendency of the work is already apparent in the title: the author wishes to write a history, a chronicle, and not a work of entertainment.

The feature distinguishing this book from other satirical works directed against certain social groups, works which are not rare even in the older European literature, is the systematic and almost scientific accuracy with which the author portrays a wide range of types belonging to the class against which his work is aimed.

Taking as his starting-point the traditions of the storyteller's novel, to which we shall return in a different connection, the author—like Mao Tun—removes from the traditional stock of literary requisites all exclusively aesthetic appurtenances, as, for instance, traditional lyrical elements, subtle complexities of plot, appeals to human emotions such as eroticism, horror, and so on, and his style is straightforward and unadorned. Moreover, particularly noticeable is the diminished dramatic character of the plot, the muted quality of the conflicts described. In all these respects we should find direct affinities between this work and Mao Tun's novels, even to the complex system of episodes which is designed to provide the whole broad canvas on which the selected area of social reality is to be portrayed. The work of Mao Tun vibrates, however, with the gigantic struggle being waged at the time it arose and of which it is the culminating expression—and in this respect it differs from its older model.

On the other hand, however, *Ju-lin wai shih*, like the work of Mao Tun, is the fruit of deep feeling, of the author's moral indignation at the class to which he belongs. His book is not merely an objective record of certain indifferent facts, but above all accusatory material in the form of stories so selected that on the groundwork of their evidence he may pass his verdict of "Guilty" on the class here pilloried. This then is the organizing force unifying what otherwise would be a mere agglomeration of facts. But just the lack of a scientific viewpoint, which naturally Wu Ching-tzu could not have in his day, prevented him from building up with the material at his disposal that logically articulated picture of contemporary life such as is represented by the novel of Mao Tun, the linking up of the individual episodes remaining more or less mechanical and accidental.

Nevertheless we must say that, as with Mao Tun, the sharp focusing of attention on reality, combined with the striving to evaluate

that reality and pass judgment upon it, led to a re-evaluation of traditional expressive means and to the creation of a new kind of literary
genre—a very special form of the social novel, which still exists in China
today, its last important offshoot being the notable novel by Ting Ling,
from the period of post-War reconstruction of rural life.

This type of novel became very popular in China in the first years of
the present century, when this art form was favored by writers from the
ranks of the rising bourgeoisie in works criticizing the imperial bureaucracy. In imitation of *Ju-lin wai shih* arose the works of Li Po-yüan, Wu
Wo-yao, and others. But here is apparent the danger of this whole genre,
with its predominantly intellectual and, one might almost say, anti-
aesthetic tendency. The works of these authors cease to be carefully
thought-out and artistically designed structures, in which reality is,
though soberly, yet artistically recast, and become merely an amorphous
mass of carelessly and haphazardly linked-up material, a tangle of stories,
anecdotes, isolated facts and incidents, heard or read somewhere or even
invented, where all that remains of the traditional respect for fact is the
disinclination or inability to weld these facts into an artistic whole of a
higher order. Here the aversion of the literati to the creation of more
complex artistic structures, which always presumes some measure of
distortion of facts, goes hand in hand with the traditional dilettantism of
the Chinese literati, who always rated higher spontaneous, impulsive
production than a carefully thought-out work of art, based on the
mastery of certain professional methods and procedures. And so the
author allows himself to be carried away by his feelings, especially by his
moral indignation, and, without a pre-conceived plan, without detailed
study, he pens a series of pictures, as they rise associatively in his mind.
It is clear that such a method will not produce good literature, and this is
evident in the low artistic level of a great part of the works by novelists
writing at the beginning of this century. But not even modern literature
is safe from this unhealthy spontaneity. The early works of Yü Ta-fu and
of Kuo Mo-jo suffer from it and, especially, the whole œuvre of Pa Chin
and Shen Ts'ung-wen.

I said above that in the production of the literati the recording of
facts is very often accompanied by their lyrical evaluation and exploitation. The author aims at raising the facts from the common rut of
everyday reality into the realm of poesy, into the realm of aesthetic
experience. And so we might look upon that intellectualizing tendency
which gave rise to the Chinese social novel and which obliterates from its

pictures all aesthetic elements, striving only to achieve an accurate rendering of reality, as an extreme tendency, as a kind of deviation, alongside of which must naturally exist other trends of development.

It is an extreme tendency also in respect of its relation to purely epic literature, to that verbal art which has its roots in the storytelling tradition, of which we made mention above. A number of studies have been written on it and a large body of examples from it have been translated into European languages, so that it would be quite superfluous to attempt any characterization of it here. I shall only draw attention to several aspects which are basically relevant to our present subject. As the main point of difference noted above I posed, in contrast to the reservations and restrictions always present in the production of the literati, to the fear of cutting loose from the basis of fact and the terra firma of reality, Goethe's *Lust zum fabulieren*, which most aptly characterizes the storyteller's art. In the popular love of storytelling, in the free play of fantasy, the oral narrative tradition has its origins and an innate narrative sense is its essential driving force.

There can be no doubt that at the heart of this antithesis between the production of the literati and the storyteller's epic is the inherent difference between the written language of art literature, which had to be laboriously learned, for which reason it could serve only to communicate reality at second-hand, reality already expressed and formulated—in the written language we have what is substantially a system of ready-made formulas—and the living language of everyday speech, which continually adapts itself to every new reality, never remains quiescent, but is constantly undergoing change and rejuvenation.

As opposed to the static precision of the language and production of the literati, there is in the spoken language an ever-present tendency toward dynamism, deformation, exaggeration, inventiveness, liveliness of expression, and so on. This freedom, which may end in complete imaginative license, leads, in respect of the attitude to reality, to the narrative absorbing uninhibitedly ever new aspects of reality, and to an expansive tendency, not only in the sphere of fantasy, but also in the sphere of reality. Where the littérateur's inner voice constantly warned him not to use this or that fact, as being unsuitable for a serious work of art, the storyteller had no such inhibitions. We know from our own experience that in narration realities and words that are anything but aesthetic may be much more effective than those which are. Thus the storyteller's narrations were notable from the very beginning of their development for the way in which they penetrated into the broad sphere of social life, overlooked by the writers of art literature as too vulgar for their consideration, and made it the subject of their tales. This greater freedom in the choice of subject and in the range of artistic expression (the use of grotesque, caricature, etc.) gives this stream of Chinese prose the advantage over the prose of the literati. And even when the lack of restraints and the free play of the imagination in the storyteller's epic led to purely fantastic productions, where the artist moved in a purely imaginary world, as, for instance, in the novel *Hsi yu chi*, "Pilgrimage to the West," this fantasy retains as its basic matter empiric elements (as cannot be otherwise in any human creation), but altogether recast, in a different context and deformed. It is, however, just this deformation of experience, its fantastic caricature, that can often tell us more about reality than its literal reproduction. In monstrous dimensions we see traits scarcely perceptible in reality and a certain shift in the angle of observation can throw new light on a relation which we had always considered perfectly natural, but which now appears grotesque, stupid or whatever. Here the possibility is opened up of quite a new vision of the world, which no mere reproduction of facts can achieve. Such a possibility, fully exploited by the storytellers, was on the whole closed to the literature of the literati.

Yet another advantage lay in the fact that the folk artist striving to heighten the aesthetic effect of his narrative was able to experiment and introduce into his work, without any feeling of embarrassment, all or any of the artistic means available in his day, and so they created works of a synthetic character, in which epic, dramatic scenes and lyrical passages are linked up to form a single whole. In this respect, their works undoubtedly signify an important stage in the advance toward modern literary art.

One aspect of this storytellers' production, however, suffered from a certain handicap which prevented it from becoming the main expressive medium for the newer literature. Apart from its too popular character, which was an obstacle to its serving as a vehicle for the expression of a deeper, philosophical evaluation of the world—tradition had made it above all a means of entertainment for the masses. But a far more serious impediment was that every work in this literary genre was conceived as the work of a professional storyteller, in which respect this literature was true for the whole duration of its existence to its storytelling origins. The professional storyteller—formerly in fact and later at least formally—

was not the author and the author was never completely identical with him. The storyteller was merely the fictive organizer and commentator of the narrative who expressed by far not so much the author's views and feelings as rather general moral judgments and evaluations. Hence the lack in this literary genre of what is the most important thing in modern literature, namely, the direct expression of the author's feelings, the direct confrontation of the projected reality with his view of the world, the contradictions between the world of the hero or the objective world and the subjective world of the author, the expression of his personal visions and moods. Here, it seems to me, we are at the root of why only in exceptional cases the storyteller's narrative could become the vehicle of higher artistic expression, and, at the same time, we see what a synthesis was necessary in Chinese literature before a truly great modern work of literary art could arise. It was essential that the subjective, often lyrical and, at times, intellectual attitude to the world, which was proper to the production of the literati, should merge with the flexible, lively, adaptable form of traditional epic for which every aspect of reality was grist to its mill. That was the necessary premise for the new literature. This synthesis was achieved in the eighteenth century in the best works of the old Chinese novelists: In *Ju-lin wai shih* and its author, Wu Ching-tzu, the intellectual attitude came out uppermost, associated with which was a certain aversion to the imaginative elements, this combination then giving rise to an imposing work of great intellectual power, encompassing reality to a greater breadth and depth than any earlier work, but losing in the process something of the colorfulness, spontaneity and emotional vitality which was an inherent part of the storyteller's production. Alongside of this novel, there arose another work which is perhaps the happiest combination of all the elements reviewed above.

We have already noted that, in the old literature, factography was always saved from the dull uniformity of everyday reality by the insertion of lyrical passages which served to invest it with the aesthetic qualities of a work of art. It would seem that for the literati the only way to overcome the grey mass of isolated and unorganized facts of life, the only way to their artistic working-up and welding into a new and higher order of living unity, to recreating from the elements into which the world disintegrates in the process of its intellectual analysis and cataloguing a new and artistically unified image of the world, was a personal gesture, personal empiricism and experience, as providing the new force capable of organizing all the components of a work of art. The path leading, by way of personal experience, to reality, to the correlation of the outer world of isolated facts with the inner world of their absorption, is the only path to success for the Chinese artist striving to create a new art, adequate in form to the new vision of reality.

And so, somewhat later than *Ju-lin wai shih*, arose the greatest Chinese prose work, *Hung-lou meng* "Dream of the Red Chamber." In it, personal experience, the tragedy of the author's life, becomes the organizing force welding the immense quantity of facts, personal and general, into unity, so that we have in this novel the most perfect picture of Chinese feudal society as it existed shortly before its break-up. Here lyrical sensibility, which inspired the greatest works of Chinese literature, permeates the epic structure, giving to it that soaring quality, that weightlessness in which the gravitational drag of life's grey uniformity is no longer operative, possessed by only the greatest achievements of world literature. The personal character of the tragedy narrated by the writer intensifies the dramatic character of the work—it is not a tragic play presented by a cast of disinterested actors, but the heartrending cry of personal misfortune and despair. At the same time the old epic tradition made it possible for the author to give his pictures the greatest plasticity, along with monumental breadth and force. And it was just this Proteus-like freedom and adaptability of traditional epic to incorporate in his work any part of the contemporary scene and freely link up his own experiences with stories told by his relatives and friends. The ability freely to reshape facts is testified to, for instance, in the way he would take over a certain episode or story, as it actually happened, and then change it, at the request of his friends, should it, e.g., seem to them too cruel. Moreover, the stressing of the imaginatively inventive element, as opposed to the emphasis on the noetic, intellectual values more commonly associated with the production of the literati, and which is also evident in *Ju-lin wai shih*, is observable already in the introduction to this novel, the author presenting his story as a mythological fable, although we know that at least a considerable part of the story is autobiographical and many details besides are based on actual fact. The writer thus exalts the "empty" as compared with the "full," to return to the distinction made above, clearly showing his preference for the traditions of imaginative folk literature and having no use for the "truthfulness" of the literati. It is clear that he was well aware of what is necessary for the creation of a true work of art.

I think that it is very significant for Chinese literature that the greatest work of the pre-revolutionary era arose out of this linking of personal experience with the storytelling traditions. It is a pointer to where we must seek the main trend of development of the new Chinese literature and, at the same time, it helps us to understand how it is that modern Chinese literature has so quickly mastered all the achievements of contemporary European literature. In my previous studies I have repeatedly drawn attention to the high level of artistic maturity which is so notable a feature of the new Chinese literature. Nor, as I have shown above, is it an accidental phenomenon. Contemporary European literature differs from that of the nineteenth century in the exceptional stress it lays upon the author as the dominating factor in literary production. It is not a matter—to use a comparison from painting—of depicting a certain reality as anybody in my place might see it (which in any case is nonsense), but to emphasize the way in which I see it, as being different from the way anybody else has seen it before me. Personal experience, personal vision, self-confession and judgment, are held to be the only approach to reality, the only criteria of value, in the assessment of a work of art. Here Chinese literature was able in many respects to link up with the accumulated experience of its traditional literature, even though in its initial phases it often failed to realize it. Certainly the fact cannot be disputed that just as the shaping of personal experience gave rise to the greatest work in the old literature, the same is true of the new literature. Lu Hsün found his way to reality along the same path of personal experience as did the author of "Dream of the Red Chamber" and created an immortal work. The literary situation of the time and, perhaps, a certain native disposition prevented him from making full use of the traditions of the storytellers' literature, which may also explain certain limitations in his work. So far the traditions of the storytellers' literature have been exploited in the new literature in a novel and original fashion only in the work of Lao She and then in the works arising during the war in the Liberated Areas, such as the earlier works of Chao Shu-li. But even then, and especially after the Liberation, the storytelling tradition often becomes a mere mannerism, rather hindering than facilitating the adequate expression of the new reality.

I hope that my contribution may at least have thrown some light on the complex antinomy between reality and its artistic expression. A stressing of the factographical aspect of a work and even an overrating of the perceptive function of literature may prove as great an obstacle in the development of literary production as may, on the other hand, too little experience of life and knowledge of the facts of life, or a disregard for the objective laws governing reality. A proper balance between the mass of facts and their proper interpretation, evaluation and artistic presentation, can alone provide a firm foundation for realistic art. The smallest deviation in the one or other direction may spell disaster for a work of art. It is natural that every critical and historical work dealing with literature must investigate both these aspects of the literary work of art which is neither a mere documentation of reality nor an irresponsible toying with linguistic material. And our literary scholarship must prove itself equal to the task.

V

Lu Hsün's "Huai Chiu": A Precursor of Modern Chinese Literature

This is not the first occasion on which I have considered the emergence of a modern literature in China.[1] There can be no more fascinating subject in the history of Asian literatures than the profound rift separating the modern from the traditional literature and an examination of its causes and significance. Analysis of the nature of this cataclysm dividing two epochs also enables us to penetrate more deeply into the essence of the phenomena surrounding it.

My earlier considerations of this subject dealt with its more general aspects, such as the change in the role of the author in the literary process, the new attitude toward the heritage of the past, i.e., to literary tradition, and the new approach to reality found generally among the modern writers; in this paper I have taken a narrower and therefore more concrete question, the actual character of the changes in the literary structure to be observed during this process of transformation from a traditional to a modern literature. I have chosen the plot as the object of my study, in an attempt to answer the question whether it is possible to distinguish changes in the structure of the plot in the new literature compared with the traditional structure. I would emphasize that it is only the structure of the plot, and not the choice of subject, that will

Paper read at the XVII Conference of Orientalists at Ann Arbor, Michigan, 1967. Published in *Harvard Journal of Asiatic Studies* 29 (1969), 169–176.

[1] See "A Confrontation of Traditional Oriental Literature with Modern European Literature in the Context of the Chinese Literary Revolution, Literary History and Literary Criticism," *Acta of the Ninth Congress of the International Federation for Modern Languages and Literature* (New York University Press, 1965), pp. 165–176; *Studies in Modern Chinese Literature* (Berlin: Akademie Verlag, 1964), Introduction, pp. 1–43; etc.

concern us here. We shall not discuss the well-worn question of what subjects were chosen by the writers of the new epoch; I feel that analysis aiming at the very essence of the literary work can tell us most about the nature of the change that came over literature at this time and the main forces that brought it about.

I shall limit my investigation to a single modern Chinese writer, Lu Hsün, and primarily to a single work, the story "Huai-chiu" 懷舊 ("The Past"), written in the winter of 1911 and published in the periodical *Hsiao-shuo yüeh-pao* 小說月報 under the pseudonym Chou Ch'o 周⊙ (for this rare graph, see Morohashi, *Dai kanwa jiten*, No. 38947). Lu Hsün himself probably forgot that this story existed, and so it was not included in any of the collections of his stories. It was reprinted for the first time in the seventh volume of his collected works in the "Collection of Items Not Included in Any Collection" (*Chi wai chi shih-i* 集外集拾遺).[2]

This story was written eight years before the May Fourth Movement began and is thus an isolated phenomenon which cannot be explained in terms of the general tendencies of the time. This fact of uniqueness makes it a "pure," one might almost say a "clinical" case for study; it is not bound by relationships which would limit it to a certain context and force us to interpret its features in accordance with those relationships. The story is written in *wen-yen*, the traditional literary language, so that not even in this respect is it comparable with the literature produced under the influence of the May Fourth Movement. Nevertheless, as we read it we feel quite clearly that it is a work entirely of the new modern literature and not the literature of the preceding period.

I shall not discuss here the fact that although this story is purely literary, and not factual, it is cast in the form of a personal reminiscence. In the older literature this form was used only for the record of actual fact from a historical point of view; the author noted down facts which he felt might interest future historians. Here, as we shall see, we are not dealing with facts at all. We are concerned with an imaginative story, although one of a very unusual type.

The first difference between this and traditional stories lies in the structure of the plot. This is the reason for our choice, since the story is

---

[2]See *Lu Hsün ch'üan chi* 魯迅全集 (Peking: Jen-min wen-hsüeh ch'u-pan-she, 1958), VII, 257–264.

a good illustration of certain more general observations. Both the stories drawing on the old narrative traditions *(hua-pen)* and therefore written in the vernacular for a broader public, and those inspired by the *ch'uan-ch'i* of the literati of the T'ang dynasty, to which P'u Sung-ling gave new life at the turn of the seventeenth and eighteenth centuries, are based on a definite plot, the solution of which provides the end of the story. The scope of the story is thus consistent with the peripeteia of the plot. There is no need to quote examples of this, for any collection of Chinese stories offers them in abundance, for instance the *Chung-kuo tuan-pien hsiao-shuo chi* 中國短篇小說集collected by Cheng Chen-to 鄭振鐸(Shanghai: Commercial Press, 1933).

What is the plot of Lu Hsün's first literary effort? It opens with the narrator recalling an unpleasant teacher under whom he had suffered as a child and describing the bad methods of teaching used. (We shall not discuss whether the narrator and the author are to be presumed one and the same, as it is irrelevant here.) The teacher expects the boy to compose parallel couplets although he has not explained to him the principles involved and the need for the tones of the words to correspond. The boy has no idea of the differences in tone between the different words. The finishing touch to this portrait of a pedantic and unpleasant creature shows him bending his bald and very shiny head so close to the book that, dampened by his breath, the paper tears. Thus, instead of a plot we have reminiscences of childhood and the evocation of a mood.

Not until well on in this description do we meet with anything that could be called a plot. The lesson is interrupted by the local rich man, a miser no less objectionable than the teacher and stupid into the bargain, incapable of understanding even ordinary expressions. The teacher treats him with great respect, however, for when by the age of twenty-one the miser had not yet produced an heir, he bought three concubines; in the teacher's view the worst sin against filial piety is to remain without descendants.

The miser brings frightening news that the "long-haired rebels" are approaching the city. At first the teacher doubts that this can be so, since the T'ai-p'ing rebellion (of the long-haired ones) had been crushed forty years before; but when the rich man declares that he has heard the news from "the third gentleman," the teacher drops his disbelief; he respects "the third gentleman" more than the sages of old.

The rich man and the teacher take counsel how to gain the rebels' favor. In this the former is carrying on family tradition, for his father had earned the favor of the T'ai-p'ing rebels and served them as a cook; in the end he had amassed a large sum of money which had founded the family fortune. The teacher advises him to try to gain the favor of the rebels, but not too openly, because that might lead to trouble with the government troops if the rebels are defeated. The wisest thing would be to manoeuver carefully between the two extremes. Panic breaks out in the town and everyone tries to flee. A servant describes how the rich man's women got ready for flight as though it were a spring picnic, their appearance taking up most of their thoughts.

Soon the dramatic action which the rich man's news seemed to have sparked fades out. While servants are retailing horror stories from the days of the T'ai-p'ing rebellion, the terrified teacher appears, followed by the rich man, and announces that it was a false alarm and had been only a band of refugees from famine-stricken parts. They all laugh happily, the teacher goes off to soothe his terrified family, and the usual evening calm returns beneath the *t'ung* tree *(Aleurites cordata)* before the gate. The old servant Wang and Li the nurse recall tales of cruelty when the villagers fled from the T'ai-p'ing rebels and then again when they pursued them, gathering up riches in the form of silver and gold coins flung down by the rebels to delay their pursuit. It starts to rain and the gossipers go home. The boy falls asleep and dreams he is talking to the teacher, while the nurse dreams of long-haired rebels.

It is clear that the action of the plot is hardly developed at all. It is not unlikely that Lu Hsün took the idea of a false rumor sending the town into a panic and revealing the gentry in their true character from Gogol's "Inspector General." A similar theme occurs in another of Lu Hsün's stories entitled "Feng-po" 風波 ("Storm in a Teacup").[3] The idea seems to have attracted Lu Hsün constantly. If our hypothesis is correct, it is remarkable how undramatic Lu Hsün's treatment is when compared with Gogol's play. Not even the obvious explanation, that Gogol's sharp conflicts and dramatic action were called for by stage performance, suffices to justify the subdued tone of Lu Hsün's story, for there are dozens and hundreds of writers of short stories who tried to give their work the same dramatic structure as the pre-Chekov playwrights. Analysis of other stories by Lu Hsün shows that he deliberately repressed dramatic effects; we know, for example, that in the story "Pai

---

[3] Published in the collection *Na-han* 吶喊, *Lu Hsün ch'üan chi*, I, 52–60.

kuang" 白 光 ("White Glow"), also included in the collection *Na-han*, the portrait of the mad old scholar, Ch'en Shih-ch'eng 陳士成, is considerably toned down from the real-life model, the teacher Tzu-ching 子京 who lived near Lu Hsün's home.[4] It is clear that Lu Hsün's interest lay elsewhere than in the creation of exciting plots to arouse the fantasy of his readers.

Turning to the central problem of this study, we can consider Lu Hsün's approach to his plot as one of simplification, a reduction of the plot to its simplest components, and an attempt to present his subject without the framework of an explanatory story. The author wants to go right to the heart of his subject without the stepping-stone of a plot. This is what strikes me as the specifically modern feature of the new literature; I would even formulate it as a principle that it is characteristic of the new literature to play down the function of the plot, even to the point of dispensing with it altogether. I would compare it to the trend in modern painting which from the time of the Impressionists at the end of the last century has declared as its aim to "paint" and not to "illustrate episodes."

In my article "Quelques remarques sur la nouvelle littérature chinoise" in *Mélanges de sinologie offerts à M. Paul Demiéville* (Paris, 1966, pp. 208–223), I made this point in connection with Lu Hsün's story "Shih-chung" 示 眾,[5] in which the plot has completely disappeared, and the whole story is a definite and painful picture of the reality to which Lu Hsün wants to draw the reader's attention. There are a number of similar examples in the work of Lu Hsün, so that this weakening of the function of the plot can be considered one of his fundamental principles.

In this same article I quoted an exact parallel to this method in a story by the Czech writer Karel Čapek, "Story without Words," ("Povídka beze slov") from the collection *The Cross at the Crossroads (Boží muka)* (Prague, 1924). It is significant that this story comes in a volume which includes other experiments in the short story form. For a writer who devoted great attention to well-worked-out plots (the detective short story was one of Čapek's favorite forms), we can assume that suppression of the plot was a literary experiment, a symptom of new tendencies beginning to sprout in world literature. That Čapek was right in

---

[4]See Chou Hsia-shou 周遐壽 , *Lu Hsün ti ku chia* 魯迅的故家 (Peking: Jen-min wen-hsüeh ch'u-pan-she, 1957).

[5]Published in the collection *P'ang-huang* 彷徨 , *Lu Hsün ch'üan chi*, ɪɪ, 67–72.

thinking that this suppression of plot was one of the trends in modern prose is shown, too, by the fact that about the same time the Soviet literary critic V. Sklovskij devoted a whole chapter of his book *The Theory of Prose* (Czech translation by B. Mathesius, Prague, 1933) to "Literature outside the Plot." Šklovskij deals here with three books by the writer Rozanov, which he describes as a completely new genre, featuring journalistic articles broken up and inserted one into the other, snatches of autobiography, scenes from the author's own life, photographs, and so on. It could thus be said that Rozanov put all kinds of new material into his books, without attempting to fit it into the framework of a plot.

This to some extent was what Lu Hsün tried to do; he substituted sketches, reminiscences, lyrical descriptions, etc. for the traditional belletristic forms of China and Europe. These tendencies shared by the work of Lu Hsün and that of modern European prose writers could, I believe, be called the penetration of the epic by the lyric and the breaking up of the traditional epic forms.

We shall not consider here how far this tendency in the work of Lu Hsün was determined or at least stimulated by the peculiar nature of the old Chinese prose in the classical language, where prose without a plot was predominant. All we shall say is that even in his early work this Chinese writer was making use of devices that European prose did not discover until much later. From this I think it is clear enough that the emergence of a modern literature is not a gradual process involving the adaptation of various foreign elements and the gradual change of the traditional structure, but that it is fundamentally a sudden process, the emergence of a new structure under an impulse from without. This new structure need not in any way resemble the structure whence the impulse came, since the imponderabilia of personality and local tradition play a major role.

As I mentioned above, the second part of the story (and it is almost half) is taken up with what the servants recall about the T'ai-p'ing rebels. These reminiscences, although they are formally justified by the rumor of long-haired rebels approaching the town, have very little to do with the central theme of the story. We have already noted that the presentation of the story in the form of remembrance of childhood experience, and the obviously deliberate intention of *not* developing the plot, are quite novel elements; the greatest difference between this story and the traditional form of the Chinese story, however, is to be seen in this recording of insignificant conversation. In the old form of story, dialogue was an important instrument for the development of the plot and determination of the structure. Here the dialogue is quite autonomous, not even serving the purpose of more precise characterization as it does, for instance, in Wu Ching-tzu's *The Scholars*. It is simply a form of presentation of a certain atmosphere, a certain situation, or a set of human relationships, such as we frequently see in the work of such modern writers in the West as Hemingway, Joyce, or Faulkner. Fragments of conversation bring the character before us without any direct description, demonstrating relationships that could not otherwise be described, and revealing the mind of the person, his vacillations and indefinable nuances of thought, in a way straightforward description could never do. Basically it is the principal way of revealing the inner mind of the characters. This makes it all the more interesting to note that in Chinese literature it is Lu Hsün, writing in the old classical language, who sets out in this new direction, one which calls for very sensitive use of living language and the instinctive ability to hear and give expression to every tone and shade of feeling.

This leads us to another conclusion: that the fundamental requirement for the emergence of a new literature is not language, as Hu Shih believed when he declared: "My purpose . . . is simply to suggest the creation of a literature in the national language and a national language suitable for literature. Our aim in the literary revolution is merely to create in China a literature in the national language. A national language may be established only after we have produced a literature in the national language,—only after we have established a national language suitable for literature."[6] Without wishing to deny the importance of a new literary language close to and freely drawing on the colloquial language, we must admit that the fundamental requirement was not a new language, but a new writer brought up in a modern way and capable of looking at the world with modern eyes, endowed with a new and very different interest in certain aspects of reality. A revolution had first to take place in the minds of writers, and then it could find its expression in their work.

The whole atmosphere of the story we are considering here shows the affinity of Lu Hsün's work to the newest trends in European

---

[6]"On Constructive Revolution in Chinese Literature," *Hsin-ch'ing-nien* 4.4 (April 15, 1918),289–306.

literature. As we have already said, it is presented in the form of reminiscences and the mood is at moments very lyrical. This emphasis on the autobiographical, reminiscent aspect recalls the words of one of the greatest epic writers of our own times, Thomas Mann, who asks in his book *How I Wrote Doctor Faustus* (Czech translation, Prague, 1962, p. 62) whether "what we have to consider in the field of the novel is not what is no longer a novel," quoting in his support Harry Levin's comment on Joyce's *Finnegans Wake* that "the best writing of our contemporaries is not an act of creation but an act of evocation peculiarly saturated with reminiscences."[7]

Even a brief glance at Lu Hsün's work shows that Levin's judgment can be applied to the whole of his literary production beginning with "The Past." The predominantly reminiscent and lyrical character of his writing brings Lu Hsün, not into the tradition of the realists of the nineteenth century, but into that of the markedly lyrical prose writers of Europe between the two wars. This is further confirmation of our view that in Asia the new literature was a sudden growth, and that the sequence of its types and patterns in time was not the sequence of their Western models.

---

[7]Harry Levin, *James Joyce* (New Directions, 1960), p. 222.

VI

The Changing Role of the Narrator in Chinese Novels at the Beginning of the Twentieth Century

In my paper for the Ninth Congress of FILLM in New York in August 1963, I dealt in general terms with the main features of that great revolution in the history of mankind, the emergence of modern Asian literature during the last and the present centuries. This revolution was the outcome of the impact of the literature of Europe at that time on the traditional literary structures of Asia. I sketched the chief aspects of these changes in the latter structures, pointing out the change in the degree of significance attached to the personality of the author in the new literature, the weakening attachment to literary tradition and to the set of literary standards hitherto accepted, and lastly the greater awareness of reality, which led to fundamental changes in subject matter. I suggested then that "new works do not arise as the end-product of successive changes in the traditional structure, but all at once, as new and complete structures qualitatively different from the works belonging to the previous period." I made the passing suggestion that "certain changes which it is possible to explain as the result of contact with European literature are already to be found in works preceding the literary revolution," but that examination shows ". . . that these changes in the traditional literary patterns do not in reality imply any true departure from the general character of the older literature, and that all such works belong, in character and substance, to the old literature." In 1963 my observations were of a general nature, and it was not therefore possible to demonstrate them and put forward any considerable literary evidence.

Lecture given at the XI. Congress of FILLM in Pakistan in September, 1969. Published in *Archiv Orientální* 38 (1970), 169–177.

In my paper for the seventeenth Conference of Orientalists at Ann Arbor, Michigan, now appearing in the *Harvard Journal of Asiatic Studies*, I argued the thesis that new literary structures appear suddenly, as the creation of new writers with a new literary conception and gifted with a new artistic sensibility. I set out to show how as early as 1911, even before the literary revolution, Lu Hsün was writing works which were modern in every respect and in some ways even in advance of the corresponding European writing of the time.

Today I would like to approach the subject from the opposite pole, and show how changes in some elements of literary structure, even if they are sometimes the result of foreign literary influence, do not give rise to any new literary structure. Our considerations will have close bearing on the immanence of literary development in the sense that we must observe to what degree certain changes in individual elements of literary structure, and the tension caused up by them in that structure, can bring about a fundamental change in the whole structure. The material I present would appear to give a negative answer to the question, but it should not be overlooked that the Chinese writing I shall be analyzing is taken from the short period of about ten years only. Naturally fundamental changes would need a series of successive changes over a much longer space of time.

In what follows I trace the development of the function of the narrator in Chinese novels at the beginning of this century, in the conviction that changes in this function can be considered a fairly accurate pointer to changes in the literary structure as a whole, and that they have a great deal to tell us about the causes and motives of those changes. I make a distinction here between the term 'speaker,' the concrete and clearly defined person who recounts some or all of the story in a literary work, and the term 'narrator,' which is much broader. The latter is the organizing principle of the narration, which may sometimes coincide with the actual author, and at other times be no more than the indetermined and changing subject of the narration. This distinction is sufficient for what we have to consider; those interested in pursuing the subject further can refer to the extensive material in European literay theory and history.

A comparison of Chinese and, say, English literature at the beginning of modern times, and particularly in the seventeenth and eighteenth centuries, reveals a striking difference in the development of the character of the speaker. In older European literature, too, fiction was generally presented as the narration of a specific speaker; this is so in Boccaccio and in Chaucer, and it was so in the Indian narrative cycle of the Arabian Nights' Entertainment, which became known in Europe through the medium of Arab literature. In the Spanish picaresque novel of the seventeenth century, as in the English novels of adventure of the same period (Daniel Defoe), the person of the narrator, usually without individual features (Chaucer was an exception in this respect), was replaced by a speaker using the first person. The work is then conceived as the memoirs or confessions of this speaker. At the same time there are attempts to replace the simple chronological narration by an elaborate construction, drawing the reader's attention away from what is told to the manner in which it is told (Sterne). Here, at the very outset of the modern epoch, a new conception of literature appears, treating it as an art form, indeed as a deliberately artificial construction.

The eighteenth century in China was the age of the flourishing of fiction, and perhaps we shall come to the conclusion in the future that developments in Chinese fiction were more penetrating, or at least more profound in their character, than the corresponding changes in European fiction at that time. Wu Ching-tzu (1701–1754) developed a consistent and very exactly applied method in his writing, enabling him to present a broad and perspicacious view of the social class to which he belonged. He stressed the intellectual and cognitive nature of his writing, suppressing almost everything that would serve only to entertain his readers. There can be no doubt that in many ways Wu Ching-tzu came close to the methods of the nineteenth century French realists, searching purposefully for the "humble vérité" about the life of his own class, as his French fellow-writers did a hundred years later. Even more significant was the achievement of Ts'ao Hsüeh-ch'in (1715–1764), whose "Dream of the Red Chamber," *Hung-lou meng*, was an attempt to present a vast metaphor of life, based on his own and his uncle's experiences, and referring both to his own personal life and to human life in general. His combination of personal experience with a detailed objective description of the life of the time has probably no equal in the literature of the period anywhere. It is interesting to see, however, that these artistic efforts, which were made possible by the unusually high intellectual attainments of the writers concerned, opening up for literature entirely new fields of personal and social experience, fields which were not mastered in European literature until much later, were not correspondingly successful on the formal literary level. Like the whole of Chinese fiction from the twelfth century onwards both these Chinese novels were conceived in the form of a performance by an anonymous professional narrator who begins with the conventional phrase: *hua-shuo*, "There is a story. . . ." It was of course absurd to present a series of subtle portraits of scholars of the time as though it was told by a professional narrator to the crowds in a bazaar somewhere; and it was even less felicitous to present in this manner a description of the over-sensitive young members of the highest aristocracy, seen, in addition, as a symbol of the vanity and transience of human life altogether. In the former case the professional speaker should have been replaced by some form of account by an impersonal "narrator"; while the latter subject called for the form of personal confessions or reminiscences.

The fact that no such change in conception occurred in Chinese fiction proves on the one hand the strongly conservative character of Chinese literature and probably of Chinese society altogether, and on the other hand it shows the unusual strength of the creative genius of the Chinese professional storytellers, who had impressed the form of their tales on Chinese fiction so effectively that it lived on without any basic changes for seven centuries and that it took the literary revolution of 1919 to break away from it, and not even then completely.

Even the clearly political novels written at the beginning of our own century still kept to the form of a storyteller's narration, although this form was obviously already felt to be out of date; almost all these writers attempted to modernize it, changing the traditional elements and adapting it to the new conception of a literary work as they saw it. A study of these attempts allows us to trace the effect on the whole structure of a change in one element and to analyse the degree of stability of a given literary structure. The next stage provides material for the study of whether literary development is immanent, whether it is realized by the tension originating between the elements of one and the same structure, or whether a fundamental change of structure requires to be set in motion by extra-literary impulses, or at least impulses lying outside the given literary structure.

As I have already said, we shall now trace the changes which took place during the first ten years of this century, in the function of the narrator, or the speaker, in the Chinese novel. It should be noted at the outset that all the fiction of this period is markedly political; the political struggle determined the subject and the attitude of all these works. The relation of the author to the reality in which he was writing was therefore exceptionally intense. Most of the works concerned turn away from the private life of the author and of the characters in his book, to concentrate on problems vital to the whole of society. This reflects the situation in China on the eve of the gigantic revolution of which the first phase was the abolition of the old Chinese monarchy in 1911.

In the first of a series of critical social novels which date from the first decade of the twentieth century, "The Exposure of the Official World," *Kuan-ch'ang hsien-hsing chi* 官場現形記 by Li Po-yüan 李伯元 or Li Pao-chia 李寶嘉 or as is sometimes given, Li Pao-k'ai 李寶凱 (21. V. 1867–7. IV. 1906), there are very minor changes in the traditional structure as codified by Wu Ching-tzu in his *Ju-lin wai-shih*, "The Scholars." Like "The Scholars," this critical novel is presented in the form of a traditional narration, consisting of a series of rather loose episodes linked together by character A, hitherto the chief character, meeting character B, who them becomes the chief character, and so on *ad infinitum*. The same construction was used by other authors too; apart from the practical advantages of this loose construction, most of the novels of the period being published serially, it offered the writers the possibility to incorporate into their works documentary evidence concerning recent history. This idea was well expressed by Tseng P'u 曾樸, another of the leading exponents of the method. According to Tseng P'u,[1] description of the main events should be avoided; the writer should concentrate exclusively on trivial anecdotes and incidents not recorded in history, thus bringing into proper relief the background of the main events.

In the work of Li Pao-chia, however, a weakness of this method of which Wu Ching-tzu was not yet aware already becomes apparent. The traditional narrator, into whose words the story is put, played a passive role—or rather, a neutral one. He simply related a story to his audience without taking up any personal attitude towards it. Where he did express an opinion, it was usually the generally accepted view—*consensus omnium*—and not his own. This suited Wu Ching-tzu perfectly, for although he set out to be critical, his aim was an objective, calm and judicious picture of his own class, only slightly colored by irony. This was not enough for Li Po-yüan, however, writing at time of rising political passions. He needed a vehicle for his hatred of the imperial officials who provided him with his subject; he wanted to rouse his

---

[1] Tseng P'u's introduction to *Nieh hai-hua* 孽海花, January 6th 1928.

readers against the corrupt bureaucracy whose sins he was recording. He wanted to rouse public opinion in order to achieve an improvement. Thus his aim is at variance with objective approach of the narrator in the traditional novel. He loads his work with author's notes, commentaries, observations and résumés which disturb the traditional epic objectivity and conflict with the established narrative form. It is clear that Li Po-yüan required quite a different form in which to present his work, with much more scope for individuality, and a far more personal narrator. This new conception of the narrator appeared in the work of another member of this group of writers, Wu Wo-yao 吳沃堯 (1866–1910), who cast his principal work "The Events of the Last Twenty Years," *Erh-shih nien mu-tu chih kuai hsien-chuang* 二十年目睹之怪現狀, in the form of personal reminiscences recounted in the first person. It is evident, however, in this case, that the transformation of the traditional narrator into a clearly defined speaker using the first person singular and presenting all the episodes as his own experience, lived through or heard, was not a functional change. The introductory chapter tries to create the impression that the author of the episodes recounted was a man anxious to give vent to even more passionate indignation at the wickedness of the world than was the preceding author. We soon realize, nevertheless, that this is only a pose and that the author had no other aim in mind than to put together a collection of stories and anecdotes to captivate and entertain his readers. The artificial framework of a writer disgusted with the world, receiving from another equally despairing soul the manuscript of the stories which follow, strikes us as an artificial and superfluous stage setting. The persistent effort to create natural situations for one or another of the episodes strikes an equally artificial note. The author could certainly have dispensed with all these artificial settings and introductions had he really recounted his subject matter in the first person, or presented it as a series of disconnected incidents. It seems to have been impossible, however, to put such heterogeneous material in the mouth of a single narrator—the author; on the other hand the author did not aim at a series of independent tales. The writers of this period seem to have been fascinated by the idea of a "great work" in the tradition of classical novels like *Shui-chu-chuan*, "Water Margin," *Hsi-yu-chi*, "Journey to the West," and *Hung-lou meng*, "Dream of the Red Chamber," 100 to 120 chapters long. They therefore made every effort to transform the series of loosely connected episodes, which is all their novels really are, and make it a homogeneous whole.

This explains the quite non-functional framework given the whole book and the separate episodes. Wu Wo-yao was a skilful though superficial writer who was well aware of the effectiveness of various literary approaches. In his crime story "A Strange Revenge for Nine Lives," *Chiu ming ch'i yüan* 九命奇寃 for instance, he begins his narrative with the culminating episode of the story, a very impressive scene describing the attack of a band of ruffians on the abode of their enemies, in the course of which eight people were burned to death, and thus gains an imposing introduction. As I showed in my paper in New York, however, this is a typical case of a formal change in structure incapable of effecting a change in the over all conception of the work. After this brilliant opening the whole novel unfolds in the simple chronological sequence used by all earlier narratives.

Nor was Tseng P'u, mentioned above, more successful in his attempt to form a new structure for the novel. His experiment was all the more significant because he was the only writer of the first decade of our century who knew a European language—in his case French—and therefore had direct access to European literature and was not dependent upon translations, which generally distorted the original form of the work. He himself translated, for instance, Victor Hugo's "93"—but this was after he had written his own novel. We can be allowed to assume that his conception of the novel was inspired by European literature; the story of the chief characters was to be considered the main axis of the novel, onto which varied espisodes and anecdotes would be linked in order, as I mentioned earlier, to present a picture of the preceding period in its entirety. There are plenty of examples, in the literatures of Europe, of the story of one or more principal characters becoming the vehicle for the description of a whole epoch. It is enough to mention "Les Misérables" by Victor Hugo, an excellent example, for even historical episodes like the battle of Waterloo or the July revolution in Paris are given a very independent status in the structure of the novel. The way Tseng P'u linked the individual story of his heroes with historical events, however, is a perfect example of how the mechanical combination of heterogeneous material ends in artistic fiasco. The axis of Tseng P'u's novel is the romantic story of two real people, the famous scholar Hung Chün 洪鈞 and the no less famous courtesan Ts'ai-yün 彩雲 better known as Sai chin hua 賽金花 Sai-chin-hua played a certain part in the Boxer rising of 1900, becoming a popular character both in folk tales and in literature. The story of this great couple, the well-known scholar who was China's ambassador to the courts of Berlin and Petrograd, and the famous courtesan, provided the novel with an interesting and romantic subject. The author revealed stylistic skill and showed that he had learned some of the European techniques by which to express the mental state of his heroes. Unfortunately his attempt to insert into this unified and romantically conceived narrative incidents showing the struggle of different nations for freedom was an utter failure. All these episodes remain alien elements artificially tacked on to the main plot. Tseng P'u, for example, had an excellent excuse for introducing the story of the Russian revolutionary Sarah Aizenson into his narration when one of his chief characters, Count Waldersee, and his friend were preparing to attend her trial. Instead, he interrupted the story (Chapter XVI, p. 101) and began a completely fresh episode: "But we shall expose in detail the history of Sarah. Her name was Aizenson. . . ." Equally forced is the inclusion of the story of the Korean Party of Eastern Learning 東學黨 while that of the Chinese revolutionaries under Sun Yat-sen is chronologically misplaced in addition. Into what was an interesting and skilfully written romantic story of a glamorous couple the author has clumsily inserted a number of episodes that have nothing to do with the plot either in fact or in spirit. The main weakness of the book is thus the great disparity we feel between the two unharmonized elements. The romantic story of an exceptional couple, and the style used, with its archaic turns of phrase and passages of poetry, in the manner of the old "romantic tales of strange things," *ch'uan-ch'i* 傳奇, goes ill with descriptions of patriotic Japanese gangsters and fanatic Annamese "black flags." In the mind of the author the unifying element was probably his admiration for heroes of all kinds, but he did not manage to find adequate literary expression for this admiration. It is clear that in this case, too, the attempt to create a new literary structure—perhaps inspired by the social and historical novels of Europe—was not successful.

In my opinion the only writer of the time who succeeded in moulding different components into a relatively homogeneous work was the fourth of the notable names of the first decade, Liu O 劉鶚 (1857–1909). He achieved this not so much by the inner logic and causal unity of various parts of the plot, but by infusing into his work a single sensibility and giving it a unified conception, what Lev Nikolayevich Tolstoy in 1894 considered the fundamental requirement for artistic unity: "People little sensitive in matters of art often think that a work of

art forms a simple unity because in it the actions of one and the same
group of people are described, because everything pertains to one and
the same plot, or because the life of one and the same man is recounted.
That is not correct. It is the impression of a very superficial observer.
The mortar which binds a work of art into one single unity and creates
the illusion that it is a reflection of life itself, is not the unity of
characters and situations, but the unity of the specific relation between
the author's conscience and his subject." In themselves the elements
which went to make up Liu O's novel *Lao Ts'an yu-chi* 老殘遊記, "The
Travels of Lao Ts'an," are even more diverse than those in the other
novels discussed here. Around the simple description of the wanderings
of Lao Ts'an, the old type of doctor, through the hills and towns of the
province of Shantung, Liu O has gathered descriptions of an enthralling
performance by folk singers, a poetic description of the scenery of the
Clear Lake in Chi-nan-fu, the story of the cruelties perpetrated by the
regional governor, a description of the Yellow River in flood, philosophical discussions in a mysterious palace in the mountains, a lyrical scene
by moonlight on the banks of the frost-bound Yellow River, a detective
story about finding the true culprit in a case of mass poisoning and
setting the innocent suspects free, climbing the holy mountain of the
east, T'ai-shan, the love story of a nun who overcame the temptations of
the flesh, etc. The author does not even try to minimize the contrast
between these various elements; on the contrary, he stresses it, in
accordance with his view of the world as a constant conflict between
opposing elements alternating contrasting episodes. Yet as we read his
book we do not get the impression of a jumble of disparate elements, but
seem to move in an atmosphere of one single mood. This is certainly
partly due to changes in the structure of the work: the author holds to
the traditional presentation of his work as a narrator's creation, introduced by the conventional "There is a story . . ." and even at some
points follows the habit of interrupting the story to divide it into
chapters at the moment of greatest tension—occasionally artificially
worked up—but otherwise the traditional convention plays the role of an
insignificant cliché here. The intergrating function of the whole work is
given to the hero, Lao Ts'an, who is hinted at in the Prologue as
representative of the author. Not in the sense that he is identified with
the author, of course, recounting incidents from his own life; Lao Ts'an
is a novel character in his own right, with his own invented life which
differs considerably from that of the author. The creation of this link

between his character and himself, however, enabled Liu O to look at things with his own eyes, express his own views and feelings, and put his own experience into his book. The artificial barrier which exists between an author and a completely fictitious character, in novels where the hero has no connection at all with the author, has disappeared. This approach enabled Liu O to give his whole work a highly subjective atmosphere which is particularly strongly felt in the lyrical scenes, which make a far more authentic impression than those conceived as objective reports on matters outside the scope of the author's personal experience and purely artifically constructed. Considerable sections of this pre-revolutionary work are not certain but evocation, in the sense of my remarks on Lu Hsün's first writings in 1911 in the paper mentioned above. How powerful this subjective atmosphere and unity of mood is, impressing a unified character on the whole work, can best be seen in those parts where the author for reasons of his own replaces his hero by another character, without our feeling any break in the spirit of the book. Only this single sensibility and single approach enables Liu O to introduce real people into his book, adapting them to his fundamental conception, and making their stories an integral part of his work.

Of all the works of this period the "Travels of Lao Ts'an" is probably the closest to modern literature, and this is probably the reason why it was most favorably received in the West and repeatedly translated into many languages. Yet even this book is essentially a work of the old era, very different from the writings of the May Fourth Movement of 1919, when modern Chinese literature really came into being. This is all the more interesting since there was an interval of no more than seven years between Liu O's book and the work of Lu Hsün. The emergence of a new literary structure is not only a question of genius, but a new social and literary situation.

All the changes I have tried to describe in this paper were essentially formal in nature; they were to change, improve or get rid of those features in a literary structure which were felt to be unsatisfactory, and replace them with others or with a combination of others. Although these changes in literary structure took place against a background of lively political change, we cannot seek their origin outside the literary sphere. Our discussion has remained within the bounds of Chinese traditional fiction. We may ask ourselves whether these changes in the traditional literary structure would have led to its transformation and to the creation of something quite new and quite distinct. We can put our question this way: would the phenomena which emerged from the literary revolution and the imports from the West from 1918 onward have appeared even without that revolution, as the result of the immanent literary development? We cannot give an answer to this question, but the sudden appearance of new structures fully developed and perfected, emerging not as strata evolving in a different period but as works written practically in the same period but differing in a qualitative sense, would suggest that the formation of a completely new structure is probably impossible merely as an immanent development in one sphere of culture, without external impulses.

VII
Mao Tun and Yü Ta-fu

(1) Mao Tun

Mao Tun's endeavor to seize and communicate reality is characterized by his preoccupation with topical reality. Few are the number of great writers in the world whose *oeuvre* is so closely and constantly bound up with the immediate present, with important contemporary political and economic events, as is that of Mao Tun. As the subject of his narrative, Mao Tun takes for the most part events from the just receding present and molds into a work of art happenings whose first immediate impression has not yet faded from the minds of his contemporaries. Thus his first trilogy, *Shih* 蝕 or "The Eclipse," recording experiences from the Great Revolution, was written a bare few months after its bloody suppression by Chiang Kai-shek, in April 1927. The first part arose in August 1927, the second in November and December, and the third part in April to June of the following year. Mao Tun created the picture of one of the most revolutionary events in Chinese history less than a year after it was over. His greatest work, the novel *Tzŭ-yeh* 子夜 or "Twilight," depicts in a broadly conceived fresco the clash of economic and political forces in China in the spring and summer months of 1930, a work which occupied him from October 1931 to December 1932. Again between the events described and the taking in hand of the work there is an interval of little more than a year. Similarly, too, Mao Tun's third major work, *Fu-shih* 腐蝕 or "Corruption," which was

From *Three Sketches of Chinese Literature* (Prague: The Oriental Institute in Academia, 1969), 10–98.

published in 1941, describes life in Chungking in the period immediately preceding. The same is true of the majority of his short stories, which regularly deal with recent events. And even when Mao Tun writes historical tales, it is evident that it is not the past that attracts him as such, but its value as elucidating certain contemporary tendencies. The work of Mao Tun is firmly linked with the most topical events, as if he wanted to record on the instant the stormy times through which his country was passing.

This close connection in time between the rise of his works and the events described in them shows us that Mao Tun's aim is, above all, to record the immediate experience, as long as it is fresh and undimmed. To grasp reality instantly and with the utmost accuracy, before it becomes history, is the basic principle of Mao Tun's art.

I think it is necessary to give deep thought to this trait in the work of an artist so extraordinarily sensitive and so well versed in literary theory as is Mao Tun. If we find this tendency represented so strongly in just his work, we must presume it to be a striking symptom of the time, the expression of a certain necessity, which put its mark on the whole of this generation. I think that what is behind this striving to give artistic form to events that are just passing is, above all, that feeling so excellently expressed by Wen I-to in his critique of Kuo Mo-jo's *Nü-shen* 女神 or "Goddess."[1] It was the need to find outlet for the feelings and impressions of which this generation was so full and which would have driven them to madness had they not been able to give them expression. It is, indeed, cogent proof of how suggestively and overwhelmingly Chinese writers of that time were affected by reality. This is apparent especially in Mao Tun's first work, the trilogy "The Eclipse," in the feverish haste with which the work was written.

It is probable that this need to express experience at once and directly also explains why the new Chinese literature as a whole was hardly affected at all by the various fashionable Western literary trends of the time such as deeply influenced, for example, Japanese literature. The principal Western literary trends then prevailing paid special attention to the manner of presentation, stressed the role of the subject and method of narration, and pushed into the background the question of how best to seize the typical features of reality. In fact, in the attitude to

---

[1] *Wen I-to ch'üan-chi*, Shanghai 1949, Vol. III. *Shih yü p'i-p'ing* 詩與批評, p. 185, *Nü-shen chih shih-tai ching-shen*.

reality expression is often given to the uncertainty and subjectivity of all perception, to the importance of who is observing reality and on the basis of what experience and to the manner in which it is expressed. The relation between the artist-subject and the object of his creation appears to be something extremely complex and is solved by a variety of artistic methods determined by the equally varied philosophical trends professed by this or that author.

In opposition to this shifting attitude characteristic of Western literature, Mao Tun consistently upheld the view that perception, insights, are both possible and necessary, and emphasized the need for scientific preparation for the work of authorship. In an article published as early as 1922, he writes: "We must learn from the naturalist writers the need to make use in the novel of the laws revealed by science. Otherwise we shall hardly be able to avoid superficiality and shallowness of thought."[2] A deep study of old Chinese literature and of European theories made it clear to him that the weakness of the old literature lay above all in an insufficiently developed ability to depict reality objectively, and so Mao Tun strives first and foremost to achieve a strictly objective presentation of his experiences. And even though his work—as we shall see—is as much an explosive unburdening of his spirit as the work of his more subjectively inclined contemporaries, Mao Tun aims at maximum objectivity in the presentation of his materials.

Mao Tun's striving after objectivity is apparent in the painstaking care with which he excludes the author's person from the narration. There is no trace of the story's being related by anybody. The author's aim is for us to see everything, feel and experience everything directly, to eliminate any intermediary between the reader and what is described in the novel. The reader participates in the action of the story, as an eyewitness of all that goes on.

This method, employed mainly in the pre-War period of his production (of which "Twilight" is the high point and, at the same time, his greatest novel) may also be characterized as the consistent application to the Chinese novel and short story of the method of the European classical realistic novel and the novella. Our description of Mao Tun's work corresponds exactly to the description of European realistic classics as summed up by our literary scholars: "Classical prose was based on

---

[2] O. Král, *Mao Tun's Quest for New Scientific Realism*, Acta Univers. Carolinae 1960—Philologica Suppl., p. 98.

epic objectivity, strove after a preservation in the epic work of the greatest possible measure of objectivity in the presentation: facts, whether 'material' or psychological, are presented to the reader as if he actually saw them. It would seem—though it is not so—that the narrator has at most the function of *a photographic lens in a camera or of an accurately recording instrument.*"

The method employed by Mao Tun is the exact opposite of the old narrative method prevailing in the old Chinese novel and short story. We might say, too, that the narrator's role, clearly expressed and stressed in the old novel (but weakened following the appearance of the classical Chinese novel in the eighteenth century), is taken over by the modern epic first person, not bound to a single person or place, but omnipresent, omniscient and allseeing, and with a constantly shifting viewpoint.

At the same time Mao Tun's method is also the absolute reverse of the tendencies generally accepted in art literature, namely, that literature should be the propagator of a philosophy and ethical code or an expression of feeling. What Mao Tun aims at, however, is the rendering of reality and he altogether eliminates from his work the author's feelings or views, or rather, he expressed them not directly, but only through the medium of his pictures.

The third main trait in Mao Tun's writing is his remarkable powers of description, especially the gift of creating a scene charged with action and evoking the perfect illusion of reality. It is closely bound up with the two preceding characteristics: in drawing attention to the moment which, so to speak, is just passing and therefore, the main weight in artistic creation must be placed on the description of each individual scene and on the suggestive force with which the given moment is recorded. The same aim must be pursued by the artist consciously substituting for subjective narrative the creation of objective pictures and the rendering and presentation of reality.

Mao Tun carries the description to a new high point along the path on which Chinese literature entered at the beginning of the twentieth century, in the domain of the critical novel. Already in the *oeuvre* of Liu O we find exceedingly well worked up and complicated descriptions, in which the author seeks to present the most diverse aspects of reality. Liu O's descriptions are, without doubt, one of the milestones on Chinese literature's road to modern realism, to the analytical rendering of many-faceted reality. Mao Tun's work then represents the crowning of this endeavor and we may say also its surpassing. Mao Tun, in respect of the art of description, had a complete mastery of the procedures of the European classical novel, as exemplified for instance in the works of a Tolstoy, and even carries them farther. It is also an example of how amazingly rapid and telescopically contracted was the rhythm of cultural life in China at this time.

In order to demonstrate the quality of Mao Tun's descriptions, I shall first cite several characterizations of modern description in novels and then give at least one example of how Mao Tun makes use of the same literary devices. The Czech literary scholar, L. Doležel, in attempting to characterize the basic tendencies in modern prose, speaks of "the activization of inner monologue."[3] The effect of this activization of the characters is, in his view, "the subjectivization of the narrative, in the sense that it is transmitted through a certain character, is coloured by that character's participation and aspect, passes through the prism of that personality. In other words, a certain figure takes over to a certain extent the role of narrator." And so modern narration is broken down into a number of sections and "each of these sections has a different subjective coloring," the sections of the story being narrated from the point of view, and with the participation of, the various characters figuring in it." The linguistic device employed in this kind of subjectivization is "mixed speech," in which the voices, or more exactly intonations, of the various subjects are interpolated into the narrative stream. This leads to a constant intermingling of inner monologue with narration, which implies a "constant confrontation of 'outer' epic reality with the 'inner' spiritual world of the character, and it is in this confrontation that the tension is constantly charged and discharged between the character and the milieu in which it moves." "Inner monologue interwoven with narration makes it possible for the character to react instantly to epic reality." The inner monologue is as a rule expressed in semi-direct speech.[4]

This constant oscillation between the objective description of a reality, the description of the same reality, as seen by a character in the work, and then the inner monologue of the same person, is well

[3] L. Doležel, *O stylu moderní čínské prózy* (On the Style of Modern Chinese Prose), Praha 1960, p. 151.

[4] Under semi-indirect speech we understand what in French is called "styl indirect libre"; in German, "Verschleierte Rede" or "erlebte Rede." It is a form of speech which is on the borderline between narration and the spoken utterances of the characters. Grammatically it is in conformity with narrative passages, its connection with direct speech is indicated by stylistic and semantic elements.

illustrated already at the beginning of the novel "Twilight," where the drive is described of the father of the principal hero, the manufacturer Sun-fu, through Shanghai at night, after flight from the village where he lived.

Let us begin our analysis at the point where a brief sketch is first given of the life story of the father, old Mr. Wu. The story is presented in the form of an objective piece of information, but into it already signals enter from the old man's sphere of thought and expression, especially signals of a subjective, emotional evaluation.

It is stated in connection with the relation of the old man to his son that it would have been better if his son had died than for him to lead such a "wayward and rebellious life"—*li ching p'an tao* 離經叛道. This traditional phrase is at once identifiable as belonging to the vocabulary of a conservative man of letters. The stream reproducing the old man's thoughts is in confrontation with the stream of Sun-fu's thoughts, ending with a sentence in which is clearly audible a note of self-justification: "After all, this is also a son's duty." There follows a short section of objective narration expressing the old man's views. (Here already we see how in a single narration two contrasted streams of thought proceed from two participating characters, so that a kind of imaginary dialogue arises.) "The old man, however, did not believe in robbers or in any Red Army,"—and alongside this description, without any intonational or syntactical division, is set this passage in semi-direct speech: "that they could in any way harm him, an old man, who so highly esteemed the divine Wen-ch'eng and had acquired such merit through his piety! But what could he do, dependent in every movement on human help and himself unable to make the smallest step? He had no alternative but to let them carry him out of his castle, place him aboard the paddle streamer 'Yun-fei' and, finally, put him into this monster 'of which the Master never spoke'—into a car. It would seem that this accursed, half-dead body . . . was now again the reason why he could not accomplish his pious work. . . .

"But he still held in his hand the Prayer to the Highest, his talisman, and above all he had at his side his fourth daughter, Hui-fang, and his seventh son, A Hsüan. With this pair, a 'boy of gold,' and a 'girl of jade' beside him, he was not yet obliged to renounce altogether his virtuous deeds, although he had entered the 'devil's lair.'" And this inner dialogue is followed again, without any break, by objective narration: "And so the old man, having spent awhile in gathering up his spiritual forces, slowly and almost calmly and contentedly opened his eyes."

The passage that follows alternates sections recording outer reality, as seen through the old man's eyes, along with his reactions (expressed in one instance in direct speech and in the other in semi-direct speech), with sections objectively describing reality.

It at once occurs to us that here we may apply to Mao Tun's descriptions what the Soviet linguist Vinogradov wrote of the language of Tolstoy: "The author's language keeps changing its expressive coloring, as if lighting up through it the instruments of thought, perception and expression of the heroes described; thus it becomes semantically many-colored and, while preserving the syntactical unity of a single stylistic system, opens up at the same time perspectives of meaning of an unusual depth and complexity. . . . The narrative style of *War and Peace* is an agglomerate in which the author's standpoint, the author's language, mingles and clashes with the sphere of speech and thought of his characters."

This reference to the art of Tolstoy in connection with the art of Mao Tun is by no means accidental. Mao Tun himself says that as a writer he was attracted by the works of Tolstoy: "I like Zola, but I am also fond of Tolstoy. At one time I enthusiastically (though unsuccessfully, for I met with misunderstanding and opposition) propagated naturalism. But when I tried to write novels, it was Tolstoy I came closer to. . . ."[5] This shows us how the new Chinese literature arose in a context of constant comparison with the experience and achievements of the foremost European writers, especially the great novelists of the nineteenth century.

Mao Tun consistently confronts the reality described with the feelings of the characters portrayed. In illustration, I shall cite one more scene, where Sun-fu talks with his employee, T'u Wei-yü: Objective description: "But when his finger was already upon the bell, Sun-fu suddenly drew back his hand and looked at the young man." Subjectivized description: "Intelligence, composure, strength—all that was reflected in his face." Monologue in semi-direct speech: "Only get them onto the right track and these young lads would go far. Sun-fu felt that none of the clerks in his factory could hold the candle to this youth. But was he to be depended upon? These young men, the more capable, gifted and courageous they are, the more restless are the thoughts in their heads."

It should be noted in connection with this analysis of Mao Tun's

---

[5] See J. Galik, *Mao Tunove poviedky* (Mao Tun's Tales), typescript thesis, p. 14.

descriptions that the endeavor to see reality through the eyes of the person described is not wholly without analogy in old Chinese literature. I shall give an example, although a careful search would no doubt produce many more. In Ch. XIV of the novel *Ju-lin wai-shih*, or "The Scholars," the walk is described of the dry, conservative man of letters, Ma Ch'un-shang, along the margin of the famous Western Lake. First it is stressed that the scenery of the Western Lake is among the finest in the world, but then, in describing what the scholar saw, mention is made only of the unattractive country women, of the quantities of meat and various foods in the shops, of coffins bespattered with mud, and so on. The description, without a word of comment, makes it clear that the old pedant saw only single things—facts—and that the beauty of the scene had totally eluded him. The irony of the description is further under-lined by the conscientious noting of what and where the scholar ate or drank. It will be necessary to examine both the old and the new Chinese literature from this aspect in order to discover to what extent the new procedures have precedent in the old literature and, on the other hand, so as to show in what measure they became the common property of all the writers of a certain epoch.

If we stress, on the one hand, Mao Tun's striving after topicality, after recording happenings just passing, the examples of complicated descriptions which we have cited show us, on the other hand, the difference between Mao Tun's work and the method of reportage, which also registers a sequence of pictures from the immediate past, but only pictures lightly sketched in, symbolizing reality rather than accurately depicting it. As we shall show below, Mao Tun's pictures produce, thanks to their elaboration and complex build-up, a static rather than a dynamic impression, such as is the main aim of reportage. And even though Mao Tun tries to see reality in motion, from a variety of perspectives and differently subjectively colored, his method has nothing in common with Impressionism, content only to record percepts without exploring their relations.

Numerous descriptions of the inner states of persons and the frequent use of inner monologue, in short, that "activization" of the figures in a literary work of which we spoke above, show the special course which Mao Tun's description takes from outer to inner reality, to the thoughts and reflexes of the participating persons. Undoubtedly we cannot but see in this a method consciously opposed to the methods of old Chinese literature, which as a rule recorded, as noted above, merely visual and aural perceptions and did not penetrate to the spiritual states of the persons depicted. Thereby, with Mao Tun, an impression of transience is at the same time evoked, we might even say of the ephemeral character of all things, and in places the sharp line of action is weakened and obscured. Instead of a clear stream of events, instead of happenings with well-defined contours, we can discern only their shadows and reflections darkly and confusedly mirrored for a while in human consciousness, perceptions rapidly changing into feelings, judgments and moods, only to merge again into a chaos of spiritual processes and states. This method would seem to tend to weaken the epic character of the work.

The directing of attention to the inner states of the figures portrayed is a trait already clearly present in Mao Tun's first trilogy, "The Eclipse," where he gives a perfect picture of the confused and hopeless feelings of Chinese youth disillusioned by the Great Revolution. It also comes out very strongly in his last great novel of the war period, *Fu-shih* or "Corruption." There the above-described "activization" of the principal character is carried so far that the whole novel is cast as an inner monologue, the heroine of the novel communicating her experiences, recollections, thoughts and especially feelings, in diary form. The author's direct narration is confined to a brief introduction.

The circumstance that Mao Tun makes use in this novel of the form of direct narration by the principal person is not, however, any kind of retreat from the endeavor to create the most precise and objective picture of reality, that is, from realism. Mao Tun does not choose this form in order, perhaps, to bring into prominence the personal or individual manner of presentation—the formal aspect—but, on the contrary, his aim is to conjure up, with perfect fidelity, the atmosphere of the milieu he is describing. In this novel, too, Mao Tun continues to take his stand on the principles of the classical European novel, which is familiar with similar procedures, as Doležel correctly points out in the above-mentioned study: "in classical, especially realistic, prose, direct narration served above all to create the image of a narrator, clearly non-identical with the author, thereby still further strengthening the illusion of objectivity. . . ."

Nevertheless, it must be said that with this procedure, even though for quite different reasons and from a different position, namely, as the result of the activization of the character figuring in the narration, Mao Tun adopts a form which was the expression of quite a different trend in the literature of that time, namely, the tendency to express the personal experiences and feelings of the author (that is, activization of the narrator). An author striving after maximum objectivity employs a form which, as we shall see further on, was peculiar to his purely subjectively inclined contemporaries. I think we must regard it as a symptom of the time, as the expression of a general tendency toward subjectivism, as the need to express very intensive emotions. At the same time it is also a proof of the growing importance of the individual liberated from the old feudal regimentation and now devoting the closest attention to his own self. It is clear that the prevailing mood of the time leads to a preference for certain literary types. It is also necessary to note that similar trends toward subjectivization appear everywhere also in European fiction, so that there is general talk of a crisis in this literary form. It would appear that Mao Tun, sooner than others, reacted to the general trend in world literature.

On the other hand, the choice of the diary as the form of presentation is also the indication of a weakening of Mao Tun's interest in the story or plot. A diary is better suited to record impressions, experiences, is always a sequence of pictures—a form unfavorable for expressing the dynamics of a plot. Nor does it serve, despite its seeming subjectiveness, to show the continuous process of an individual's growth, but rather atomizes it, breaks it down into single experiences, impressions, percepts and feelings. And so, from Mao Tun's novel, too, we learn far more about the environment in which the heroine lives than about her personal character, in which much remains obscure and conflicting. That, however, was the real purpose of Mao Tun's novel; his aim was to give a picture of social conditions and the heroine's true function was to record, and react to, outer reality.

All that we have so far said shows that Mao Tun's interest was focused first and foremost on a certain situation, on a certain characteristic phenomenon and not on an individual happening or personal story. He depicts rather than narrates.

Confirming this basic tendency in Mao Tun's art is also the fact that a number of his books are presented as unfinished or without a conclusion. Thus the novel *Hung* 虹, or "Rainbow," as also "Twilight," remain torsos, Mao Tun himself saying of the latter that it is only "a rough outline, which failed to receive a careful working out and that his original plan was much more comprehensive. . . ." But Mao Tun's finished novels are also in the form of stories without an end. An example is the novel "Corruption," cast in the form of a diary ostensibly found by the author in an air-raid shelter and breaking off at the moment of highest tension, when only a matter of hours or minutes will decide whether the girl-author of the diary and her protégée will escape from the net of the Kuomintang secret service or whether they will be trapped in it. Equally abruptly, and with no intimation of "how it ends," are concluded all three parts of the trilogy "The Eclipse," and also the majority of Mao Tun's short stories. It is, as it were, a kind of parody of the traditional scheme of Chinese novels, when the story always breaks off at the moment of greatest tension and the reader is directed in a conventional phrase to the next chapter, where he will learn all. Only with Mao Tun there are no further chapters.

Still, it should be noted that the reader of Mao Tun's novels, whether "unfinished" or "without conclusion," does not feel them to be uncompleted in the sense of something being missing. The exceptional force of the author's descriptions, the suggestive quality of each scene, makes the reader feel as if he was present and taking part in it, as if the happening were in the true present, and so it does not even occur to him to ask "how it turned out" or what happened then. The reason must be sought in that actualization of which we have spoken, that focusing of attention on the section of the plot or happening described, or on the scene taking place which, like every moment of living experience, is complete in itself without any reference to what comes after, if anything does.

A detailed analysis of the *oeuvre* of Mao Tun shows that not only his novels as a whole have no end, but that the same is true of the greater part of the strands of which the plot is made up. The author picks up one such strand, carries it forward for a while and then, suddenly, lets the story and its heroes drop out, as if forgotten, thus leaving a loose end. This is the fate, for instance, of almost all the figures in the novel "Corruption," whether they be the victims of persecution by the Kuomintang secret service or its agents. All take the stage, become the actors in some plot, but before they finish their role the author's lens turns away and we see no more of them. The same procedure is followed in "Twilight," where one strand after another is taken up and then dropped, till suddenly the novel comes to an end: in this case, however, the main strand in the plot, the story of the industrialist Sun-fu, is carried to its conclusions, that of financial ruin on the Stock Exchange.

This method of letting the strands of the story drop before they have worked themselves out strengthens still more the impression of the transitory character of all happenings—they are like film strips carried forward to the present moment, or seemingly carelessly snapped off. . . .

And it is just this breaking-off as if by a higher power that gives us the impression that the story after all is not of any great significance, or, more precisely, that the actors in the story are handicapped by a certain weakness and impotence. They are not the contrivers of the plots in which they figure, they appear and disappear without their decisions having seemingly much effect; one cannot help thinking that matters would have taken the turn they did, even if they had done the exact opposite of what they did do. If we examine all Mao Tun's major works, from his first trilogy, "Eclipse," and follow them through "Twilight" and his outstanding trilogy of tales from village life, *Ch'un-ts'an* 春蠶 or "Spring Silkworms," *Ch'iu-shou* 秋收 or "Autumn Harvest" and *Ts'an-tung* 殘冬 or "Cruel Winter,"[6] to the novel, "Corruption," we discover that this presentation of the plot is the basic scheme and ground plan of his works; I should say that here we are at the true emotional source of the author's personality from which his whole art springs. Let us give one example: In "Twilight," one of the main strands in the plot is the social struggle in the factory of Wu Sun-fu. The women workers are asking for a raise and go on strike; the owner on the other hand makes use of every means to break the strike, for he must keep his delivery terms. He manages to end the strike by means of terror, but the Stock Exchange collapses and Wu Sun-fu, reduced to bankruptcy, closes the factory. The whole struggle was decided at a higher level—in the domain of financial speculation. But the fate of this speculation was not decided alone by the struggle of a group of industrialists fighting the financiers, but factors affecting the end result included the penetration of American capital into China, the world economic crisis, the expansion of Japanese industry, the agrarian revolution in the Chinese countryside, and others. These are the decisive forces that determine both the fate of individuals and of whole collectives; it is they who put the actors on the stage, assign to them their roles and sweep them aside when they are no longer needed. They are the true actors of the piece, and the stories which the author narrates only *illustrate*—let us note this word which will recur again and again in our further analysis—the might and

---

[6]*Mao Tun tuan-p'ien hsiao-shuo chi* 茅盾短篇小說集   , Shanghai, K'ai-ming shu-tien 1949, Vol. 1, p. 159; Vol. 2, p. 3, p. 36.

omnipotence of these forces in the background. As compared with them, the individual and his strivings are insignificant, his fate transient as the flowers of the field.

Thus it would seem that Mao Tun's *oeuvre* springs from the same roots as the tragedies of Antiquity, from the feeling of the tragedy of human life, crushed between the grindstones of fate, against which it is vain for the individual to protest or revolt. Moreover, this feeling of tragedy is raised to gigantic dimensions by the fact that it is never the fate of an individual or of a single family that is at stake, but of immense human collectives, of whole classes, and even of a whole nation. Mao Tun, as a rule, describes whole collectives, and even when he tells the story of an individual human fate we always feel that it is the person-ification of the fate of a whole group, that the situation is typical not of the one, but of the many. The story of Sun-fu in "Twilight" is the story of a whole class of Chinese industrialists, and the same is true of the women workers in his factory, of the peasants in the village of T'ung Pao, the principal hero of the "Village Trilogy," to give only a few examples. What Mao Tun depicts in his works is the fate of the hundred millions of China. Nor can there be any question that he has succeeded perfectly in bringing out, in an acutely observed and realistic picture, the features characterizing the whole of contemporary Chinese society.

We must draw special attention to this feeling for the tragic aspect of life, which was typical of the literature of the time and undoubtedly colored the outlook of the new intelligentsia. Here Mao Tun, with superlative art, expressed what a whole generation felt, and so his very first work, the trilogy "Eclipse," was an immense success and placed the barely thirty-year-old author among the most notable Chinese writers. This new tragic feeling, as we pointed out above, is what divides most sharply the new literature from the old, it is the result of "seeing through" the "daring rebel" of which Lu Hsün speaks in his sketch *Tan-tan-ti hsüeh-hen chung* 淡淡的血痕中, or "Faint Traces of Blood."[7]

It would seem, too, that this feeling for the tragedy of human existence, when men are crushed by forces often incomprehensible, or at best inadequately explained—a typical example of this non-understanding of reality is contained in Mao Tun's "Village Trilogy," where he describes the feelings of the chief character, the conservative

---

[7]*Lu Hsün ch'üan-chi*, Jen-min wen-hsüeh ch'u-pan-she, Peking 1956, p. 208.

farmer T'ung-pao—points to a certain affinity of view with the naturalistic perception of the world. The naturalist also believed that life was
determined—usually tragically—by forces far higher than the human
will, only with the difference that he believed these forces to lie in
biological determination, in heredity. For this reason their attention was
focused on individual cases, on individuals or on a family, and their
observations and insights could not be generalized, or where such
generalizations were made, as in Zola's "Earth," they are altogether wide
of the mark, for they are based on false premises.

On the contrary, Mao Tun, who from the first was a near-Marxist
and soon was politically active in the Communist Party, seeks the forces
determining the fate of the individual and also of whole collectives not in
natural determination, but in social reality. And, indeed, we can explain
the whole development of Mao Tun's art in terms of this dialectic of the
individual and social forces, and the striving after their ever more
adequate presentation. In the growing precision with which he lays in
that background, the social forces determining the course of history in
the China of that time, we can follow on the one hand the maturing of
his art and then also his political development, his striving after a
Marxist interpretation of reality.

In the trilogy "The Eclipse," these forces still form a kind of vague
background atmosphere, the feeling that everything is in dissolution, that
there is no certainty, that the traditional order and values are breaking
up, leaving behind only overwhelming chaos. What can the individual do
in this world of upheaval and overthrow, in these streams and currents,
so dark and unfathomable, which swallow up everything and carry it
away no one knows whither? Bewildered and terrified by the general
confusion and disintegration, Mao Tun's heroes, all of whom belong to
the petty bourgeois intelligentsia, try to shut out this complete debacle of
their world by plunging into some adventure—whether of love or
fighting—try to fill their days with antlike industry or seek contentment
in the narrow circle of family life. All these attempts, however, are vain,
over all surges the flood—we cannot say of revolution, but rather of
social overthrow and disintegration, which sweeps away everything in its
path. Possibly in this work, at his very beginnings, Mao Tun was nearest
to the school of naturalism, with its feeling of tragedy, crushing destiny
and uselessness of all effort. It is particularly marked in the first and
third parts of the tragedy, but traces of naturalism are present in several
brutal scenes in Part II, for instance, in the description of the end of the

revolution in a small town, in the scene of the horrible killing of women workers by hooligans, of naked women tortured by soldiers and, finally, in the apocalyptic finale, where an erotic scene is overlaid by a vision of general ruin and devastation.

Nevertheless, the second part of this trilogy, entitled *Tung-yao* 動 搖, or "Vacillation," endeavors to give a more objective view of the revolution and is, at the same time, a document of the stubborn inner struggle waged by Mao Tun for a more just evaluation of contemporary reality. There already Mao Tun shows in his analyzing of the situation in the small town that all happening is not governed by mere blind forces, but that reactionary forces and also progressive forces—the forces of the people—are at work, only the National Party at that time, the Kuomintang, to which fell the role of organizing the revolution, vacillated between these forces, now sympathizing with the people, now afraid of them, and so was unable to draw upon the support of the progressive elements and put a stop to the terrible excesses of the hooligans that were threatening even the functionaries in the Kuomintang personally. They are weaklings tossed about in a storm they have not the strength to ride out. The end is undiluted tragedy: the reactionary soldiers take the little town and a terrible slaughter ensues. This, however, somewhat undermines the force and conviction of Mao Tun's analysis. The reader asks himself whether the end would have been any different, no matter what the protagonists of the revolution had done or how they had acted. Moreover, at the very end of this volume the question is mooted: was all this necessary, was there any sense in unleashing this storm?

Like the greater part of Chinese youth, Mao Tun, too, was stunned by the terrible end to the Great Revolution, an end which filled him with pessimism, bitterness and loss of faith, and these feelings come out undisguised in what he wrote at that time. But just as the revolution could not be smashed by the use of terror and force, the tragedy they had gone through could not break the Chinese revolutionary writers, nor dull the sharpness of their perceptions with gloomy self-pity or despairing pessimism. A new positive will made itself felt in Chinese literature with the founding of the League of Leftist Writers in 1930; in Mao Tun's literary output, too, from 1929 onwards, we can follow the victorious struggle for an objective view of Chinese society, culminating in the novel "Twilight," of 1931–32, and in a number of outstanding short stories.

Mao Tun remains true in his succeeding works to the attitude of a

painter who accurately and uncompromisingly renders a truthful account
of the reality around him—or, perhaps, more apt would be the comparison with a surgeon who, with sure hand and unerring eye, performs an
autopsy on the social organism, laying bare all the diseases that are
consuming it. Mao Tun does not wish to delude the reader with the
illusion that the situation is, after all, not so bad and that the cure is
already at hand. Nor must we forget that the Kuomintang censorship
prevented writers from expressing themselves openly, and that especially
of the revolutionary movements among the people they could write only
indirectly and in hints. Mao Tun himself expressly states in the Preface
to the Czech edition of his novel "Twilight": "In order to bluff the
Kuomintang censorship, I was obliged in many cases to renounce direct
description and characterize my figures and certain phases of the plot in
an indirect way and by the method of allusions and symbols."

Already in "Twilight," however, forces are shown opposing this
flood of destruction and overthrow threatening to engulf the Chinese
people. In "Twilight," there appear upon the scene peasants in revolt,
workers on strike, and even—though obviously for censorship reasons in
somewhat distorted form—organizers of the popular struggle—
Communists. It is clear that the consciousness of these forces colors the
background of all Mao Tun's ensuing works, even though he continues to
show how people are crushed by the grindstones of economic and social
processes. Running through all of them is the basic conviction that any
individual effort to change a personal destiny is vain, that only a general
revolution can at the same time solve the problems of the individual. His
last great novel, "Corruption," shows on the one hand that it is impossible to live in an environment poisoned to the core by Kuomintang
bestiality, but on the other hand it is clear that the Kuomintang monster
is only running amok in a premonition of its own end and thereby
hastening its own imminent and inevitable destruction.

Mao Tun's striving to identify ever more precisely the forces at work
in society determines to a great extent the way in which he organizes his
materials. The main pillars of his literary art are carefully worked up
individual scenes documenting the operation and varied manifestations of
these basic social forces, or mirroring a certain social situation. They are,
as a rule, scenes packed with action, the culminating points in social
processes, when as in a storm all social tensions reach breaking point and
basic contradictions and antagonisms come to an open clash. Thus in the
novel "Twilight," such scenes are the taking of a little town not far from

Shanghai by peasants who have risen in rebellion, the struggle of strikers with yellow strikebreakers, the street demonstrations of May 20, financial speculation, the collapse of the Stock Exchange, and so on. I think that this concentration on moments of supreme tension is, in general, one of the main features characterizing Chinese literature of this epoch, the best works of which show a maximum concentration tending toward a single supreme moment, usually of tragedy. Writers evidently felt that only by trying to render the highlights of human destiny could they do justice to their time. Proof of this concentration is the fact that in Mao Tun's greatest work, "Twilight," a great number of themes, a wide variety of human characters from all kinds of social groups, an almost complete panorama of all the most important social processes in contemporary China, are brought within the limits of nineteen chapters, of which the last is actually only an epilogue. Thus in no more than eighteen frescos, of monumental dimensions and rendered with consummate art, a modern author succeeds in depicting the main outlines of what is the most revolutionary period in China's history. If we compare it with the 108 chapters of Wu Wo-yao's novel, *Strange Events of the Last Twenty Years*, with the sixty chapters of Li Po-yüan's *Exposure of the Official World*, or with the sixty chapters of the same author's *History of Modernity*, we see how a truly modern artist can create a synthesis, is able to "donner au particulier l'illusion du général," as the great French critic, Marcel Schwob, has put it. Mao Tun's short stories also repeatedly seize and record such high points of tragedy in the life of the individual or of whole groups. Thus, for instance, in the village trilogy already referred to a number of times, he depicts the collapse of the whole village economy as the result of a general economic crisis, of speculation, of drought and other contributory factors. We may say that if Mao Tun's works are always tragedies, the principal scenes in them describe that tragedy in its culminating phase. It is not surprising, therefore, that in Mao Tun's novels we rarely come across descriptions of nature, his whole attention being directed toward the working out of the social process, though there can be no doubt that Mao Tun had a perfect mastery of scenic description, had he wished to employ it.

The variety of the social milieu described in his novels is reminiscent, however, on the other hand, of the above-mentioned works of the old novels of social criticism of the school of Wu Ching-tzǔ. The authors of the end of the Manchu era also aimed at embracing the largest possible sector of reality and not at depicting the story of a single life, as Tseng

P'u explains in the Preface to his novel *Nieh hai-hua* 孽海花.[8] It would seem as if Mao Tun, at least in his most outstanding works, endeavored, too, to embrace the social reality of his time on as broad a canvas as possible. However, as we have shown above, the anecdotal type of story favored by these authors is replaced by extraordinarily careful and detailed scenes and mainly what, in them, is a mosaic and accidental agglomeration of details, with Mao Tun is an amazingly and skillfully contrived construction, in which every detail is drawn in with a penetrating knowledge of the basic social problems, so that the whole gives a deeply considered and exact picture of Chinese life. Unquestionably, the novel "Twilight" gives a more exact, fuller and more authentic picture of the problems relating to conditions in the China of the 1930s than even the most exhaustive study.

Reflected in this careful selection of facts and their buildup into an integrated work of art is clearly apparent Mao Tun's world outlook, his philosophical view. He shows that no individual effort is of any avail, that what is needed to sweep away all the terrible existing chaos is a widespread revolutionary rising and that only then will it be possible to live. His work is a perfect example of how a great literary work is of exceptional value for the insights it provides, often deeper and more comprehensive than those furnished by scientific investigation, and therein lies its revolutionary significance. Mao Tun, with his finely sieved and objectively presented facts, must convince every reader that the old order was doomed.

From the artistic point of view, it should be noted that this skillful construction of carefully elaborated episodes to form a whole evokes the impression of an immense fresco, as if the whole social processes were suddenly to freeze into immobility or a sequence of significant episodes peopled by a huge cast were to turn into a gigantic still-life. Despite the

---

[8]This Preface was published in the revised edition of the novel *Nieh hai-hua*, of 1927. In it, Tseng P'u explains that he obtained the subject of the novel and a sketch of the first 4–5 chapters from his friend, Chin T'ien-ke 金天翮, but stresses the difference between his conception and the original plan of his friend: "Only Mr. Chin's original manuscript devoted too much attention to the principal hero and described only [the life of] a celebrated courtesan and only lightly sketched in several events connected with this . . . My aim was quite different, I wanted to make [the life story] of the principal hero the thread [connecting up the plot] of the whole book and introduce into it, in an exhaustive way, the whole history of the past thirty years [and in such a way] that I would avoid [the description] of external events and concentrate on the small details and less well known happenings, in order thus to illuminate the background of great events and give greater breadth to the whole conception of the work . . ." See Ah Ying 阿英 , Preface to *Nieh-hai-hua*, Peking, Pao-wen-t'ang shu-tien, 1955, p. 2.

dynamism of the individual scenes, the general impression is static, being more a picture than a film. The method employed by Mao Tun is, in fact, synchronic rather than diachronic. And this follows from what we have repeatedly affirmed above, namely, that Mao Tun creates a scene rather than tells a story, that his attention is centered more often upon a typical situation than upon some single happening or individual fate. This is also borne out by the ease with which, as we have noted above, he lets some thread of action run to one or two episodes and then drops it.

Another indication of this relatively small interest in the individual and his inner development is a certain vagueness or even contradictoriness in the characters which stand at the seams of social tension. For whereas Mao Tun sharply contours the antagonistic forces in the social context and equally sharply draws in the protagonists on either side of the front—the capitalists, speculators, blacklegs on the one side, and rebel peasants, strikers, and others on the opposite side—those figures occupying a position where the fronts merge or belonging to groups not divided by a clear-cut line are not convincingly portrayed, because in their case it would be necessary to trace their inner development and demonstrate by means of their orientation and attitude to different problems the social ferment of the time. But that would probably have broken up and obscured the whole conception of the work and made it impossible to present the nexus of social problems on such an enormous scale. So these figures appear now on one side, now on the other, of the opposing fronts, seen each time from a slightly different angle, the ensuing impression remaining ambiguous and indistinct. This is true, for example, of the figure of T'u Wei-yü 屠維嶽 in "Twilight." Perhaps Mao Tun wished to show the impossibility of the intellectual's attempt to preserve independence in the struggle of classes and even to think of acting as a kind of mediator. But the figure remains sketchy.

Similarly the figure of the principal heroine of the novel "Corruption" is not altogether clear. On the one hand, she commits acts of incomprehensible callousness, as when she deserts her child, is reconciled to the killing of her lover, betrays his friend, yet on the other hand she does not hesitate to risk her own life to save a strange girl. As we noted above, for the author the figure of the heroine is above all a pair of eyes observing what is going on around her, and in this context there is no room for the analysis of complicated mental and spiritual transmutations.

It is also possible that the diary form is an attempt to overcome the system of independent episodes which tends to disrupt the unity of the work, and to give it the maximum homogeneity, while retaining the possibility of recording in it the results of a wide range of observation and experience.

I think that it is in this focusing of attention on social facts of general validity and in the small interest taken in the development of individual personalities lies the chief difference between Mao Tun's realism and the realism not only of the nineteenth century, but also of his time. We stated above that the school of naturalism was limited by its theoretical premises—though these were seemingly possessed of universal validity—to individual cases, eventually to the life stories of a small group of people. And so the author, if he was to illustrate his theses with respect to a specific human fate, would usually have to describe the whole history of an individual from the cradle to the grave, and, indeed, the history of an entire family. For this reason, for instance, Zola creates a complex of novels around the Rougon family. The method of the naturalist writer is always diachronic, as compared with the more synchronic method of Mao Tun. Similarly, we might point to basic differences in the perception of reality. Nowhere do we find in Mao Tun—or naturally anywhere else in Chinese literature—that love for material reality, that delight in the abundance and variety of nature's forms which is so notable in Zola's descriptions and which stems from the legacy of the Renaissance and, even more, from the Baroque view of the world, from the joy in shapes and colors, which gave birth to the whole genre of still life in European painting. Actually, admiration for nature and her prolific creative power, though sometimes monstrous and terrifying, is at the back of the whole body of naturalist literature, and this is a feeling entirely alien to Chinese literature, whether old or modern. Certain indications of it are perhaps present only in the work of Chuang-tzŭ.

The principal difference in my view, however, is in the stress on the individual. In the center of Zola's imaginative world is always the romantic hero who alone—and therein lies the pathos of his fate—takes up the cudgels against society. It is a reflection of the revolutionary who, with a banner in his hands and a few faithful friends at his side, defends the barricade, and it is also the expression of the time—the culminating phase of capitalism. The individual is still everything in people's minds: he leads, his enthusiasm carries others with him. On the contrary, the romantic hero has no place in new Chinese literature, individual action has had no significance in Chinese life since the 1920s, and so it has no place in the country's literature either. It is a further indication of the weakness of the Chinese bourgeoisie: the individualism characteristic of the bourgeois view of the world had no influence at all on the Chinese way of thought.

Those features which we have pointed out as being divergent in Mao Tun's work as compared with the naturalist school is true also of the great realists of the nineteenth century, especially the Russians. With them, too, attention is centered above all on the individual, and in a confrontation of his attitude to life and the reality around him is sought the key to an explanation of the social problems of the time. As a rule, the whole history of the individual is again presented. Very correctly, if we allow for a parodist's exaggeration, is this tendency in realistic literature defined by Karel Čapek, in the book *Marsyas* or "On the Margin of Literature," where he jokingly enumerates the differences between romantic and realistic literature: "Further, romantic literature tells a story, beginning with the fact that Angelica, now grown into a fair maiden, meets M. d'Evremonde; realistic literature, on the other hand, tells the story of a life, *that means, as far as possible, of a whole life*" (Průšek's emphasis). The reduction of a work to a single significant experience is typical for the first time of Chekov's art. But it would perhaps be superfluous to point out the differences between Chekov's bitterness and the tragic feeling of Mao Tun, between Chekov's stories of individuals and the collective scenes of the Chinese writer, and so on. The backcloth to Chekov's work is the growing unrest and incipient disintegration of Russian society: with Mao Tun it is actual civil war, foreign aggression, revolutionary storms. Hence the striking switchover from description to the dramatization of the whole presentation.

At the end of these thoughts on eventual connections between Mao Tun's *oeuvre* and foreign literatures, I should like to halt for a moment at the fact that in respect of a certain mosaiclike character and in the interweaving of various strands of plot, Mao Tun's works are reminiscent of the novels of certain European and, more especially, American writers of the period following the first World War, as, for example, Dos Passos. In the latter's novel *Manhattan Transfer*, the texture is made up of several threads of plot, a device enabling the author to bring within its compass the exceptionally wide span of city life in New York. But apart from the quite different use of reality—with Dos Passos it is the expression of the actually physical, that is, mainly the biological, feeling for life—the reasons for such a complicated structure are altogether divergent in the two authors. With Dos Passos, it is the endeavor to overstep the tradition of a unified and oversimplified single-rail plot, and also perhaps the striving to render adequately the polyphony of city life, combined with the desire to create a more complex composition; in the work of Mao Tun, the main purpose is to show the principal forces determining the course of history in China. His motives are, first and foremost, political and analytical.

An analysis of Mao Tun's *oeuvre* shows us clearly that both the content and form of his works are determined primarily by his attitude to reality and not by his attitude to the preceding literary tradition or to foreign influences. It is important to establish this for, as we have stressed more than once, it would be difficult to find any other writer so thoroughly acquainted with the whole of European literature and European literary theories—and of course with his native literature—as was Mao Tun. Having mastered the possibilities and gained from the experience of European literature, his work occupies a place of equality in world literature, but on the other hand he did not succumb as a writer to the influence of any particular European school, but found his own original attitude to, and view of, reality, as the basic ingredient of his work, and shaped in his own way his experience and insights into a work of art.

(2) Yü Ta-fu

In certain respects the work of Yü Ta-fu provides the sharpest contrast to that of Mao Tun, and the comparison of the output of these two writers brings out sharply the basic differences between these two trends in new Chinese prose and, on the other hand, also certain traits symptomatic of the whole epoch.

It would seem at a superficial glance that no two artists could be more dissimilar than Mao Tun and Yü Ta-fu. Opposed to the extreme objectivism of Mao Tun's work stands the extreme subjectivism of the work of Yü Ta-fu. Whereas Mao Tun almost completely excludes his person from his works, the subject matter of Yü Ta-fu's writings is almost exclusively his own experiences and feelings. And we shall discover more such differences.

On the other hand, we shall also ascertain a number of features which they have in common: the work of Yü Ta-fu draws, as does that of

Mao Tun, on personal and still fresh experiences; he, too, tries to record the reality that is just passing. In a number of his works, a living experience is immediately transformed into a work of art. Thus, for example, the short story *Shih-i yüeh ch'u san* 十一月初三 , or "November the Third," describes the happenings of what was the author's birthday, and was written the very same day.[9] Similarly, the story *I-ko jen tsai t'u shang* 一個人在途上 , or "A Lonely Man on a Journey,"[10] was inspired by events just experienced, and this is true of a large part of his literary production. It is probable that, as in the case of Mao Tun, so also in that of Yü Ta-fu, we must see in this urge to record the fleeting reality around them a strong personal identification with reality, though each with a different kind.

I think that we may speak in connection with Yü Ta-fu also of a striving to record reality as objectively and truthfully as possible, of his endeavor to achieve objective truth and true understanding. Because the subject of his artistic insight is, especially, his own self, he approaches it with the same determination to lay bare the naked truth as does Mao Tun. And if we compared Mao Tun to a surgeon dissecting the diseased body of Chinese society, the same comparison is equally apt for Yü Ta-fu, who, however, dissects his own mental and spiritual world. None of his own living experiences, his habits, weaknesses and passions is too humiliating or shameful for him not to speak of it with complete frankness. He writes repeatedly of his drunkenness, of how his lusts turn him into a beast and drive him to visit brothels, of how he was tortured to the point of exhaustion by his erotic perversities, describes his masochism, finding satisfaction in letting himself be kicked and beaten by the woman to whom he is attracted, and in a passion of erotic desire drives a needle into his face. He imagines for himself the role of a thief, sees himself in the part of the most despicable of human beings. The openness of these confessions have earned him the condemnation of a number of critics, as reflected, for instance, in the study by van Boven.[11] On the other hand, his works are full of descriptions of the beauties of Nature, sympathetic observation of the finest nuances in the workings of the human soul and especially in the psychology of women, lovingly

---

[9]*Ta-fu ch'üan chi* 達夫全集 , Vol. 1, *Han-hui-chi*, Shanghai, Ch'uang-tsao ch'u-pan-pu 1927.

[10]*Ta-fu ch'üan chi*, the end.

[11]Henri van Boven, *Histoire de la Littérature Chinoise Moderne*, Peiping 1946, p. 75.

understanding descriptions of the child mind and, mainly, few can rival
him in the delicacy of the pictures he sketches not so much of love as of
erotic desire, of erotic dreams and visions.

Undoubtedly the most characteristic trait in the personality of Yü
Ta-fu and in his writings is the instability of his temperament, which is
forever running through the whole gamut of emotions, from the lowest
and most pitiable to the highest delight in beauty and the nobility of
self-sacrifice. This peculiar disposition enabled him to "get inside" his
characters, especially female characters, for whose psychology he
showed a quite remarkable understanding, and so he has created several
splendidly sketched portraits of women, for instance, in the short stories,
Kuo-ch'ü 過去, or "The Past,"[12] and in *Ch'un-feng ch'en-tsui-ti wan-shang*
春風沈醉的晚上, or "Intoxicating Spring Nights." The interest of Yü
Ta-fu, as of Mao Tun, was directed above all toward man's inner life,
except that with Yü Ta-fu, in keeping with the general subjective
coloring of his work, it is actually introspection.

This focusing of attention on his own inner self, on his own
feelings, spiritual states and mental processes finds a commensurate form
for its expression. Yü Ta-fu repeatedly makes use of the diary, notes,
letter—all forms specially suited for direct communication and, actually,
nonliterary, being vehicles of expression designed for his own use or for
that of a very intimate circle. These forms themselves point to the
subjective bias of his work, the author implies that he is presenting his
experiences, so to speak, "off the cuff," without an eye to any reader and
without any editing for his benefit.

On the other hand, the fact that the author himself—and immediately after writing—publishes these things confirms that they were
intended from the first for a reader, that they are not real diaries, notes,
and so on, as was the case in the old literature, but merely a form
designed for a reader, just as is any other. Moreover, in Yü Ta-fu's work
a striking trait is observable. A. Vlčková has shown that a great part of
his literary production is of autobiographical character, that it works up
his personal experiences and that we can relate every work, also in
respect of content, to a certain phase of his life and to events affecting
him personally.[13] But this basically same material is treated in two
different ways:

---

[12]*Ta-fu tai-piao tso* 達夫代表作, Hsien-tai shu-chü 1933, p. 235 et seq.

[13]A. Vlčková, *Pokus o zhodnotenie Yü Ta-fuóvej tvorby a náčrt jeho vyvoja so zvlá*ᵛ
zretelom k autorovu dielu do roku 1930 (Attempt at an evaluation of Yü Ta-fu's work and a

A number of these works are presented in the first person—as diaries or notes—whereas others are written in the third person, thus having the form of a narrative or even of a novella. More striking still is the fact that the majority of Yü Ta-fu's works, which we should regard from the point of view of European literary forms as the most perfect works of art, as perfect examples of the short story or novella are related in the first person; those which remain in rough sketch as notes recording experiences are often, on the contrary, in the third person. Without a detailed knowledge of Yü Ta-fu's life, we should say that he wrote, on the one hand, perfect novellas, in the form of *Ich-Erzählung*, on the other, freehand sketches, probably with strong subjective coloring, sometimes in diary form, or again as a report of the experiences as a literary hero. I think that this statement entitles us to speak of the *belletristic* processing of personal experiences as the basic artistic principle of Yü Ta-fu's creative output. The author's intention was not to record his experiences for himself or for his friends, as did certain old Chinese authors—of which more below—but to shape them into works intended for an anonymous reader. Therein, as we shall see, exists an important difference between the works of Yü Ta-fu and similar works in old Chinese literature.

First we shall give an example of a work presented as a diary or body of notes. The work we have chosen is the sketch "November the Third" which arose the same day in Peking and so we can suppose that in it the link between the experience and its recording is exceedingly close. First the contents in brief: The author awakes and calls to mind his wife, her care and love. The recollection plunges him into a mood of sadness and despair: He is alone, deserted like a telegraph pole gleaming in the cold wind, he has not a single friend, he has an empty heart, whose fire has gone out, he would need to change to stone, deaden all his feelings, in order to become like other people. The description of his feelings becomes ever more passionate till it ends in a cry of despair.

He discovers that it is his birthday. He is shaken by new feelings of despair. It is the birthday of a scurvy frog, of a dog that mumbles a few phrases, he is not even written into the family tree. He compares himself with the man in the tale his friend gave him, and finds that he is much more unhappy; he wanders through the streets and recalls the words of a Russian revolutionary, that a man if he is to be content in life must

---

sketch of his development, with special reference to the author's work up to 1930), typescript thesis.

devote himself to religion, or make a revolution, or drink. And so he goes and drinks, but alcohol cannot dissipate his bitterness and grief.

He goes to the theater, listens for a while to the play, and then begins to think things over. He realizes that most of the people here to entertain themselves are, in reality, as sad as is he. His thoughts are interrupted by a blast of music. He leaves the theater and is considering where he should go. At that moment a car stops in front of the building and a woman steps out, elaborately made up and bejewelled. He says to himself—here comes another swine to sell herself in small change. A new spiritual crisis breaks out.

A lovely description of an approaching sandstorm follows. Another crisis in the rickshaw. The author plays with the thought that if all the world were a stage everybody would be an excellent actor; he alone would be ch'ou 丑 , a despised clown, buffoon, the partner of servants, serving as the foil for the beauty of the principal players. His own ugliness is others' good fortune. He shouts out that he praises this role of a small clown assigned him by fate. He then likens himself to one half of a pair of scissors of which the central screw has been lost. Thus rendered useless, it eternally seeks the other half, but it is nowhere to be found. He exclaims that he would speak of love, only that it no longer exists.

Let us halt here for a moment. We see that so far the narrative consists of a stream of specific experiences, punctuated by outbursts of emotion. A special characteristic is then the lovely lyrical description of Nature, which colors the mood of the narrative and creates a sharp contrast to it.

We have no reason to doubt that the author in this sketch records the spiritual states through which he passed, that his inner life was continually shaken by these passionate outbursts, that emotionally he was extremely high-strung and was constantly slipping into moods of despair and depression and self-torture.

But on the other hand we cannot overlook the fact that his works written in the third person are composed in a similar way, that, indeed, the emotional gradation is still steeper. Already Yü Ta-fu's first such "story," *Ch'en-lun* 沈 淪, "Drowning,"[14] ends with the tragic culmination of a spiritual crisis, with the hero's suicide. Even though we may concede that the author's production was also determined by his natural

---

[14]*Ta-fu ch'üan-chi*, Vol. 2, *Chi le chi*, Ch'uang-tsao ch'u-pan-pu 1927, beginning.

disposition, that he projected into it his spiritual states and depressions, the example of "Drowning" shows us that in his work this trait is intentionally underlined. We might speak of the strong *dramatization* of these narrative strips, spiritual experiences are always presented as a dramatic ascent culminating in an outburst of despair or even in a suicidal mood. It would seem that this construction which he employed in his works of a series of waves, where narrative alternates with descriptions of dramatic spiritual crises, aimed to introduce into the diary-form notes action and life, create sharper contrasts and so enliven the stream of prose, which lacks any real theme. The same end is served also by descriptions of Nature, which also break up the simple relation or record. I think that here we have one of Yü Ta-fu's methods of recasting in belletristic form what is noted down or entered in a diary so as to make it interesting for the reader.

We can point to a whole group of Yü Ta-fu's works employing exactly this method. A single explosion of despair is, for instance, the sketch *Ling-yü-che* 零余者 , or "A Superfluous Man."[15] Its content is nothing else than a reproduction of the moods he passes through on a walk outside the ramparts of Peking. (The tale was written on January 15, 1924.) The author etches in the picture of a winter evening, the grey ramparts, the frozen-over river, the empty sand-blown fields and a few gaunt trees. He imagines to himself how splendid it would be if his body could melt away like a heap of snow in spring. He has lived his life and all that remains is a feeling of emptiness. As he walks on the thought comes to him that he is a superfluous man, a useless man, as he says, using the English expressions. He has done nothing, he is no good for anything, he is not even of any use to his family; had he not married his wife, somebody else would have done so, another man would have begotten his son. He shouts for a rickshaw, jumps into it, drives he knows not whither, and is furious that the rickshaw man does not go quickly enough.

The work which illustrates most strikingly this method of dramatizing personal experiences is the long stream of memories entitled *Huan hsiang chi* 還鄉記 "Reminiscences on Returning Home,"[16] to which the author then wrote a continuation.[17] It is in the first person and describes

---

[15]*Ta-fu san-wen chi* 達夫散文集 , Shanghai, Pei-hsin shu-chü, undated, p. 125.
[16]*Ta-fu tai-piao tso*, p. 65.
[17]*Hou-chi* 後記, id, p. 109.

the author's return from Shanghai to his native Fu-yang, in Che-chiang, not far from Hang-chou. Let me give at least one example of his typical dramatization of a personal experience. The author, seeing at the station how every traveler is accompanied by his family or friends, is overcome with sadness at the realization of his own desolateness. He pictures to himself that he is waiting for a lovely girl who is coming to see him off. His vision is so vivid that it makes him wish to help a girl with her luggage who is going by the same train. But her surprised gaze confuses him, fills him with panic and, with a hasty inward apology, he flees from her. Afraid she may catch sight of him again, he does not even dare to buy his ticket. In his agitation, he then buys a second-class ticket and sneaks into the train. Here a small incident is worked up into a quite complicated spiritual drama. And so one experience after another is dramatically recast. The author reproduces a dream in which he acts the part of a thief, enters a woman's bedroom and steals a pair of satin shoes and a handbag, attempts to commit suicide, when he compares his futile life with the happiness of a peasant family. Plunged in the dark mood of an evening on the ramparts of Hang-chou, he declares that all that was lacking was the sound of bells and he would have thrown himself down from the battlements, and so on. The narration keeps oscillating between the objective description of things and scenes and agitated monologues, spiritual confession, rhetorical questions, the author apostrophizing people and things around him and carrying on with them passionate and stormy dialogues. The actual incidents of the journey are practically submerged beneath this truly fantastic whirl of emotions and imaginings. Again and again we get flashes of the sharp contrasts between the real or imagined picture of others' happiness, the contented fulfillment of peasant life, the beauties of Nature and the author's feelings of despair, between his own outbursts of almost ecstatic joy and the deepest plungings into despair. We find here, too, the romantic dramatization of his own fate, which as we shall see is so characteristic of the work of Kuo Mo-jo. On the margin of the Hang-chou Lake, the author weaves a dream-story of his meeting in his youth with a lovely girl, of their falling in love and the amazing happiness they enjoyed until, having lost all his money, he was deserted by her, too. On returning to that place, old and in rags, he caught sight of her once again, more beautiful than ever, splendidly robed and in the company of a rich man.

In the chaos of emotions which continually convulse his soul, we hear occasional sharp words of contempt for the intelligentsia who serve the militarists, and of hate for those who destroy the happy life of ordinary folk.

The style of this narrative strip is in keeping with its contradictory character. On the one hand, we have very complex and artistic descriptions, whether of natural scenery or of the author's dreams and visions, for which the vehicle is a configuration of complicated sentences. These well-balanced and effectively modeled descriptions are then interrupted by a whole battery of exclamations, rhetorical questions and interjections, from which it is clear that Yü Ta-fu is still seeking his own path to self-expression and is still experimenting with different expressive means.

On comparing this stream of reminiscences with *Mang-mang yeh* 茫 茫 夜, or "Deep Night,"[18] which is cast in third-person narrative, but under an easily discerned pseudonym, we find no great differences. Again it is a rosary told over by the hero of his own spiritual dramas, perhaps described with greater objectivity and a greater effort at a still more accurate description of the settings and of the incidents described. On the other hand, this narrative strip descends most deeply into the obscure domains of the human psyche. In it the author describes his love for a man, the ecstasies of masochism and the beastlike instinct which drives him to the brothels. A number of scenes end abruptly with his hero leaving the brothel he has sought out; the deserted streets evoke in him the picture of a "Dead City," and with it the image of himself as a "living corpse," as he says to his friend in English.

To use a simile, Yü Ta-fu's experiences and those of his friends are like the balancing feats of a tightrope dancer; every time he sways he risks a fatal fall into the abyss that yawns beneath him, and we realize that any stronger tremor will end his desperate attempt to keep his balance, and actually, perhaps, spell for him his release. This consciousness of danger underlying the states and incidents described, creates a certain dramatic tension and stimulates the reader's attention, thus providing a substitute for the tension achieved elsewhere by subject-matter and intricacies of plot. Whether intended or not, this tension is a notable means in the belletrization of personal experiences, of which we spoke above.

We might add that this feeling of the imminent tragedy of life lived continually on the brink of disaster and destruction is yet another link

---

[18]*Ta-fu ch'üan-chi, Han-hui-chi*, first tale.

between the work of Yü Ta-fu and the atmosphere that permeates the work of Mao Tun. With different means and in another context, Yü Ta-fu tries to express the same feeling of life's tragedy as is expressed in the work of Mao Tun. Only in nuances that are passive, more despairing and more hopeless, for Yü Ta-fu's subjectivism is lost in the misery and confusion of contemporary life, the author being unable either to analyze the happenings around him or see the forces which are preparing to emerge from the surrounding darkness and usher in a brighter future.

But let us go back to the prose piece "November the Third." Placed in immediate juxtaposition to the author-hero's wanderings through the unlit city and his outbursts of despair is an episode completely different in character from anything that has gone before. Because the rickshaw man does not wish to take the author to some brothel outside the Ch'ien-men Gate, he goes with him to his house beside the P'ing-tse-men Gate. He wants to see once more the home of the girl from Hung-mao-kou 紅茅溝, or the Ditch of Red Rushes.

And now the author unfolds the story of how he laid eyes on the girl the previous autumn when he first came to Peking and was suffering from repeated attacks of nervous depression. Once on a moonlight night, shortly before daybreak, he stole away to the P'ing-tse-men Gate and out of the city. Everything was covered with a thick layer of hoarfrost and thin ice. He saw the bare fields, the cairns, the gaunt trees, heard the sound of the wind in their tops, and how the whole earth seemed to breathe. He was approaching a group of well-kept buildings when, on the ridge beside the winch of a well, he saw a girl of about fifteen. She was simply, but tastefully, dressed. The newly risen sun lit up her beauty, and no Beatrice or Mona Lisa could have been more beautiful. The author describes this beauty in detail and stresses that she had a Greek nose. The girl carried away her bucket of water and, on entering the gate, looked around, whereupon a light blush colored her cheeks. The author goes to the well, looks down into it and he imagines he sees there the girl's reflection. He goes to the house, looks in at the window and only the whirr of a pair of birds in flight brings him back to earth again.

Once more he caught a glimpse of her in spring, when he stopped there on his way to a friend. He went up to the window and saw her. He was inexpressibly happy. Now he was going there and such a sandstorm was blowing that he thought he would have to turn back. But the wind subsided a little, a crescent moon appeared in a clear sky and it seemed to him that, on such a night, the dead might well rise from their graves. At the house, he found the shutters closed, nor did any ray of light shine through. He stood there until driven away by the barking of a dog. Full of grief he returned home, remembered and longed for his wife, and wrote this piece.

Here, a string of freely linked episodes, dramatically punctuated by explosions of feeling, is followed without transition by a romantic scene of great beauty. From the point of view of literary craftsmanship, it is a masterly grouping of carefully laid in and inwardly related pictures, forming as a whole what is really a highly artistic novella. Its structure is determined by the fact that there are projected into the single level of a present experience a number of other levels created by past experiences. Each level has its own emotional sphere, is differently emotionally colored and is related to a different point of time and pattern of relations. Thus arises a kind of web of many-colored threads and this is the basic structure of Yü Ta-fu's psychological prose. Or, to use another simile, they are like the various gleaming facets of a cunningly cut stone, their varying coloring contrasting one with another and at the same time adding depth to the whole. The author, without attempting to develop his motifs into some connected story, by the mere art with which he stratifies his reminiscences and weaves them into the situation he has just experienced (which also forms the framework in which they are mounted) creates a highly organized and unified composition.

Thus, alongside autobiographical strips, enlivened and interrupted by emotional outbursts, descriptions of Nature, recollections, thoughts, dreams and images, we see another much more complicated method in use, one designed to work up personal experiences into an elaborately constructed complex, which we are fully entitled to call a novella. This is the author's alternative method of giving his personal experiences belletristic character. At the same time the "Reminiscences" show how a few small motifs suffice Yü Ta-fu for the creation of a picture full of profound inner meaning and perfectly evoking a certain keenly felt experience. Undoubtedly, this concentration on a certain experience through which he has passed and its suggestive description while it is still fresh in the memory can be linked up with the thought expressed in the "Reminiscences," namely, that life is made up only of experiences that we have just passed through and that we must try to taste their flavor to the full.

The most striking example of this method of complicated stratification of various time and emotional levels is Yü Ta-fu's perhaps most tragic story, issuing from the deepest springs of human feeling, *I-ko jen tsai t'u-shang* 一個人在途上, or "A Lonely Man on a Journey," telling of the death of his little son, Lung-erh 龍兒. Let us list here at least a number of these levels:

. (1) Setting of the story—train from Peking to the south. Situation: the author has just bidden his wife farewell.

(2) Recollections: teaching in the south. News of his son's illness, return to Peking and meeting with his wife, who informs him of their son's death.

(3) Recollections of his family life, with wife and son. His departure, return, parting again, the last time he heard his son's voice. Various personal happenings and his return to Peking after his son's death.

(4) Recollections of his little son, projected into his present sorrow.

(5) His wife tells him of his son's illness.

(6) Sequence of recollections of the time before the boy fell ill and his waiting in vain for his father's return.

(7) Description of the author's state of mind during this relation.

(8) Recollection of times when he struck him.

(9) Continuation of the description of the child's illness. His wife thinks that the child cannot die, because he is waiting for his father, and herself begs him to stop breathing.

(10) Recollection of his meeting with his wife after his return from Peking. They return to their home and see the boy's things. They go to visit his grave. The recollections gravitate to the time of his departure and to the moment when the novella is born.

Each of these motifs is a fragment of heartbreaking grief and highly sensitive observation. For instance: when the boy was alive the author used to shake down dates for him from the tree in the courtyard. After his death, when he is lying in bed with his wife, he is afraid of the sound of falling dates. He and his wife go to their son's grave to burn pictures of money, as the custom is. But his wife remembers that they have only banknotes, and what good are they to a little child? So she goes to buy pictures of little copper coins.

We noted above that a characteristic feature of old novels and tales, as well as of other popular productions, was their small degree of homogeneity, for they broke up as a rule into a series of independent episodes, inwardly unrelated. Our example then shows how a modern author is able, on the contrary, to work up into a single whole a great number of motifs, situations and time levels. He weaves them into a unified tapestry of emotions and moods, in which each detail is related to all the others, supplements and colors them, and, at the same time itself first acquires full meaning and significance in the context of the whole. The work of Yü Ta-fu shows a similar striving after compactness and homogeneity in the new novel and short story, as we remarked in the work of Mao Tun, a striving which culminated in the great achievement of Lu Hsün.

There can be no doubt that, by means of this complex interlining of a variety of motifs belonging to different timestreams to produce a unified texture, the writer creates a picture rather than an epic sequence, the resulting impression being static rather than epic. Here again we come across a characteristic which we discovered in our study of the work of Mao Tun, namely that the strongly emotional quality of these pictures would entitle us to speak of a *lyrical picture*. We shall do no more here than state the fact, to a discussion of which we shall return later.

The integrating method described above both strengthens the homogeneity of the picture and, at the same time, loosens its connections with the rest of the context. This comes out very clearly in the previous "Recollections . . . ," in the description of the meeting with the girl. This episode, linked only very loosely with the preceding chain of narrative could, indeed, very well stand by itself. But through this inner completeness the scene is isolated not only from the given context but from any context at all; it ceases to be fixed in time or space; its meaning need no longer be sought in relation to any other reality, but solely in itself. Figuratively speaking we might say that all the levels of the picture aim to converge at the center and do not tend toward some outer point, whether in time or reality. The picture ceases to be part of a narrative action and becomes a symbol which may be brought into connection with any reality. By this procedure, Yü Ta-fu points the way to the creating of pictures with many planes of significance, such as Lu Hsün was then to paint with such supreme skill.

A very instructive example of this procedure is Yü Ta-fu's prose piece *Li ch'iu chih yeh* 立秋之夜, or "A Night in Early Autumn."[19] First there is sketched in very suggestively the mood of some dark deserted

---

[19]*Ta-fu san-wen chi*, p. 49.

corner of a city, shrouded in almost complete darkness. Here two friends meet, one dressed in a Chinese robe, the other in European clothes, and that is all that we are told about them, except that both are unemployed. Twice they exchange the same questions, to which the interrogator never gets an answer. The circumstance that everything else is suppressed, that the scene is literally enveloped in darkness, so suggestively described that it is almost palpable, every moment, every word, is endowed with special significance compelling the reader to try and plumb its hidden meaning. Our first impression is of an impressionistic picture deftly sketched in, as if the author aimed only at the very precise recording of a visual phenomenon. But then the fact of the friends being unemployed links up with the obvious aimlessness of the two men's movements and the scene acquires a new significance: the symbol of the vague, aimless trailing about of the unemployed intelligentsia. Further on, these movements in the obscure gloom evoke the impression of the aimlessness of human life lost in darkness, its traces covered up by windblown sand. It is an excellent example of the method generally favored in the new literature which, by leaving part of the picture in darkness, evokes the impression of tension and of a number of layers of meaning, eventually of mystery. Each fills in the detail of the picture for himself and interprets its symbolism in his own way. It is a method employed with remarkable success by Lu Hsün.

The methods described above acquire special significance when Yü Ta-fu applies them not only to his personal experiences, but to a certain social reality and so opens up a new approach to its expression.

A similar procedure to that we described in our analysis of the piece "November the Third" is followed in the tale "Intoxicating Spring Nights." Here, too, the recording of a sequence of dark and gloomy personal experiences, punctuated by the usual outbursts of despair, builds up to a picture of exceptional beauty, purity and refinement. Only what in "November the Third" was a skillful interplay of moods and delicately tinted perceptions, in this contact with the most cruel living reality, rendered with unusual expressive force, becomes charged with quite new meaning.

The tale is extremely simple: the author, having fallen into the most hopeless poverty, is obliged to live in a derelict garret in the Shanghai slums, its sole furnishings being a heap of old books. Separated from it by a thin partition is another in which a young woman worker from a tobacco factory lives and to which access is only through the author's garret. Only twice do they come into closer contact; the first time the girl invites the author to a poor little meal, the second time he invites her in return on receiving some small fee. Both meetings are limited to a short conversation: in the first, the girl tells of her lately deceased father, a worker in the same factory where she is employed, of the terrible conditions of work, of the foreman's lewdness, and so on. The second time she tries to persuade the author to start a new life, for she suspects him of going out at night to work with thieves. The real reason, however, for his nocturnal habits is that his clothes are already so shabby that he dare not show himself in the streets in daylight. The author explains this and also that the money he got was for a translation. The girl weeps with compassion and the author, who then spends the night walking the streets, realizes more poignantly than ever his utter misery.

It is difficult to imagine a more simple episode, and yet the whole narration is illuminated with a strange brightness and reaches almost metaphysical heights. Above the unmitigated misery of a Shanghai hovel, above the dirt and brutality of life, above the hopelessness of the author's existence, spent the whole day in a dark hole lit by a candle in gazing into emptiness, with hunger gnawing at his vitals, a picture of flawless purity lights up of a human being, full of deep feeling and goodness, always thinking of others, who, in the midst of misery and filth, strives to preserve her humanity and human dignity. Truly pathetic is the care with which the girl tries to make the kennel of a lodging into a decent and homely place, and with which she prepares a few poor dainties for her guest.

Here again we meet with the romantic antithesis of poverty and despair on the one hand, and the cherishing of a high ideal on the other. The author, on comparing himself with the girl, is overcome by despair, in a fit of self-humiliation he would wish to take his own life, recalling how the bus driver had cursed him for a yellow dog. But the antithesis to this is not a vague chimera of womanhood, the beauty of a Beatrice or Mona Lisa, but a factory worker. The author in his descent to the lowest depths of human society comes into contact with the Chinese proletariat and draws with unusual art, sensibility and truthfulness a picture of its representative. The girl's portrait acquires symbolic meaning: only in the purity and honesty of the proletariat, in its dignity and labor, is salvation to be found, and release from present misery and gloom.

A. Vlčková has shown in her study how Yü Ta-fu worked his way through to a Marxist view of literature. In this prose piece, we see his sensibilities being trained in this direction. For him the path to the artistic representation of the proletariat was not by way of theoretical abstractions, but above all, through his own living experience. Yü Ta-fu lived among the Chinese proletariat, himself more miserable. The realism to which he attained in these tales, through the mists of romanticism and the slough of his personal decadence, is the outcome of bitter firsthand experience; he not only wrote about the proletariat, but he knew the life of the proletariat, because he had lived it.

I have repeatedly pointed out similarities between the work of Lu Hsün and Yü Ta-fu, which at least in part explain Lu Hsün's liking for him. These correspondences are particularly striking in the narrative *Po-tien* 薄奠, or "A Humble Sacrifice."[20] I have not here in mind the similarity in subject matter with Lu Hsün's *I-chien hsiao shih* 一件小事, or "An Insignificant Incident,"[21] but rather the approach to the theme. Like a large part of Lu Hsün's tales, this tale of Yü Ta-fu's is presented in the form of a reproduction of reminiscences. In this case it is the reproduction of reminiscences of three different meetings of the author with a rickshaw man. All that we learn about the rickshaw man stems from the reproduction of three short talks with him, one of which is nothing more than a recollection. Everything else is enveloped in obscurity. The story is reduced to a minimum and fragments of it are almost submerged in the author's emotional outbursts. These not only provide a contrast to the narrative action, as in his other stories, but also contain a false interpretation of the facts which the author learns about the rickshaw man's life, and so add force to the shattering impression of the final exposure.

First we are confronted with the rickshaw man's remarkable kindness. Although he is driving the author at night for a fare that another rickshaw man would not accept, he returns him the money, saying that after all they are neighbors. Only after long insistence will he take the fare. The author envies him: the rickshaw man has a proper job, is now returning home and the author pictures to himself the happy family scene no doubt being enacted. The discovery of how far from the reality were the author's illusions comes out later, when the author happens to be passing the rickshaw man's house and he hears a noisy bickering and the rickshaw man pouring out abuse. The author finds it strange,

---

[20]*Ta-fu tai-piao-tso*, p. 175 et seq.
[21]*Lu Hsün ch'üan-chi*, p. 43 et seq.

knowing him for an extraordinarily kind man. Into this tense situation, the author mounts as a reminiscence a description of the rickshaw man, his account of the poverty with which he wages a ceaseless struggle, for all his profit is swallowed up by the rent for the rickshaw, besides which his wife, so he says, is not a good housekeeper and he cannot save money to buy his own rickshaw. The author would like to jump down and embrace his poor friend.

It is yet another example of that skillful interweaving of various timestreams and various motifs in a single piece, so that, instead of a series of loosely linked episodes, a homogeneous whole arises such as we spoke of above.

Then the author relates how he entered the rickshaw man's house and saw how angry the rickshaw man was with his wife for having spent three of the dollars he had laid by on a piece of material. The author secretly leaves him his silver watch, but the rickshaw man brings it back to him. The author is then ill for a long time. When he gets better and goes for a walk for the first time chance takes him past the rickshaw man's house. Outside a crowd is gathered and the sound of sobbing comes from inside. The author thinks that there has been a quarrel again and wants to help them. This time he has money. On going inside he finds the rickshaw man dead. He was drowned in the floods at South Swamp. His wife had also wanted to drown herself, but they saved her. And now she laments bitterly: Her husband had always longed to have his own vehicle and now she hasn't even enough to buy him a paper rickshaw and burn it on his grave. The author buys a paper rickshaw and takes it to the grave. The gaze of the idle onlookers infuriates him: "Their staring curious eyes maddened me. I cursed them inwardly, and felt a feeling of almost irresistible rebellion rise within me. Oh, those rich people in their cars, and the uncaring passersby! 'Swine! Dogs!' I wanted to shout. 'Do you know what you are looking at? We are going to the grave of a poor rickshaw man, my friend, who was driven to death by such as you! It is his memorial you are staring at!'"

This emotional outburst, provoked not by a personal feeling of despair, but by indignation at the injustice of the world, concludes the story.

As in Lu Hsün's stories, the actual tale forms only a kind of *pentimento*, visible only in its main outlines. Those parts of the story which show through evoke in us the impression that what remains hidden is possibly much more terrible than what we see, that we know only a small part of the whole tragedy. Somewhere in the shadows is a whole vain life, full of toil and hardship. We do not even know how the rickshaw man met his end, nor is it impossible that he may have committed suicide; at least the possibility is hinted at by his wife. A terrible mystery surrounds everything. Against the dark background of this ghost picture, certain features stand out in highlighted contrast: the extreme kindness and honesty of the man, and this notwithstanding, after a whole life of labor, not enough remains for a paper rickshaw to be burned on his grave! And this tragedy is matter to gratify the vulgar curiosity of a gaping crowd. Another point that underlines it is that, in his wife's mental picture, the rickshaw man is to remain a rickshaw man even beyond the grave—with the one difference that he will own his vehicle!

His aim, like that of Mao Tun and also of Lu Hsün, is not to tell a story, but to throw light on a certain typical social situation, which reflects the whole state of society at the time. It is an illustration of how a certain historical situation leads to the rise of a certain literary method, and also of how a certain artistic method is not the work of an individual, but constitutes the common work of a whole generation, if not of whole generations. It is necessary in this connection to stress especially the realism of the story, or more precisely, the fact that the story is an exact reproduction of reality: nothing is added or changed, and yet the story is not a kind of impressionistic genre picture, but embodies in a simple tale the whole essence of contemporary reality. This piece of narration is undoubtedly a quite exceptional testimony to the artistic and ideological maturity of the literature of the period to which it relates.

The piece is also instructive as demonstrating the author's approach to reality. The narrator in Yü Ta-fu's stories is not an unidentified and all-knowing epic first person, as in the classical realistic European novel or as in Mao Tun, but always the author himself, or the person who represents him in stories narrated in the third person. For this reason, we can speak of the markedly subjective coloring of his work, for the author—or his representative—is almost always the principal hero of the story, the plot being based as a rule on his personal experiences, and the subject of his narrative are his own spiritual processes, everything being described from his subjective angle. We learn no more about the other characters and the milieu in which they move than the author or the author-hero knows or sees. We can take any story related in the third person in confirmation of this; for instance, the story "Drowning," where we see and experience everything from the standpoint of a hero who is anonymous—and that is typical. In the tale "Deep Night," the chief actor of the piece—the author—is concealed beneath a very obvious pseudonym, Yü Chih-fu 于質夫. Even in the historical tale *Ts'ai shih chi* 采石磯, or "The Colored Cliff,"[22] the action is centered on the poet Huang Chung-tse 黄仲則, whose whole character is, as it were, that of the writer's double, and everything is seen through his eyes. I think that it is in general characteristic of Chinese fiction that we know very precisely who relates and what he relates and what he can know. Either the author speaks in his own person, or he is the narrator, sometimes the chronicler who, however, makes no attempt to conceal his role, but rather stresses it, as we noted above. The Chinese author does not as a rule try to obscure the fact that in every story, no matter what attempt is made to evoke the impression of reality, it is always a matter of reproduction, the reflection of a reality (usually complexly), and not the reality itself.

By presenting the narrative as the author's personal experiences or recollections, or those of his double, in spite of its not seldom complicated character, to which we drew attention above, it usually forms a unified whole, actually a single monologue, into which are mounted reminiscences, descriptions, the speeches of other persons recalled by the hero or interpolated by him. Everything is viewed from a single angle; that ever-shifting dynamic perspective which we discovered in the work of Mao Tun has here no place.

We might define the whole artistic development of Yü Ta-fu as the creative endeavor to reshape personal experiences in increasingly artistic and homogeneous wholes. At the beginning of this path stand freely linked episodes describing the stream of the author's feelings and impressions, as in "Drowning" or "Reminiscences on Returning Home," and culminating in complex psychological pieces such as "A Lonely Man on a Journey" or "The Past." At the same time Yü Ta-fu works his way through to an understanding and expression of social reality, whence arise those works which are a significant contribution to modern Chinese realistic literature, such as "Intoxicating Spring Nights" and "A Humble Sacrifice."

This process is very clearly reflected in the development of his style. Naturally, we can only touch on this question, for without previous

---

[22]*Ta-fu tai-piao-tso*, p. 20 et seq.

analytical studies we cannot do more than indicate several obvious traits. We have already said above that these narrative strips are strongly dramatized and that in keeping with this, too, is the style, in which the even tenor of the description of some reality is constantly interrupted by a barrage of highly emotionally colored sentences, rhetorical questions and often direct exclamations. It is evident that the author is aiming at the greatest possible liveliness of style, whose dynamism is designed to overcome the monotony of diary-form notes; he seeks sharp divisions and contrasts. His style is marked by pathos and rhetoric, with the accent on personal, emotional elements.

On the contrary, in his stories, his style throws off to a considerable extent the ballast of these emotional elements, or at least limits them to mere inserts occasionally interrupting the flow of the narrative or concluding it. It has a clear tendency toward objectivization, strives after the greatest possible homogeneity and avoids sharp breaks. A characteristic feature of this tendency is the reduction of the dialogue to the reproduction in direct speech of the utterance of one person, whereas the replies of the second person are summarized in the description. This is the procedure repeatedly adopted by the author, for instance, in "Intoxicating Spring Nights" (pp. 168–172, the second conversation of the girl with the author).[23] Only the girl's talk is reproduced, whereas the author's replies are reported. Actual dialogue is limited to two questions and answers, throwing light on the basic facts of the situation. Thus the whole text has actually the character of a monologue: The relation is really the author's monologue, the girl's speeches are monologues to which the former link on.

Another typical trait of the same tendency is the insertion of direct speech—usually only short sections—into the unified stream of the narrative. This is the case in the repeatedly cited piece "A Lonely Man on a Journey," which is altogether presented as the author's reminiscence—that is, as monologue. This monologue is interwoven with the recollections and recounting of his wife, the latter in its turn containing the reproduction of their son's utterances. We see that the wife's reminiscences are, for the most part, incorporated in the stream of narrative as the simple stating of certain facts; sometimes indirect speech is used and the reproduction of the son's utterances is limited to short sections, really exclamations, which do not break up the unified stream

---

[23]*Ta-fu tai-piao-tso*, p. 147 et seq.

of narrative. I cite here at least a fragment from the most deeply affecting passage to illustrate the method, the punctuation being left as in the original: "My wife told of how for five days preceding his death, after several nights in the hospital, he cried out, Daddy, Daddy! When she asked him: 'Why are you calling for Daddy,' he made no sign of having heard and very soon began crying out again. Then on the third day of the fifth month, according to the old calendar, he seemed to have fallen into a death stupor, and when the doctor took a marrow specimen, all he could do was call out, 'what are you doing?' The tube in his larynx gasped for breath, his eyes were starting out of his head, a little white foam trickled from his mouth, but his breathing did not stop. His Mummy, weeping, called to him: 'Lung! Lung!' Tears streamed from the corner of his eyes and then his Mother, seeing how he suffered, said to him: . . ."[24] Only then does a longer speech by the wife follow.

It would be necessary to confront with this description the psychological novella composed by Liu O in the second part of his novel *The Travels of Lao Ts'an*[25] to show what a remarkably long distance Chinese literature had covered in the twenty years separating the two works. Liu O's novella takes the form of a narration by the young nun, I-yün, of her unhappy love and initiation. Interpolated into the nun's monologue in direct speech are long speeches of her lover and of other persons, also in direct speech, and within these again are cited the words of yet other persons, so that in spite of all the freshness and charm of the narration an extremely unnatural construction arises of a whole nest of inserts, yet despite the complexity of the construction the text is not adequately varied and articulated.

An interesting attempt to achieve a smooth transition from narrative to the reproduction of speech is a passage in the tale "Humble Sacrifice," where the author recalls his meeting with the rickshaw man. There, separated from the narrative section by a row of dots, follows a group of sentences reproducing the rickshaw man's speech. All the sentences are introduced by the same formula, *t'a-shuo* 他 説, "He said," thereby stressing their uniformity and continuity and indicating that they are sections of a single homogeneous stream. This series of reproduced

---

[24]Op. cit., p. 7.
[25]*Lao Ts'an yu-chi erh chi* 老殘遊記二集, Shanghai, Liang-yu kung szu 1946. Partially translated into English by Lin Yutang, under the title *A Nun of Taishan*, in the book *Widow, Nun and Courtesan*, New York 1951, p. 111, et seq. Complete Czech translation in Putování, *Starého Chromce*, Praha 1960. (The Travels of Lao Ts'an.)

statements is then linked up with the continuation of the narrative by
another row of dots.

The tendency toward homogeneity and smooth flow in the relation
is apparent also in the way one sentence is linked up with the next,
which is particularly noticeable in the tale "Intoxicating Spring Nights."
In quite a number of cases we see that two sentences are separated by a
full stop, though a comma could have been used equally well. The
second sentence links up very closely in meaning and also in construction
with the first of the pair. Here at least is one example. First sentence:
"Seeing this expression of mine, she probably took me for a homeless
vagrant." Second sentence: "*Lien-shang chiu li-shih ch'i-la i-chung* . . .
piao-ch'ing . . ." 臉上就立時起了一種…表情 . . . . "And in
her face there instantly appeared an expression . . . of compassion. . .
."[26] The conjunction *chiu*, as well as the adverbial phrase *li-shih*, show
that actually it is a clause depending on the premise contained in the first
sentence. Usually the second sentence is introduced by a preposition, so
that the division is not so strongly marked as if at the beginning of the
complex sentence stood a main clause; the same effect is achieved by
beginning both sentences with the same word or word-group, as for
instance the adverbial phrase of time: *yo shih hou* 有時候, or "sometimes," which underlines their forming part of a single thought-unit.

Already in these tales we find very complex sentences, although
here the gravity and strongly emotive character of the theme did not call
for an overcomplicated style. For this reason, probably, especially in "A
Lonely Man on a Journey," short sentences predominate, the author in
general not departing from the style of simple narrative.

On the other hand, where Yü Ta-fu goes back to the recording of
personal experiences, where the story as such practically disappears and
the author's main preoccupation is with the creation of a certain atmosphere, we find a singularly complicated style, characterized by elaborate
periods. This we can illustrate by means of a seemingly very simple
sketch or tale entitled *Yen-ying* 煙影, or "The Shadow of Smoke,"
written in 1926.[27] The tale begins with a sentence which no translation
can fully express. We shall try only to reproduce the individual sections:
"Every day he thought about returning, thought about returning. But for
one thing he had a terrible cough, so that he was afraid that as soon as he

[26]Op. cit., p. 157.
[27]*Ta-fu tai-piao-tso*, p. 215.

moved it would precipitate some catastrophe, and for another the fee for several sheets was not sufficient to cover the expenses, so that in the long run he remained in his lodging on the first floor, in front, with a family that had somehow come down in the world." This complicated sentence pattern is really only a group of relative clauses, in attribution to the subject. The subject and predicate then follow: "Wen p'o, on this afternoon, again languidly and aimlessly set out on his lonely walk in the street, K'ang-ma t'o-yeh, full of whirling grey dust."

Two things stand out in this sentence: first of all the remarkable number of facts incorporated in a single semantic and syntactic whole. It is, in fact, a whole story told as it were in a single breath, a single sentence. We are given here a brief character sketch and history of the hero-author, the milieu in which he lives comes to life and he is pictured in a certain situation. Secondly there is a clearly marked tendency to obscure the hierarchy of the sections of this complex sentence. The subject of the whole sentence is completely submerged beneath an accumulation of attributes and also by a fairly complex predicate. Thus no part has a predominating position, all are somehow reduced to a single level, all being equal parts of a single complex. Thus a configuration arises with a balanced intonational pattern, the first part coupling up with the second without any sharp breaks in the rising intonational line, and not until the end of the whole complex sentence do we reach the full conclusion.

The basic structural units of this text are long complex sentences of this kind, with an occasional shorter sentence. As a result, the text acquires a high degree of homogeneity, further supplemented by the methods mentioned above, such as the reduction of the dialogue and the suppression of all direct affective expression in passages strongly charged with emotion. Unlike the earlier dramatized narrative strips, Yü Ta-fu makes no use here, not even in the most agitated passages, of exclamatory sentences or rhetorical questions, but presents them as a mere statement of certain facts. For instance, on page 4 of our sketch, he relates that the hero cannot leave for the north because everywhere hordes of soldiers are on the rampage, and adds: "If Wen-p'o, who under normal circumstances was not too careful of what he said, had set out for the north, heedless of the dangers of war, there is no doubt he would have been killed by the ravaging troops. True, the question of life or death was not, in Wen-p'o's view, one to be regarded as terribly important. . . . But rather than be murdered by these Chinese soldiers,

worse than beasts, it seemed to him more glorious to die of snake-bite.
. . ."28

I think that this endeavor to build up unusually complex sentences, containing in a single unit a great many facts of very varied and dissimilar character, so that a very condensed and uniform context arises, has its origin in that tendency to belletrize personal experience of which we spoke above. In this case, however, the author tries to achieve his aim by a method which is the exact opposite of that which he uses in his narrative strips. Here he attempts to overcome the chaos of atomized percepts and impressions which personal experiences always in essence are, merge and shape them into an artistic whole and so create, instead of a mere stream of notes and entries tending to flow on unendingly, a carefully worked out and structurally perfectly integrated psychological novella. It is yet another example of the striving to supersede the free structure of the old literature and replace it by more complicated forms. Stylistically it assumes the preference for more complex sentence units in place of the earlier parataxis and rhythmization.

It is also probable that the author wishes, by the use of a more complicated style, to raise the theme—a purely personal experience—to a higher level, to give it weight and importance, to make it of general interest. There is no doubt either that he has succeeded in his aim; out of purely individual experiences arises a tale laying bare with a fine probing touch the whole gloom and tragedy of the old family life. The ever-darkening mood enveloping the description of the journey home from Shanghai concludes with a shattering scene in which are reproduced only the drunken babblings of his mother, who thinks of nothing but money, and the warring conflict of feelings experienced by the hero, in whom revulsion at the miserly, vulgar old woman contends with the natural love of a son. If some of Yü Ta-fu's sketches sometimes remain material in the raw, elsewhere he creates narrative pieces of subtlety and refinement, perfectly reflecting changing nuances of mood and reminiscent in this respect of the work of Katherine Mansfield.

Finally, it remains to be noted that the descriptions of the author's emotions remain on the traditional level of logically expressed feelings. So far as I know, we do not find in Yü Ta-fu any attempt to penetrate to the domain in which emotions are generated, to the domain of the subcon-

---

28Op. cit., pp. 218–219.

scious and of not more exactly definable feelings such as modern literature seeks to describe.

The tragic schizophrenia of Yü Ta-fu's nature, the permanent tension between the ideal and the beautiful, seen by him in revealing flashes, and the dark stream of lusts into which he bogged down, between his desire to sacrifice himself for a cause and the feeling of the futility of all effort, indeed of the futility of life itself, the ever-present shadow of death that falls on all his work and life, these would justify us in speaking of expressly romantic traits in his creative personality. His work, and also his life, recall figures in European romanticism of the beginning of the nineteenth century—a Byron, or a Czech Mácha, including their tragic end. And perhaps it is just Yü Ta-fu's end that hints at the still more cruel circumstances under which his life ran its course, and at the reasons why his work has also a different quality. Whereas Byron died of an illness contracted in making a supreme gesture in which was summed up his lifelong rebellion against any form of bondage, whereas the Czech poet was cut down by an equally chance illness, Yü Ta-fu was murdered, far from his native land, unknown, and even the circumstances of his death are wrapped in obscurity. Perhaps that is why the romanticism of Yü Ta-fu has only a tragic aspect, the consciousness of the futility and the vanity of life, and why only seldom do we hear the note of revolt and never is he able to give his personal tragedy a universal perspective, project his personal time-bound fate into infinity. The life he lived was too cruel for a man weak and sick, and the individual in the social chaos of the China of that time was of little or no account.

The Preface to his collected tales, *Han-hui chi* 寒灰集, or "Cold Ashes," of 1926, is permeated with feelings of impending dissolution: "I am thirty this year and this spiritual suffering, suffering for the destruction of my intellect, is never absent for a moment from my consciousness. Moreover, since last year when I contracted lung disease my body has become daily weaker and thinner. . . . In the mutability of human life, death is something very common and, so far as the Chinese are concerned, living as they do in constant chaos and confusion, for them death and annihilation are the best fulfillment of their wishes the gods can grant them. But such despair at the destruction of one's intelligence before the body perishes, is the greatest punishment, worse by far than hell itself, and one to which it is difficult for a man to reconcile himself. Half my life has been altogether needlessly wasted. I have done absolutely nothing of benefit to humanity, to society or to myself. What will my dissolution, the dissolution of my spirit, signify in this world of millions . . . ?" And in order to underline this almost pathological preoccupation with the thought of death and dissolution, he cites in the original a long poem from the book *The Autobiography of Mark Rutherford*,[29] in which the author revels in the physical image of his own body lying cold in the grave, making food for worms.

Another ingredient in the work of Yü Ta-fu is the usual romantic contrast between the misery of town life and the happy life of country people, as we saw in the above-mentioned sketch, "Reminiscences on Returning Home." The feeling of the emptiness of an intellectual's life is one that is voiced in Yü Ta-fu at every meeting with working people, whether peasant, worker or rickshaw man. Here the consciousness comes into sharp relief of the loneliness of the intellectual and the longing to overcome it by closer contact with the working people, which was undoubtedly one of the factors that drew the intelligentsia into the ranks of the Communist Party.

Important for Yü Ta-fu and, indeed, I think, for the whole situation in Chinese literature at that time, is the fact that the romantic consciousness of the estrangement between the writer and Nature, between the life of the intellectual and country life, does not lead to a sharp opposition of individual and society, to individualism and solipsism, as among the European romantics. Already in his first tale, "Drowning," where Yü Ta-fu expressed perhaps most strikingly the antithesis between the individual and his milieu, he explains this opposition not on individualistic grounds, but on social or, eventually, pathological grounds, thereby blunting its sharpness. The environment which the hero feels to be hostile is created by the Japanese, who look upon the Chinese with contempt, and the hero himself is an obviously pathological case, suffering from a persecution complex. The writer clearly wanted to express the then undoubtedly important conflict between the individual and society, a conflict perfectly natural in an anti-feudal revolution, yet he felt the necessity partially to disguise it. Thus in "Drowning" he stresses and even exaggerates the conflict between the hero and his elder brother who, it is affirmed, assumes the right to decide about the hero's life. The conflict is given pathological coloring. Proof of the very real importance

---

[29]*The Autobiography of Mark Rutherford* is the work of the writer William Hale White (1831–1913), and was published in 1881; its continuation is *Mark Rutherford Delivered*, 1885.

of this problem in the contemporary social context was the exceptional popularity of "Drowning," which cannot be attributed solely to its artistic qualities.

The above-mentioned scene in "Reminiscences on Returning Home" then shows us how, in the mind of Yü Ta-fu, the romantic contrast between himself and happy country life is at once interpreted as a social phenomenon, in keeping with the general tendency of the time. Along with the picture of the peasant's happy life, Yü Ta-fu sees in his mind's eye those who ravage this happy life—the politicians and soldiers—and he abuses and shows his contempt for the intellectuals who toady to them. It is evident that not even for Yü Ta-fu did the front of that time divide the individual and society, but rather the individual is driven into isolation by the general misery and chaos, the blame for which he lays at the door of those who at that time wielded power in China.

We have dealt more widely with the work of Yü Ta-fu, because in many respects he seems to us to be typical of the literary situation of his day. We have seen that even as objective a writer as Mao Tun employs a form usual in works bound up most intimately with the person of their author, namely, the diary, and the infiltration of personal, subjective and autobiographical elements into the literature of the time is characteristic of all contemporary writers. We shall have opportunity to return to this point in connection with Kuo Mo-jo; the close tie between Pa Chin's most notable work and his personal experiences has been shown by O. Král;[30] M. Boušková has demonstrated the subjectivity of the work of Ping Hsin in a study devoted to this author;[31] the form of a diary is also used by the woman writer, Ting Ling,[32] and elsewhere I have already drawn attention to the exceptional fondness for autobiography and personal reminiscences in the literature of this period.[33] I think that this fact is deserving of special attention.

It is particularly striking that this trait is not only characteristic of Chinese literature, but was a mass phenomenon somewhat earlier in the

---

[30]O. Král, "Pa Chin's novel, *The Family*," *Studien zur modernen chinesischen Literatur*, Berlin 1964, p. 97 et seq.

[31]M. Boušková, *The Stories of Ping Hsin, Studien*, p. 113 et seq.

[32]Ting Ling, *So-fei nü-shih jih-chi, Hsien-tai Chung-kuo hsiao-shuo hsüan*, Shanghai, Ya-hsi-ya shu-chü 1929, Vol. 1, p. 1.

[33]"Subjectivism and Individualism in Modern Chinese Literature," *ArOr* 25 (1957), p. 261 et seq., especially p. 266.

literature of Japan. There the spread of autobiographical literature was linked up, at least by some scholars, with the influence of naturalism. Thus Yoshikazu Kataoka, in the Preface to his book *An Introduction to Contemporary Japanese Literature*,[34] maintains that Japanese naturalism, "instead of developing into a thorough-going objectivism burying the author's ego, tended largely towards autobiographical or confession literature, which sought to project the writer's sincerity. Inevitably, it became to a marked degree a vehicle for rendering the author's personal affairs into subject matter, eventually producing the sort of result wherein the term naturalism came to be associated in one's mind with an author's miscellaneous notes respecting his private life. At the same time, even in a case of taking a broad view of phases of life, the Naturalist writers were incapable of objectifying them purely as *social* phases. The consequence was that they descended to articulating, for the most part through the medium of their own feelings, merely the conflict of harmony or sentiments. Accordingly, instead of achieving objective thoroughness, they constantly wrote narratives of exclamation, describing their individual sentiments."

The character of these tendencies in Japanese literature, as defined by the Japanese scholar, certainly calls to mind several traits which we have observed in the work of Yü Ta-fu and which are proper to the works of other authors of this epoch. If we remind ourselves that a considerable number of Chinese writers studied in Japan at a time when these tendencies were very much to the fore in Japanese literature, we might well suppose that the Japanese environment worked upon them, that Chinese parallels are the reflection of Japanese patterns, or at least that Japanese influence possibly strengthened certain leanings already existing in Chinese literature.

On the other hand, it seems to me that the interpretation of the Japanese scholar oversimplifies the situation. The influence of naturalism can explain a certain liking for sexual themes, for the portrayal of uprooted characters and persons with a hereditary taint, for dark and gloomy coloring, such as characterize several works of this genre in Japan, for example, some of the works of Katai Tayama, Doppo Kunikida, and others, and in some measure also the *oeuvre* of Yü Ta-fu, as we saw above. We could hardly, however, attribute to the influence of the writings of Zola, Maupassant or the Goncourt brothers—the writers

---

[34]Edited by the Kokusai Bunka Shinkokai, Tokyo 1939, p. XII et seq.

whom the Japanese scholar holds to be the patterns of Japanese naturalism—that tendency "towards autobiographical or confession literature," referred to in the passage cited above. The works of the French writers just mentioned are rather an example of attempts to give the most objective possible picture of reality, and it is, after all, Kataoka himself who reproaches the Japanese representatives of naturalism with insufficient objectivity and as lacking the ability to make a scientific study of reality. I would only add that his further criticism of these authors as turning their works into "miscellaneous notes," as he puts it, stresses the formal looseness of structure of these works. But that, too, would speak against an overestimation of the influence of naturalism on this literary genre, for it is certainly not possible to observe in the works of the French naturalists any tendency away from structural cohesion, rather the opposite.

A marked tendency toward the conscious breaking up of the traditional literary structure is, however, observable in European romanticism, whose whole significance after all rested in a revolt against the artificial, stylized and petrified art of the end of the feudal epoch, represented by fussy Rococo and the sober regimentational tendencies of the Age of Enlightenment. The free play of feeling, the natural and spontaneous new way of life of the rising middle classes, were reflected in literature and in art, in a rejection of all convention, regularity and prescribed rules. It seems to me that, alongside the undoubted influences of European naturalism, we must see in this fondness for a literary work, with strongly subjective coloring and having the form of a free expression of feelings and emotions or of a record of personal experiences, above all, the very palpable influence of European romanticism; or, more correctly, a similar social situation evoked similar literary tendencies. Indeed, the Japanese scholar, too, points to the "marked emotional and egoistic tendency" of this genre and attributes it to romantic influences which were pushed into the background by the predilection for the naturalistic school.[35]

We called attention above to the very strong romantic elements in the work of Yü Ta-fu; undoubtedly his works are the expression of the same *Weltschmerz* that permeates those of the European romanticists. In respect of formal aspects, we can then find numerous parallels between the records of Yü Ta-fu's various experiences, punctuated by emotional

---

[35]Op. cit., p. XI.

outbursts, and the classic of European romanticism, *Die Leiden des jungen Werthers*. There, as we know, the story of young Werther is in the form of a collection of heterogeneous materials in which the hero's letters preponderate. It is thus the freest of forms and aims to create the impression that these are documents left intact by the author. There is no doubt that in *Die Leiden* we have the prototype of those subjectively colored "miscellaneous notes" of which the Japanese scholar speaks. *Die Leiden* was translated by Yü Ta-fu's fellow writer, Kuo Mo-jo, when he was still in Japan, and the book was tremendously popular among Chinese youth.[36] It is not unlikely that it also made a great impression on Kuo Mo-jo's close friend, Yü Ta-fu. It is, indeed, probable that the whole "Creation" group grew up under the strong influence of romanticism, as we shall show in our study of Kuo Mo-jo. It would probably not be difficult to find parallels in mood and structure between *Die Leiden* and Yü Ta-fu's "Drowning" and other early works. Again and again Yü Ta-fu returns to the description of the aberrant mental states of a young man and also the tragic conclusion of "Drowning," motivated only by emotional disturbance and gloomy moods, recalls the suicide of young Werther. It seems to me, too, that we could find a certain connection between Yü Ta-fu's production and the *oeuvre* of the great Russian writer Turgenev, who, as A. Vlčková has shown, was one of Yü Ta-fu's favorite authors. Especially striking are the analogies between Yü Ta-fu's tale *Kuo-ch'ü* 過去, "The Past," and Turgenev's novella "First Love," in the portraying of women of strong personality, dominating their environment and especially their admirer, who subordinates himself to their will with devoted humility. And then also the predilection for describing love's craving and dreams rather than an actual erotic experience is a further link between Yü Ta-fu and the Russian author. We may say that these connections appear especially in the romanticist elements of the work of the two authors and that they confirm our view of the strong influence of European romanticism of Yü Ta-fu. But Yü Ta-fu lived in the twentieth century and so we could equally well find in his work naturalistic elements, as for example in the daring dissection of perverse and pathological human states and, finally, in links with the whole legacy of the nineteenth century.

It should be noted here that by literary influence we mean only that

---

[36] I pointed out in my article "Subjectivism," p. 263, how highly Chinese youth valued this book and saw in it a direct reflection of their own feelings.

foreign literary production shows an author certain possibilities and paths for the solution of his own problems and the problems of his time. If the artist is not faced with the same questions and tasks as was the artist or whole artistic school of a different time or place, no "influence" will be truly operative; at best it will only be a formal imitation, without deeper significance for the receiving literature. This is very well expressed by the Czech poet Vítězslav Nezval: "This alone is what I understand by the term literary influence: it lies in this that the poem of some poet affects us deeply, because it illuminates and verifies for us at the same time, from a position outside us, our most intimate and deepest insights and experiences and because it teaches us to try and seize and give expression to them ourselves."[37] And so, if we wish to explain the connection between the literature of the China of that time with European romanticism, we must in the first place see the similar social situation, which made a certain part of the Chinese intelligentsia—and evidently also of the Japanese—accessible to the influence of moods which beset European youth at the turn of the eighteenth and nineteenth centuries and which achieved prominence in the literature of the whole first half of the nineteenth century.

As I have already said above, the soil out of which, in both Europe and Asia, such romantic moods developed was the struggle for the liquidation of the feudal order. In Europe, this struggle is exclusively the business of the bourgeoisie, which drew over to its side the whole mass of the national collective in opposition to a narrow aristocracy. It is an economic and political struggle, which is particularly strongly reflected in the domain of the arts; there the antithesis between feudal regimentation and the unrestrained outbursts of a free man comes out very sharply. In the Far East, a similar struggle was being waged, but its aspects diverged considerably. The main difference lay in the weakness of the Chinese bourgeoisie. In Japan, the bourgeoisie never succeeded in winning the victory over the old gentry and what emerges is a symbiosis of monopolistic capital with the top stratum of the aristocracy; in China, the fight against the old gentry was not fought out by the bourgeoisie, but by the working class under the leadership of the Communist Party and having the support of the masses of the peasantry. That in itself means that bourgeois ideals, especially in strong individuals, not feeling bound by any considerations or obligations, could not develop at all, or

---

[37]Vítězslav Nezval, *Z mého života* (From My Life), Praha 1959.

could not mature into the various extreme forms in which they appeared in Europe, from the early romantic rebel and outlaw, by way of the solipsism of German romanticist philosophy, to all those types of superman evoked by the degenerate moods of the end of the nineteenth century. In the Far East, the individual intellectual still felt much more that he was crushed and threatened by his environment, in which he never found any support for his revolt so long as he remained in his own class, in that of the petty bourgeoisie, eventually in the small gentry. The first support he found was in the revolutionary working class and, later, in the revolutionized peasantry, but that meant accepting quite a different, nonromantic ideology, and substituting for the ideal of individual revolt the theory of class struggle and the class-conscious proletarian revolution. The wave of individualistic, romantic revolt of the individual could thus only be something of a passing character, only the blaze of a prairie fire which rapidly spreads, but equally rapidly dies down. And so in China, too, the romanticist writers of "Creation" soon moved over to the Marxist position, as did Kuo Mo-jo, and indications of a similar trend of development are observable, as we saw, in Yü Ta-fu.

On the other hand, it must be stressed that the questions of the individual life, of personal happiness and of individual morality were much more urgent at this time in the Far East than in Europe in the epoch of romanticism, for in the Far East feudal oppression and regimentation were inseparably bound up with patriarchal oppression, in which the whole life of the individual was determined, step by step, by the will of parents, husbands and brothers, older people and superiors, and all these demanded from those to whom the individual was subordinated, blind obedience to the point of complete self-immolation. These patriarchal ties, *wu-lun*, "the five human relationships," were the main pillar of the feudal order for they turned people into obedient automatons and were the heaviest fetters constricting the life of the individual. Moreover they were hallowed by a thousand-year-old Confucian ethic and etiquette. It is important here to realize that this morality was based on completely fallacious ideas about human beings. It maintained that children *joyfully* sacrifice themselves even for evil or worthless parents and older relatives, that a wife endures *with love* every brutality and villainy on the part of her husband, herself being without any needs, and that every subordinate longs for the opportunity to sacrifice himself for his superior.[38] It was not possible to consummate the revolution against

---

[38]Evidence of the propaganda of this feudal morality is to be found in the greater part

feudalism without destroying the patriarchal family and, especially, without utterly rooting out all these false ideas about human nature on which patriarchal morality was based. We must bear in mind that an important part of the anti-feudal revolution in China was the breaking up of the patriarchal family and the complete emancipation of women. It is my belief that in the revolt against the old morality and false ideas about man lies the main significance of this autobiographical, subjectivist stream in the literature of China and of Japan, and therein, too, the chief importance of the work of Yü Ta-fu, as well as of the similarly keyed works of Pa Chin, Ting Ling, and others. It was necessary to show that the individual has his own life, his personal needs, that his conduct is often determined by forces which are stronger than his will. The task was to show man as he really is, light up his inner life and probe its most hidden corners. This was not only necessary for literature, so that it should be capable of describing the intricate psychology of the human being, which so far it had not been able to do adequately, but it was a necessity for society to be able to check up on, and reassess its ideas about, human nature and create a new conception of morality based on a realistic knowledge of human psychology.

It is clear that, even though this trend was stimulated by impulses from outside, its true origins were implicit in a certain social situation.

Moreover, not even in the domain of literature did the main filiations of the trend lead abroad, but to the native literature, and this not only in China, but also in Japan, where it linked up with a very rich literary tradition. In many respects, however, though of course at a newer and higher level, it is a continuation and culmination of the preceding literary output in the written language, *wen-yen*. In my article "Subjectivism and Individualism," I tried to determine the main features of this literature and here I shall therefore confine myself to an enumeration of its characteristics. I shall leave out of account the tales, notes and anecdotal episodes which were only part of the marginal output of the literati and were not included in their *chi* 集, or "collected works." I have in mind their poetical works and then those designated in the collections as *ku-wen*, old art prose, even though this term rightly applies to only a single trend in this genre. The main hallmark of this literary production is its subjectivism. The author's personal experience, his views, thoughts and feelings, are the sole source of its inspiration. A considerable part of

---

of the tales written by the literati for the people, with the one aim of spreading this morality.

the work of the old literati are notes written down for personal communication, diaries, letters, and so on—works of the most intimate
nature. The outer world figures in his work only as the object of his
personal perceptions. Another trait is the lyrical quality of this literature.
In it is always expressed only a percept, a feeling, a single picture or
experience. Plot, story, epic, has no place in it.[39] Connected with this,
undoubtedly, is its limited scale. These works are, as a rule, shorter
pieces, which for the most part appear in various collections, but not
linked up to form a work of larger dimensions. The character of this
production is purely static and not dynamic, it is always a single picture
or emotional complex, which does not unfold in time. Everything in this
literature is strongly stylized and normative: the choice of vocabulary
derived exclusively from the old written language, the rhythmic layout
of the text, the fixed structure of the whole work, whether poem or prose
essay, and then also the selection of theme—nothing ugly or coarse, at
least in theory, was admissible in this literature. This normative and
artificial character goes hand in hand with a certain degree of improvisation and dilettantism; the author, having learned his craft with boundless
industry and over many years, then turns it to account on a single
occasion, under the impression of a deeply felt experience, and sometimes actually to order. This quality of improvisation no doubt also
explains the limited scale of these works, in which, as we pointed out
above, a short poem and a very concise essay or sketch predominate.
These productions are not designed for some anonymous reader, but as a
rule only for the author himself or a very small circle of friends. Beyond
this circle, and when the impulse that called them into life vanishes, they
lose their significance and meaning. For the most part it is literature of a
purely intimate, non-heroic character. The author speaks of himself
usually with a certain irony, the portrait he paints being of a man weak,
sick, poor, and beset with many troubles and hardships. We can point to
a number of sociological and philosophical reasons for this kind of
autostylization; as far as its literary significance is concerned, it seems to
me that it is part of the tendency to evoke the impression of intimacy, of
spontaneity. It is an attempt to enter into the closest possible emotional
contact with the reader and so compensate for that stylized and norma-

---

[39]See Hirth, *Das Formgesetz der epischen, dramatischen und lyrischen Dichtung*, 1923, p.
194: " . . . die lyrische Situation ist eine Schau, ein Bild, aber die Sachlage ist nicht anders
zu umschreiben, denn lebendige Verhältnisse können nur geschaut und in Bildern darge-
stellt werden."

tive character which produces a cold and impersonal impression. (Let us not forget that the literati wrote not in their own personal, natural style, but in a style they had acquired and into which they could introduce little that was personal. We may also add that this strong subjectivism also begins to color the Chinese novella and novel, when these genres become the main vehicle of expression of the Chinese literati in the eighteenth century. To this, too, we have drawn attention in the above-cited study.)

As regards literary structure, we can note that in this genre we commonly find the combination of a lyrical tableau with the record of a personal experience, eventually with commentary: in fact, the typical ground plan we repeatedly find in the works of Yü Ta-fu.[40] In this genre, too, there exists a very artfully constructed novella, expressly lyrical in character, where tension is achieved by the contrast of various emotions, and unity is maintained by means of a basic thought, which is successively illuminated from various angles, and by a unified mood or atmosphere. Examples are furnished by the crowning works of Ou-yang Hsiu, such as *Ch'iu sheng fu* 秋聲賦, "Ode on an Autumnal Note,"[41] or of Su Shih 蘇軾, for instance his celebrated *Ch'ih-pi-fu* 赤壁賦 or "Excursions to the Red Wall."[42]

The culmination of these tendencies in the old literature, in *wen-yen*, is the rise of the lyrical autobiography, represented by the work *Fou-sheng liu-chi* 浮生六記, or "Six Stories of Transient Life," by Shen Fu 沈復.[43] And even though several parts of this autobiography have outspokenly narrative, epic character, as cannot be otherwise in autobiography, the whole is not organized as a unified epic work, borne along by the stream of events, but rather as what is actually a catalog of mainly lyrical pictures and diverse notes. The material is, namely, divided according to the content into six "relations," *chi*. (For a more detailed analysis, I refer the reader again to the above-cited study.) Nevertheless,

---

[40]A typical example is the description of a festival on Tiger Hill, Hu-ch'iu 虎丘, by Yüan Hung-tao 袁宏道 (1568–1610), see *Yüan Chung-lang ch'üan-chi* 袁中郎全集, Shanghai, K'ai-ming shu-tien 1935, *Yüan Chung-lang yu-chi*, p. 1. There the description of the festival is all at once linked up with a relation about personal problems and considerations.

[41]See G. Margouliès, *Le Kou-wen Chinois*, Paris 1926, p. 259 et seq.

[42]Op. cit., p. 292 et seq.

[43]Shanghai, Hsin-wen-hua shu-she, undated. For a full survey, see *Šest historií prchavého života* (Six Tales of a Fleeting Life), translated into Czech by J. Průšek, Praha 1956.

the work is not a sheaf of quite unrelated pieces, as were the old "collections"—*chi* 集 or sketches—*pi-chi* 筆記, but is held together by a single central motif, the death of the author's wife. This tragedy is the *ostinato* running through all the parts, giving them a new significance and binding them into a unified whole. It is characteristic of the situation in Chinese literature that the creation of such larger units is not achieved by epic processes, but above all by lyrical processes, by imbuing the parts with a unifying mood. It is the same method as we discovered in the works of Yü Ta-fu.

Still more important is the fact that in the "Six Stories" we also find sharp transitions from feelings of greatest tragedy and despair to outbursts of unrestrained gaiety, the contrast between the unsullied beauty of Nature and the grief of human life, dreams of escape into the mountains and of a hermit's life opposed to the misery and dullness of everyday life. All this would entitle us to speak, too, of the strongly romantic coloring of this autobiography. Here we may note further that romantic moods inspire a great part of Chinese poetry, beginning with the poet Ch'ü Yüan.

All that we have said so far justifies the statement that if Yü Ta-fu's work and similar works of his contemporaries are influenced by European romanticism, they had their roots, at the same time, firmly in the old production of the literati. I think it is typical of the then situation in Chinese literature that an author who was so well versed in European literature and whose thought was so saturated with European ideas and pictures should show in his work such strong ties with the traditional native literature. In Yü Ta-fu, we find the diverse forms of literature cultivated by the literati—the diary, notes and the letter; his work is strongly subjective and romantic in character, permeated with lyricism and frequently contrasts the magnificent beauty of Nature with the petty misery of the life of the individual, as in the aforementioned works of the old literature. However, the fact that the shackles of feudal morality had fallen enabled the modern author to render in his work a whole scale of feelings and experiences which for the old writer were taboo. Inspired by the example of naturalism, he was able to investigate those obscure corners of his subconscious which formerly were strictly out of bounds. His work thus acquired strong dramatic and dynamic force as well as increasingly epic character.

One trait, however, must be particularly stressed in this confrontation of Yü Ta-fu's work with old traditions: Yü Ta-fu, like the older literati, conscientiously limits his artistic production to the circle of his own experiences, fights shy of pure fantasy, even should it be based on experience and observation. For him something imagined is something "empty"—*hsü*, as the old literati defined it. And so if he wishes to penetrate to reality, the one path open to him is by way of personal experience, what he writes of must be known from first-hand, not merely grasped by the intellect or conceived by the imagination. In this, too, is something of that honesty and truthfulness which characterized the notable works of the old literature and which we come across especially in Lu Hsün. Here, too, we find the requirement so often demanded of the contemporary writer, namely, that if the writer is to grasp the new reality, he must live it, must change his way of life, that the decisive factor for his art is his living experience, not merely cognition or fantasy.

Finally, it must be made clear that these traditional elements acquire in the new environment also a new significance, their aim is not to evoke some moment experienced either by the author or by his friends. These works are above all an appeal to the public, and the most intimate experience serves as propaganda against the misery and poverty of contemporary life. An instructive example of a change of function in a certain order of literature is Yü Ta-fu's *Kei i-wei wen-hsüeh ch'ing-nien-ti kung-k'ai chuang* 給一位文學青年的公開狀, "An Open Letter to a Young Writer."[44] With biting irony, Yü Ta-fu shows the uselessness of education in contemporary society, an educated man can at best pull a rickshaw or be a thief. Instead of the intimate thoughts which the old literati expressed through the medium of a letter, with Yü Ta-fu even a letter becomes a public indictment of social evils. At the same time this letter reveals the deep bitterness with which the society of his day filled him, a bitterness which had brought him into the ranks of Leftist writers.

---

[44]*Ta-fu tai-piao-tso*, p. ͻ01 et seq.

VIII
Yeh Shao-chün and Anton Chekhov

It would be a presumption on my part were I to wish to remind this esteemed gathering of the immense dimensions of the changes which are taking place today everywhere in countries outside Europe and, indeed, also in Western countries. I should only, too, be repeating a well-worn phrase were I to add that human history has not so far recorded such a tremendous revolution, both as regards its geographical extent and in respect of its depth and intensity, and that there is no critical investigator who does not feel that his powers and also the traditional methods of study are inadequate to the task of understanding and describing the process unfolding before our eyes. We shall, then, not be so lacking in modesty as to suppose that we could make some substantial comment on this world phenomenon, but confine ourselves to documenting its problems by means of an almost microscopically small section on which we have done some research, namely, the problems connected with the rise of a modern Chinese literature.

There can be no doubt that the rise of a new Chinese literature after the first World War was one of the reflexes of the revolutionary ferment that made itself felt throughout the whole of Asia and is, at the same time, also a part of this world-wide phenomenon, so that through an analysis of it we can augment and give some precision to our ideas about the causes and forces which set the process in motion. In China, the rapidity and thoroughness of the transformation of the literary structure

Lecture delivered at Stockholm University in December 1969 on the occasion of receiving the degree of Doctor Honoris Causa. Published in *Archiv Orientální* 38 (1970), 437–452.

have earned it the designation of a "literary revolution," and it is perhaps truly the only epoch in the history of literature to which the term can, in full justice, be applied.

It seems to us that hitherto—insofar as scholars have made a study of this process—they have been content more with the registration of the external aspects and we may even say with the accompanying phenomena; they have studied the political and philosophical trends influencing the literature of the given epoch, they have sought the connections with the social and economic life of the time, and so on. On the other hand, they have devoted little attention to changes in the actual structure of the literature, to what are the differences between works which are the product of the literary revolution and those of the preceding epoch. Seldom, too, has the question been raised as to what actually brought about the observed changes in the structure of the works; whether we are to seek for the causes in the realities of life, in the milieu in which the literature arose, or in the state and character of the literary legacy, or whether we must, perhaps, also take into consideration the influence of foreign literatures. We are faced with a nexus of problems which may be summed up in the dichotomy: development from within, changes brought about by the tension arising between the individual components of the literary structure, and, on the other hand, changes evoked by external causes, such as national and class conflicts, economic changes, and the like.

I shall not repeat here the results of certain previous studies. I think today we may accept as a proved fact that the new literature could not have arisen without a new artistic sensibility, generated by a new way of life, a new mental atmosphere, the product of a new technical and scientific civilization. The new literature could only be created by new artists endowed with this new sensibility and so it arose suddenly as the fruit of it. But this general statement does not enable us to explain the specific quality of individual literary works or the differences between the creative output of various authors; nor does it explain why the work of Lu Hsün is the antipode to the work of Mao Tun or Lao She. It is clear that here, at work, alongside more general causes, must have been causes of a more special kind and to discover these should be the foremost task of the literary historian. On the other hand, it is almost a banality to affirm that no work exists in a vacuum, that it inevitably shows similarities and affinities with both contemporary and past works and that it cannot be regarded as an isolated product of its author, to be explained only on the basis of his individual disposition. We believe that a work of art can only be fully comprehended if we look upon it as part of a certain context, with which it has certain traits in common; these traits it is our business to ascertain and describe and then attempt an explanation of them.

Under the term, 'literary revolution,' we must understand, above all, certain radical changes in the traditional literary structure. Our primary aim will be to establish whether the changes we discover are the result of tensions in the traditional literary structure or whether they were induced by contacts with foreign literary structures, or even whether the influence of extraliterary reality was of decisive significance. Our task must be the precise analysis of mutually interacting influences, of the individual elements operative in the literary process.

I deal in one of my more recent studies with some aspects of the revolutionary changes comprehended in the term 'literary revolution,' as observed by us in the opus of one of the greatest names in the new Chinese literature, that of Lu Hsün.[1] There I stated, too, that one of the principal attributes of one branch of the new narrative prose, as compared with the narrative prose of the preceding period, was the attenuated role of the *sujet:* the plot or story as such loses its significance to the point of vanishing entirely, its place being taken by the straightforward record of a certain segment of reality. I noted also a certain analogy to this phenomenon in European literature, but did not seek to discover its deeper roots.

I think that certain questions which occurred to us in our study of the work of Lu Hsün might be clarified by the study of the work of one of Lu Hsün's contemporaries—Yeh Shao-chün 葉 絡 鈞 , otherwise known as Yeh Sheng-t'ao 葉 聖 陶. This writer is little known in Europe, no more than a few short stories and his autobiographical novel *Ni Huan-Chih* 倪 煥 之 (*Yeh Sheng-t'ao wen-chi* 葉 聖 陶 文 集 , Jen-min wen-hsüeh ch'u-pan-sheh, Peking 1958, Vol. 3, pp. 119ff.), so named after the principal character), having, to my knowledge, been so far translated. In China, however, Yeh Shao-chün is among the foremost personalities in new Chinese literature and his work has always been rated very high. He also took part in the founding meeting of the Society for the Study of Literature—Wen-hsüeh yen-chiu hui—in 1921, when

---

[1]Lu Hsün's "Huai Chiu," *A Precursor of Modern Chinese Literature*, Harvard Journal of Asiatic Studies, Vol. 29, 1969, pp. 169–176.

the new writers made their first appearance as an organized group, and later he contributed to various literary periodicals and collaborated with important publishing houses, such as Commercial Press and K'ai-ming shu-chü. Yeh Shao-chün was somewhat younger than Lu Hsün, his birth-year being 1893 or 1894, whereas Lu Hsün was born in 1881. Nevertheless, both belong to the same group that aimed to give its hallmark to the first products of the new Chinese literature, and, indeed, their works show striking similarities. And so Yeh Shao-chün's work, like the work of Lu Hsün, offers a suitable opportunity for tracing more precisely what the literary revolution really signified and what new features not present in the old literature characterize the products of the literary revolution.

In the same way as Lu Hsün makes his literary début with a short story in the written language, entitled "A Recollection"—*Huai-chiu*, which we analyzed in the above-mentioned study, Yeh Shao-chün also writes his first surviving tale in the written language. It is the short story *Ch'iung-ch'ou* 窮 愁 , "The Sorrow of the Poor," dating from 1914 (*Wen-chi*, Vol. 3, pp. 110). It is obvious that the old traditional education, which consisted mainly in acquiring a knowledge of classical writings in the written language, determined the first literary attempts also of the new literary generation. Even in the later productions of Yeh Shao-chün, already composed in the colloquial language, we still feel the strong influence of the written language, tending always toward a parallelism of expressions and a rhythmic balance between the individual sentence clauses.

At this point, however, we must pose the question of whether the influence of literature in the written language was only involuntary and whether the authors wrote in a style which long training had made second nature to them, or whether the old hierarchy of literary genres and styles also played a part. "High" literature, as opposed to folk or popular literature, was always composed in the written language, and now, when writers aim to create literary works they hope will be regarded as "high" literature, they make use of elements, clichés and a style traditionally associated with high literature, quite overlooking the fact that the old novel and short story were always written in the colloquial language. But, of course, in the eyes of the literati that was not "real literature."

Links with the old prose are apparent both in our author's above-mentioned earliest extant short story, and especially in his first collection, published in 1922, entitled *Ko-mo*隔膜"Barrier" ("Misunderstanding," *Wen-chi*, Vol. 1, pp. 103–109), with a hint at the author's program, but also indicating the new *Lebensgefühl* with which the new authors are filled, namely, the feeling of loneliness. Nevertheless we can trace connections with the old literature alike in the lyrical sketches—the genre closest to the old literature—and in stories from life such as was his above-cited first short story. In his lyrical sketches, we find affinities with the old literature even in the choice of theme, on reading, for example, his sketch, *Han-hsiao-ti ch'in-ko*寒曉的琴歌"Song of a Lute on a Cold Morning," (*Wen-chi*, Vol. 1, pp. 84–85), we instantly are reminded of the well-known poem by Po Chü-i, *P'i-p'a Hsing*琵琶行 "Song of a Lute" (Pai-shih ch'ang-ch'ing chi白氏長慶集, *Wen-chi*, Vol. 1, pp. 103–109, ed. Wen-hsüeh ku-chi k'an-hsing she 1955, Pt. 2. ch. 12, pp. 56a–57a), describing the poet's meeting with a girl singer, who tells him the story of her life. It is interesting that in a modern writer's sketch there is no longer any story; there is only the description of a melancholy mood when the narrator—the short story is written in the first person—takes an early morning walk through a poor quarter of shabby little houses mostly, so it was said, inhabited by singers. The sketch records the feelings of the narrator on listening to the sad sound of a lute falteringly played and the singing of, it would seem, a very young girl, who is evidently, despite cold and weariness, trying to practice her song. We realize that the modern prose writer can do quite well without any story, all he needs is to explain the social significance of the observed phenomenon, in which he sees the reflection of the unhappy fate of certain groups of population. Here a definite shift is perceptible toward the capturing of reality, achieved not by the recording of facts, but alone through emotional coloring.

A close link with the old literature is apparent also in those prose pieces which are a kind of record of the fate of some individual. It should be remembered that the life-stories of interesting individuals, formerly, of course, belonging mostly to the gentry-class, used to be a favorite theme for literary *pi-chi*, "notes" or "jottings." We find very clear links with the old prose style in our author's earliest known short story in the colloquial language, *I-sheng* 一生 "A Single Life" (*Wen-chi*, Vol. 1, pp. 3–6), strongly reminiscent of Lu Hsün's story, "New Year's Sacrifice." Yeh Shao Chün's story is, however, much earlier, for it was written on February 14, 1919, not long after the publication of Lu Hsün's "Madman's Diary." Here, especially the opening paragraph, with its parallel phrases—"She was born in a peasant's family, she did not enjoy the luck of calling the servants and ordering the maids . . . putting on powder and applying the lipstick . . ."—at once recalls the style of the old classical literature. The tragic story of a girl who is bartered, beaten, dragged here and there, shows how the Chinese writer had the literary resources to picture the life of a wretched human being without trying to make his relation more interesting by contriving some artificial plot. He is content to give his narration the simple form of a report on the cruel fate of an individual. Although the traditional, narrative style sometimes erred on the side of baldness, the tales being sometimes more like police reports than literature, it led the writer, on the other hand, to exactness of factual description and to the expression of only relevant matter. Like the older authors, Yeh Shao-chün keeps strictly to the facts—for him, as for the old authors, creative fantasy was, we may suppose, "empty" and "void."

As we saw in our study of Lu Hsün, also the work of Yeh Shao-chün shows close links with the old written literature. Though the new writers strove to discard the old written literature of the gentry, the chief characteristic of which was the special language in which it was written, they did not link up with the popular literature written in the colloquial language, but with this "high" literature. That is one insight. Another is that in Yeh Shao-chün's early work we find no trace of the influence of European literature, except perhaps a general sensibility stimulating interest in "the downtrodden and oppressed," in the cruel aspects of life. Undoubtedly the work of Yeh Shao-chün is a good example of "literature for life," literature aiming to serve life, as proclaimed in 1921 by the Society for the Study of Literature, referred to above and of which Yeh Shao-chün was a founding member.

On the evidence of the above-mentioned prose pieces, we could characterize Yeh Shao-chün's early production as growing out of the soil of traditional literature, but already permeated with a new spirit. But in his second collection of short stories, of 1923, entitled after the hero of one of the pieces, *Huo-tsai* 火災 "Conflagration" (*Wen-chi*, Vol. 2) we come across certain short stories which are strikingly different in character from anything in the old literature and, on the other hand, call to mind Lu Hsün's short story "Reminiscence," which we analyzed in the study cited above. As the principal new feature in Lu Hsün's story I regard, as I pointed out in that same study, the almost complete lack of a plot and the fact that the dialogue has become practically autonomous, not even serving the purpose of more precise characterization. It is simply a form of presentation of a certain atmosphere, a certain situation, or a set of human relationships, such as we frequently meet with in the works of such modern writers in the West as Hemingway, Joyce or Faulkner. Fragments of conversation bring the character before us without any direct description, indicating relationships that could not otherwise be described, and revealing the mind of the person, his vacillations and indefinable nuances of feeling in a way straightforward description could never do.

The author endeavors to approach reality directly and render it without any artificially contrived context. The reader's impression should be that the author is just noting down a piece of reality, some real happening, or—more frequently—a casual conversation he chances to overhear. The collection *Huo-tsai* contains three pieces not in the form of short stories, but simply presenting certain segments of life. The simplest of these is the sketch *Hsiao-hsing* 曉行 "The Morning Walk" (*Wen-chi*, Vol. 1, pp. 113–121), written on November 6, 1921. It still has the traditional form of personal notes or jottings and is related in the first person. It describes a walk in the vicinity of Western Lake, Hsi-hu, near Hang-chou, a famous beauty spot. But besides the usual descriptions of the enchanting scenery—the author recalls, too, a previous visit to the Lake—he weaves into his descriptions conversations with the peasants he meets on his walk. Gradually the personal experience of a pleasant excursion changes into a series of scenes from the life of the peasants. The narrator describes two peasants working together at an irrigating wheel and notes that his compatriots, even when working together, pay no heed to each other, but concentrate on their individual tasks as if working entirely on their own. He reports a conversation about a plague of insects two years before; the peasants admit that it need not have been nearly so bad if they had been able to join forces in combating it. In the scraps of conversation, we get a glimpse of the cruel realities of the Chinese peasant's life in the old society: the landowner comes into the village to collect his rents—and not even drowning saves a poor man from the persecution of his family. The author's picture gradually fills in with miniature shots of the peasants' life, till finally we have before us a lifelike, complex picture of country life.

More ambitious is the story *Pei-ai ti chung-tsai* 悲哀的重載 "A Heavy Load of Grief" (*Wen-chi*, Vol. 1, pp. 122–191), written on June 26, 1921. The form is again of notes in which the narrator recalls his trip on a local boat, hauled by a small steamer somewhere in his native countryside, in the basin of the Yang-tzu. The boat could carry about forty persons, but "incomparably bigger was the load of grief it was wont to carry," is the author's comment. Distracted by the lovely riverside scenery and the noise of the engines, the narrator and his friend are unable to pass the time in reading and so observe the people around them and listen to their conversation. A middle-aged woman, "on whom seems to rest all the sadness of mankind," is telling how her children, afflicted by an hereditary disease, probably tuberculosis, passed away one after the other. Now her son is in hospital with no hope of recovery. He is looked after by his wife, whom he married during a short period of improvement. The narrator's field of vision is occupied successively by a rich man quarreling with an attendant about three coppers for a hot face-cloth, a vulgar young servant-woman from Shanghai, full of praise of the interesting and lucrative service offered by the Shanghai ladies who play ma-jong most of the day and of contempt for life in the country to which her husband is now calling her back. These film-like sequences of shots from real life are not related to any *sujet*. We are reminded of the assertion of the Russian literary theoretician and critic V. Šklovskij who condemned traditional subject-matter because "it spoils and deforms the literary material," and suggests substituting for it, among other things, travel notes. A Chinese author succeeded in realizing this thought even before it was expressed.

The best of these travel sequences is called *Lü-lu-ti pan-lü* 旅路的伴侶 "Travel companions" (*Wen-chi*, Vol. 2, pp. 170–181). A boat again provides the setting and a group of passengers the cast. But what reaches our ears is not this time a chain of loosely connected episodes—it is a profound and carefully built up picture presenting the fate and character of a queer human group. The chief narrators are two women, one older, with bloodshot eyes, and the other middle-aged; between them sits the girl called Chu-erh 珠兒. The girl is silent for the most part and the whole story is told by the two older women, especially the one with bloodshot eyes. They are taking the girl to an older relative in Shanghai, not as a servant, but as a help. From the conversation it is apparent that the girl left her home without saying anything to her father, telling only her mother. She evidently has not much respect for her father who, as we learn from scraps of conversation, is an incorrigible waster, opium-smoker and gambler, who has squandered his whole property, including house and boat. The family of six is dependent solely on the earnings of the mother, who sews for a livelihood. One day her husband, still in his bed, hears that his wife is finishing a piece of work for which she is to get the money. The husband gets up, goes to the customer and collects the payment, as if his wife had sent him. But in the evening he comes home and gives back the greater part of the money to Chu-erh; he had evidently won back something at cards. Nor does he treat his children badly: when he occasionally wins he brings them peanuts and oranges, but never does he bring anything to his wife. Nevertheless, a certain intimacy must exist between them, for although they have four children, she is again in the family way. Little by little, fragments of the women's conversation give us an insight into the psychology of a very strange group of people, such as we seldom meet with in the new literature and practically never in the old.

What is particularly new in Yeh Shao-chün's presentation is that we make direct acquaintance with these characters in the women's conversation, that we see them as their partners see them, that there is no attempt here at any description or commentary by the author. It is the same method as we find employed by Lu Hsün, but exploited for much more exacting aims, for the documenting of a certain general situation in the countryside, for the portrayal of various types of people and especially those who are the victims of a crushing fate, and, finally, this method is used to reveal the inner mind and relations of people who are clearly not normal. The circumstance that the author informs us of all these things solely through the reports of other speakers, without himself adding a word of comment, creates an absolutely objective approach to the reality he wishes to bring to our notice and so gives a sharper edge to the facts he records.

These methods, which we find adopted by Lu Hsün and Yeh Shao-chün, are not, as we pointed out above, at all uncommon among a number of Western authors. A very close analogy exists, for instance, in the works of Hemingway, but the writings of the Chinese author are, of course, much earlier than the writings of any of these Western authors. Are we to suppose then that Yeh Shao-chün himself created this method, without having any pattern or even impulse in the preceding literature? It seems to me that in one of his short stories we find at least a hint of where we might look for such an impulse. Yeh Shao-chün's third collection of short stories *Hsien-hsia* 線下, "Below the Horizon" (*Wen-chi*, Vol. 1, pp. 251ff.), contains the piece entitled *I-ko ch'ing-nien* 一個青年 (*Wen-chi*, Vol. 3, pp. 342–362), written on January 31, 1924, in which the principal character is a young man who wishes to become a writer. We have no special reason to regard this story as autobiographical, but there is one detail that seemed to us significant. On the wall of this apprentice-author hang the portraits of three writers: Leo Tolstoy, Anton Chekhov and Hans Christian Andersen. I have not the impression that we should find in the exclusively short-story production of Yeh Shao-chün any obvious traces of the influence of Tolstoy, even though we might find points in common in the religious bias of both authors — Yeh Shao-chün has a marked interest in Buddhism. But undoubtedly one of the authors whose portraits hang on the young writer's wall deeply influenced one domain of Yeh Shao-chün's production: that author is Hans Andersen, who served Yeh as a model for the writing of fairytales and stories for children; the name of one of his fairytales, Huang-ti-ti hsin-i 皇帝的新衣 "The Emperor's New Robes," speaks for itself.

We must ask ourselves whether the third of the writers for whom Yeh Shao-chün's hero had evidently a special esteem was not of some significance for the author of our short tales. We pointed out above that a striking feature of the narrative prose pieces of both Lu Hsün and Yeh Shao-chün, which we have here described, is the dominating importance of the dialogue, in which the characters appearing in the story introduce themselves, explain their mutual relations, indicate their living circumstances and situation, and so on. We need only call to mind one of Chekhov's well-known longer tales *V bane*, "At the Turkish Baths," where both episodes consist only of dialogues and the author's direct part in the narration is limited to several observations. It is possible that examples such as these, where the core of the story is embodied in the brisk dialogue, acted as a stimulus upon both Lu Hsün and Yeh Shao-chün, prompting them to try and present the characters in their narrative and express certain human relations through the medium of the conversations of the persons involved and so dispense with an author's introduction and commentary. Our hypothesis then gains in credibility when we discover other links between the works of Yeh Shao-chün and Chekhov.

It must, however, also be emphasized that between Chekhov's approach and that of Yeh Shao-chün there are certain basic differences. It is especially Chekhov's short stories, which make use of dialogue as the main structural element, that come closest to the genre out of which Chekhov's art evolved, namely, the humorous short story written de-

signedly for humorous magazines. Naturally this led to the stressing of
certain details at the expense of others and to a certain shift in their scale
of values; figuratively speaking, these stories are not a normal mirror held
up to life, but a distorted mirror, whose purpose it is to ridicule and
caricature the phenomena it reflects. This is not so in the case of the
Chinese artist who, trained in the strict traditions of Chinese "high"
literature, which required first and foremost accuracy and veracity,
endeavors to present a certain reality with the greatest possible exactness
and authenticity. Thus the dialogue-based short stories of Yeh
Shao-chün approach most closely the similarly constructed short stories
of Hemingway, with their stubborn endeavor to render as objectively
and truthfully as possible a given segment of reality. And so Yeh
Shao-chün's compositions have far sharper contours and he carves, with
firm, unhesitating hand, out of the hardest reality around him, the
portion he has chosen to present.

I believe, however, that in the work of Yeh Shao-chün we find other
traits showing affinities with the work of Anton Chekhov, so that our
hypothesis that the dialogue form of Yeh Shao-chün's, and eventually
that of Lu Hsün's stories was, in fact, inspired by Chekhov's short
stories is not just an empty conjecture. The two authors even work up
similar themes: Chekhov, in the short story *Damy*, "Ladies," tells how
the Director of National Schools in a certain government, is obliged to
discharge a poor teacher who has lost his voice, but promises him a
vacancy as secretary in a social institution. This good intention, however, is frustrated by the pressure of ladies, who fall over each other in
recommending a certain young man who, though far from prepossessing,
has succeeded in insinuating himself into the good graces of the local
ladies. Naturally, in face of such competition, the deserving teacher has
no chance. Yeh Shao-chün, in his story, *Ta pan tzu* 搭班子 "Shaping a
Team" (Collection *Ch'eng-chung* 城中, "In the City," *Wen-chi*, Vol. 2, pp.
203–213), describes the dreams of an idealistic pedagogue who has just
been appointed headmaster of a school and now plans to call onto his
staff friends whom he knows as persons of learning and culture. But soon
one outside recommendation after another make it clear that all his plans
are mere illusion. Of course, a similarity of themes may be a pure
coincidence, especially when we remember that Yeh Shao-chün was a
pedagogue and that the situation in Chinese schools was not so very
different from that at the schools of Tsarist Russia. Nevertheless, this
identity of themes, as well as a similar conception and approach, points

to a certain parallelism between the works of the Chinese and the Russian author, which is not likely to be purely accidental.

Common to both authors, for example, is a special kind of "bitter humour." It would be superfluous to cite examples from Chekhov, as these are readily accessible in any handbook; we shall give here only the most drastic example from the works of Yeh Shao-chün, which at the same time will illustrate the more tragic disposition of the Chinese author.

Positively demonic is the sharpness of the impact made by the mixture of sardonic humor with the most terrible tragedy in Yeh Shao-chün's short story *Fan* 飯, "Rice" (Collection *Huo-tsai, Wen-chi*, Vol. 1, pp. 132–140, written on September 24, 1921), localized in a village in a flooded area, where the young crops are rotting, which for the inhabitants is the presage of famine. An inspector comes to visit the school and reprimands the teacher who is not at his post, because he has gone to buy groceries for his family. The teacher humbly promises never to go again to buy groceries for his family. The children make fun of him: If his family has no groceries, they will have nothing to eat and will die of hunger. For the children, too, there is in it a kind of devilish humor, because they know from the grown-ups that they are all on the brink of starvation. The teacher's family is now in a still more precarious situation, for the inspector has imposed a fine on him equal to the greater part of his salary. One might say that here Yeh Shao-chün's humor penetrates to regions even more tragic and dehumanized than those explored by Chekhov.

It seems to me, however, that the main parallels between the two authors' works must be sought in two more general spheres: The first is a certain attitude to life, which led both writers to draw upon a similar group of themes and to regard them in a similar way; the second is the special free form which predominates in their short story production and which we find already in Lu Hsün. There we defined it as an attenuation, eventually a suppression, of the function of a *sujet* in the compositional structure.

Chekhov described very accurately his thematic bias and the purpose of his work in the short story *Kryžkovnik*, "Gooseberries": "But look at life: the baseness and sloth of the strong, the ignorance and brutality of the weak, everywhere indescribable misery, hardship, degeneracy, drunkenness, hypocrisy and mendacity . . . And yet, in the streets and in the houses, all is peace and quiet; of the fifty thousand people living in the town not a single person who would shout out a protest against it. We see those who go to the market to buy, who eat during the day and sleep at night, speak about their trivialities, get married, grow old and respectfully accompany their dead to the grave; but we do not see and we do not hear those who suffer, and what is terrible in life takes place behind the scenes. Everything is quiet and peaceful—only the dumb statistics protest: so and so many people have lost their reason, so and so many barrels have been drunk, so and so many children have died of undernourishment . . . Such a state of affairs is evidently necessary—a happy man feels happy only because the unhappy bear their burden in silence, for without this silence happiness would not be possible. Behind the door of every contented and happy man, somebody would need to stand with a hammer and by constant knocking remind him that there are unhappy people and that, no matter how happy he is, life will sooner or later show its claws, that there will come upon him evil, sickness, poverty and losses, and nobody will see or hear him, just as he now does not see and hear the others . . ."

Six of Yeh Shao-chün's collections of short stories are written in this key, though among them are not lacking pieces of a sunnier character. Let us note here, for example, the above-mentioned cruelly realistic story, *I-sheng*, "A Single Life," or the tale entitled *Ch'ien-yin-ti ai* 潛隱的 愛 "The Hidden Love," contained in the first of Yeh Shao-chün's collections (*Wen-chi*, Vol. 1, pp. 93–103), about the similarly wasted life of a woman, or the still more heartbreaking piece, *Ch'un-kuang pu shih t'a-ti* 春光不是他的, "The Glory of Spring Is Not for Her" (*Collection Hsien-hsia, Wen-chi*, Vol. 1, pp. 363–387). The last-mentioned tells of the brave struggle of a woman to acquire education and independence when her husband drives her away, but who after all her striving sees that "the glory of spring is not for her." Yeh Shao-chün is able to paint in, like Chekhov, the hopeless greyness, misery and dreariness of Chinese life, very much the same in these respects as life in Russia. We could document this in dozens of examples. In certain instances, however, I should say that Yeh Shao-chün goes farther than his Russian predecessor—that he creates pictures that could well find a place in the gallery of the most anguishing existentialist visions of hopeless despair and human loneliness—of a human being rotting away in the dark and cold, all around him the indifference and apathy of his fellow creatures. I think a story far overstepping the bounds of place and time within which it arose is that entitled *Ku-tu* 孤獨 "Lonely," or better, "Deserted"

(Collection *Hsien-hsia, Wen-chi*, Vol. 1, pp. 251–268, written on January 28, 1923), describing the gradual loss of all human contacts and the sinking into endless darkness and loneliness of an old man. After a vain attempt to find a little human warmth beside his only relative, he fails, too, in his endeavor to evoke from the little boy of his landlady any affectionate response. The child does, indeed, snatch the orange he has bought with his few coppers out of his hand, but at once he turns away from him and the landlady drives the old man back into his dark hole, among dirty rags covered with dust and soot, because his cough irritates her. It is a penetrating vision of a human being driven to the limits of the last attributes of existence. It is a work of great formal perfection, too, unified and highly organized. In it the reminiscences of the old man and his gradual decline are projected in a kind of flashback in the last stage on his path to nothingness. Not even Lu Hsün succeeded in rendering so suggestively the greyness and hopelessness of a great part of Chinese life.

In Chekhov, too, we find a short story with a subject and mood very close to Yeh Shao-chün. It is the piece called *Nachlebniki*, "The Parasites," also telling the story of a lonely old man who wishes to set out and visit his practically unknown granddaughter, in the uncertain hope that she will take him in. In order not to be hampered in any way on his journey, he gets the knacker to put down his horse and his dog, the last creatures to feel any attachment to him. And when the animals fall, he is ready himself to face the slaughterer's death-blow. The story reveals with superlative art the confused, pitiful brutality of the old man, but cannot compare with the terrifying picture of humanity drawn by the Chinese artist. It is difficult to say whether there is any thematic connection between the short story of Yeh Shao-chün and that of Chekhov, it is not even particularly likely, but it is a further proof of how the works of both authors grow out of the same attitude to life that permeates their art.

Chekhov surprised his contemporaries with the novelty of his form, or rather with the fact that his short stories seemed to lack any kind of form. The Russian literary theoretician Viktor Šklovskij cites in his *Zametky o proze russkich klasikov*, "Notes on the Prose of Russian Classics," a critical notice that appeared in 1886, in the periodical *Nov*, by the critic Zmijev, where he writes: "Short stories such as 'Conversation with a Dog,' *Jeger*, 'The Huntsman' . . . and many others are more like delirious ravings or babbling for the sake of babbling about terrible stupidities than the telling with even the slightest precision of a properly thought-out tale." I think that here is expressed in other—somewhat harsh—words, what we observed in connection with Lu Hsün's short story, namely, the weakening of the significance of the *sujet*.

The special and new feature of Chekhov's work is excellently defined by L. N. Tolstoy, who, himself a great artist, grasped exactly what was the essence of his contemporary's work: "It is not possible to make a comparison between Chekhov and earlier Russian writers—say Turgenev, Dostojevskij, or even myself. Chekhov has his own form, like the Impressionists. You look—he seems to be smearing on without thinking the colors that come to his hand, and seemingly there is no mutual connection between these strokes of color. But when you step back a little and take another look, you experience a surprising impression: in front of you is a sparkling, fascinating picture" (cited in D. J. Raichin, V. J. Stražkev and others, *History of Russian Literature*, Czech translation, Praha 1948, pp. 402–403).

Tolstoy expresses the simple fact that the old artists painted a theme, a story, an episode, a reminiscence—such as "The Birth of Venus," whereas the Impressionist artist painted a part of reality—what he saw and how he saw it, and rejected any kind of "story." We find the same attitude in Chekhov's short stories. The artist renders a certain segment of reality and does not subordinate it to any previously thought out plot. Many such prose pieces, with a *sujet*, are to be found in Chekhov's literary production; we have only to open any collection of his short stories. Let us take, for instance, the piece entitled *Archijerej*, "The Bishop," which records the last days of Bishop Peter, his officiation in the Easter rites of the Church, a visit of his mother, conversations, recollections, emotions—a sequence of pictures registering the last hours of an ordinary old man. The short story, *Na podvode*, "On the Wagon," is merely the noting down of the simple experiences of a woman teacher returning on a wagon from the district town where she has been for money. In Yeh Shao-chün's output, such stories without a plot, or with only a very slight one, comprise the largest part of his work. Belonging to this category are the short stories we have described, those constructed out of fragments of conversation overheard on a boat, those describing the sad fate of various persons, mostly women, for instance, the piece entitled *Ah Feng* 阿 鳳 contained in Yeh Shao-chün's first collection of short stories (*Wen-chi*, Vol. 1, pp. 70–74) and giving a picture of a little girl, bearing with courage and humor the hard lot of a child-bride in the family of a headservant, and, finally, those stories relating various experiences of the author. Among them is the very charming piece, *Ma-ling kua* 馬鈴瓜(the name of an excellent kind of melon); the story is contained in the author's third Collection *Hsien-hsia*, "Below the Horizon" (*Wen-chi*, Vol. 1, pp. 323–341) and tells how the author, as a boy, sat for the first State examination.

It is interesting that neither European students of Chinese literature, nor Chinese literary critics, should see in the face character of Yeh Shao-chün's short stories any innovation; rather did they see a departure from established procedures in the works of those among his contemporaries who imitated European prose of the nineteenth century. I think that the reasons for this are not far to seek. All the prose production of the old literati, insofar as it was written in *wen-yen*—the old written language—was essentially without a plot; on the contrary, a plot or story was rejected as "empty fantasy," "fanciful invention." The main part of their prosaic output consisted of various sketches, notes or jottings, often of a lyrical character, and we should find in this production a number of parallels to both the work of Yeh Shao-chün and various examples of Chekhov's art and, in general, to the modern prose arising in Europe after the first World War. The links between modern Chinese and European writers are not due so much to the direct influence of the new European literature on the Chinese, as to the closeness of traditional Chinese writing to modern European production. The tradition which determined the work of Yeh Shao-chün and Lu Hsün also explains certain traits that make the work of Chinese authors seem, in a number of respects, more modern than the work of the Russian author. One of these features is the stress on the role of the narrator in the work of Lu Hsün and also in that of Yeh Shao-chün. The greater part of their short stories is in the form of the relation of a certain narrator and is in the first person. A certain intimacy is thereby achieved which we often find lacking in Chekhov, but which is strikingly manifest in Hemingway. Again the reason for this is to be found in tradition—the notes of the literati were composed for the most part as *Ich-Erzählungen* in keeping with the predominantly lyrical character of Old Chinese literature as a whole.

In concluding my address, I should like to draw attention to one fact which, should it be confirmed, might afford a further proof of the links between the work of Yeh Shao-chün and the work of Anton Chekhov. It is the prose piece *Ch'iu* 秋 "Autumn," included in the third volume of his collected works (*Wen-chi*, Vol. 3, pp. 34–42). It is my impression that this short story is actually nothing else than a certain parallel to

Chekhov's famous play *Višnevyj sad*, "The Cherry Orchard." The theme is transposed into a Chinese context, but the basic situation remains the same. The heroine is, for Chinese conditions, somewhat unusual. Though she is already in her thirties, she is not married and earns her living as an independent woman; she is a midwife, but obviously is of higher intellectual standing. She returns from Shanghai to the country for the spring festival of the dead, to visit the graves of her family, and is immediately approached by his sister-in-law, who offers her an excellent match with an older banker. Soon, however, the young woman finds out that behind it is a very definite ulterior motive: the family wish to sell their old family house and dispossess her of the twenty *mou* of land left her by her father. The excursion to the graves, the recollection of the charm of her early life, provide the lyrical background to the tale. Confused and unhappy at the breaking-up of the home where she spent the first sixteen years of her life, the young woman returns to Shanghai. Again it would be difficult to prove that Chekhov's play did, indeed, inspire Yeh Sheng-t'ao's prose piece, but the correspondences in theme, the uncommon character of the heroine, and other parallels which we have discovered between the short-story genre of the Chinese and the Russian author make this connection probable. Nevertheless, it must be noted that Yeh Shao-chün's story is very different in tendency from Chekhov's play.

It would be an interesting contribution to the tracing of the roots of modern Chinese literature and, especially of the literary origins of the work of Yeh Shao-chün and, possibly, also of Lu Hsün. On the other hand, we must stress that, despite the parallels with the European works which we have pointed out, it seems to me that much more important for the rise of the new Chinese literature is the influence of the Old Chinese literature, especially that written in the classical language. It was necessary only to permeate the old traditions with the new artistic sensibility for them to become the fertile soil for new creations. It is worth considering whether this example of ours might not shed light also upon other domains of Chinese cultural, economic and political life.

IX

Basic Problems of the History of
Modern Chinese Literature:
A Review of C. T. Hsia,
A History of
Modern Chinese Fiction

I. General Remarks

Being myself opposed, in principle, to carrying on a discussion in the spirit of dogmatic intolerance and disregard for human dignity, I must, insofar as these qualities are present in the book by C. T. Hsia,[1] first make clear my standpoint in regard to them. Only then will it be possible to treat objectively of those parts of the book worthy of serious comment.

Admittedly it is only natural that the attitude and approach of every scholar or scientist is determined in part by subjective factors, such as his social standing, the time he lives in, and so on—in short, by those *idola mentis* of which Francis Bacon spoke many centuries ago. Still, all scientific endeavor would be vain, should the investigator not aim at discovering objective truth, at trying to overcome his personal bias and prejudices, but, on the contrary, make use of a scientific work to indulge in them. This requirement is all the more necessary if the book is designed for a wider circle of readers and deals with a subject on which the reader himself cannot form a judgment and, over and above, one he is likely to approach with a certain bias. The author's responsibility is then all the greater. There can be no doubt that a book treating of modern and the most recent Chinese literature demands a quite exceptional measure of objectivity, as the majority of readers—not excluding

Published in *T'oung Pao* 49 (1962), 357–404.

[1] C. T. Hsia, *A History of Modern Chinese Fiction 1917–1957, with an Appendix on Taiwan by Tsi-an Hsia* (New Haven: Yale University Press, 1961).

195

professional sinologists—cannot correct the author's judgments independently, as they do not possess a sufficient knowledge of the material under discussion, and certainly there is here a much greater danger of judgments being colored or even distorted by personal prejudice than if the author were to write of English, French or Russian literature.

The author of the book under review admits the need of making such demands, but only insofar as they apply to other authors than himself. Thus he censures Catholic authors of histories of modern Chinese literature for not complying with his postulate (p. 496): "Yet a literary history, to be meaningful, has to be an essay in discrimination and not a biased survey to satisfy extrinsic political or religious standards." Unfortunately, as we shall show in a number of examples, C. T. Hsia's work serves, for the most part, just the satisfying of extrinsic political standards.

It is sufficient to read the chapter headings, "Leftists and Independents," "Communist Fiction I," "Conformity, Defiance and Achievement," and so on, to see at once that the criteria according to which C.T. Hsia evaluates and classifies authors are first and foremost of a political nature and not based on artistic considerations; in other words, he commits the same sin as that for which he condemns Catholic writers. Indeed, the author himself tells us that he is not so much interested in the literary aspect of the work as in the political standpoint it embodies. On p. 498, he declares: "In my survey of modern Chinese fiction, I have been principally guided by considerations of literary significance," but immediately adds: "The writers towards whom I have shown critical approval or enthusiasm share by and large the same set of techniques, attitudes and fantasies with the other writers of their period, but by virtue of their talent and integrity, they have resisted and in some notable cases transformed the crude reformist and propagandist energies to arrive at a tradition that presents a different literary physiognomy from the tradition composed principally of leftist and Communist writers."

And here we arrive at the second general requirement for a scientist and especially for an historian. I do not think a present-day historian, notably after the experience of the last War, can adopt the old slogan, *Tout comprendre c'est tout pardonner*, but still we must demand of him normal human decency. And in this the author is very often lacking. We may differ in our opinion as to the correctness of the political views of the writer Ting Ling, we may easily differ in our estimate of her various works, but we cannot let pass without protest the way in which the author speaks of her life and character. It is repugnant to a degree that C. T. Hsia should use the most vulgar expressions in connection with this woman's personal relations, while repeating nothing more than mere gossip.

It is immediately clear with what malicious spite C. T. Hsia speaks of Ting Ling and of left-wing writers in general. Thus, for instance, he brings in the name of Lu Hsün quite gratuitously in connection with the description of this scene from a short story by Ch'ien Chung-shu (p. 434): "The hero is a duce, . . . he now lies helpless in bed, surrounded by a tearful throng of admirers. (One is reminded here of the homage the dying Lu Hsün receives; but the Writer seems more of a composite of Chiang Kuang-tz'u, Ts'ao Yü, and the early Pa Chin.)" This last sneer aimed at a group of the most deserving of Chinese writers is itself sufficient proof of a complete disregard for the limits set by good taste.

The intrepidity with which C. T. Hsia presents his judgments of various leftist writers contrasts strangely with the moderation bordering on positive laxness which he shows in connection with questions of partriotism. Not only does C. T. Hsia fail to give a just assessment of the heroism of these writers—and they comprised the great majority—who left their homes on the Chinese seaboard during the Japanese occupation and withdrew to the interior in order to help in their nation's struggle; he tries, on the contrary, to make light of it. It is difficult to grasp how anybody knowing the heroic role of the Chinese writers during the War can write the following sentence (p. 275): "With this novel [Hsiao Chün's *Village in August*], we are entering the extremely uncomfortable period of wartime patriotic propaganda," and speak in derogatory terms of militant patriotic literature.

It would be a superfluous undertaking to show how unjust are the verdicts of the author in his evaluation of the work of Hsiao Chün and other patriotic writers. I should only like to point out one thing in this connection, namely, that C. T. Hsia says not a word about the immense influence of this work upon Chinese youth and the broad masses of the people, or the immeasurable service rendered by it in the patriotic struggle of the Chinese people, facts well brought out by E. Snow in the Foreword to the English translation of the above-mentioned book (T'ien Chün, *Village in August*, Introduction by E. Snow, London 1942).

The author, on the other hand, is remarkably tolerant in his judgment of acts of downright collaboration, such as the betrayal of

Chou Tso-jen, whose contribution to the rise of a new literature is rated very high. C. T. Hsia characterizes his behavior during the war in the following words (p. 314): "Chou Tso-jen, too much in love with the culture of Peking to undertake the long trek to the interior, is content to remain as minister of education in the puppet government of North China." Only later the fact is mentioned that after the War, Chou Tso-jen, like collaborators in all other countries, was sentenced to several years' imprisonment. In the same connection, C. T. Hsia writes of another favorite author of his, whose work as an essayist and critic was closely bound up with the activities of Chou Tso-jen, namely, Lin Yutang: "Hu Shih and Lin Yutang are in America, the one as Ambassador to Washington and the other as a best-selling author purveying the charms of the old China and reporting on the heroism of the new" (ibid.). Not even in the case of Lin Yutang does it strike C. T. Hsia how great is the difference between the decision to lead a life full of hardship in the interior and a life of ease in the United States, from where—so far as I know—Lin Yutang returned only once for a short visit to China, whereupon he wrote a sharp pamphlet against the forces of resistance in the Liberated Areas. The same indulgence characterizes the author's attitude to the majority of writers whose work is congenial to him: Ch'ien Chung-shu, Eileen Chang, Shih T'o and others. The impression we get is that, for C. T. Hsia, to remain and work in occupied territory was a kind of merit, whereas those who went to the interior to work and fight were deserving of condemnation.

This curiously perverted judgment does not only point to an individual lack of those feelings and sentiments which seem natural in the citizen of any country, but shows us at the same time that C. T. Hsia is incapable of justly evaluating the function and mission of literature in a given period, of correctly grasping and showing its historical role. C. T. Hsia may deny such a view as he will, but literature has a social function and the writer is responsible for his life and work to the community to which he belongs. I think it is chiefly owing to this failure to grasp the social significance of literature that the introductory chapter devoted to the Literary Revolution does not make a correct or adequate assessment of all that has taken place in Chinese literature since 1918.

C. T. Hsia repeatedly reproaches Chinese writers for devoting too much attention to social problems and being unable to create a literature unshackled by these problems and unburdened by the struggle for social

justice, actually seeing in these the general weakness of the new literature: ". . . the generally mediocre level of modern Chinese literature is
surely due to its preoccupation with ideals, its distracting and overinsistent concern with mankind" (p. 499); this complaint is repeated
again and again. At the same time he admits that it was perhaps
inevitable, that it was the consequence of a certain objective reality.
Instead of blaming Chinese writers for subordinating their literary work
to social needs, it would have been more appropriate to show what the
necessities were which induced them to take such a course, to give a
picture of the historical situation which determined the character of
modern Chinese literature.

C. T. Hsia, in his lack of comprehension for the social function of
literature, goes so far as to censure even those Chinese theoreticians
whose worth he fully acknowledges, for their excessive preoccupation
with social factors. Thus he also reproaches Hu Shih, who he claims
declared his allegiance to "humanitarian realism," for his "narrow view of
literature as an instrument of social criticism" (p. 9). Similarly he
criticizes Chou Tso-jen and his demand for "a humane literature,"
observing that "he was as much dedicated to the task of reforming
Chinese society . . . as his fellow-intellectuals" and that "this reformist
urge . . . accounts for the shallow character of the early romanticism,"
adding that "it inevitably leads to a patriotic didacticism" (p. 21). It
would be only logical if the author were to explain the reasons for this
general attitude on the part of theoreticians and writers, not excluding
rightists; in other words, were he to describe the social context of the
literary revolution.

This, however, C. T. Hsia nowhere attempts to do, for it would
immediately be apparent that the Marxist theoreticians were right in
defining the period in which the new literature developed as a period of
revolution aimed at the overthrow of the survivals of feudalism and
against foreign imperialism. He would be forced to admit, too, that this
struggle, in which the very existence of the Chinese nation was at stake,
was waged with such fury that no writer could remain indifferent, nor
had any writer either the time or the peace of mind to be able "to engage
in disinterested moral exploration," as recommended by C. T. Hsia.

Such an analysis of the social conditions under which the new
Chinese literature arose and developed would have compelled C. T.
Hsia, moreover, to admit that, in the struggle to abolish feudal survivals,
the chief enemies of progress were certain social groups—landowners,

usurers, speculators and the compradore bourgeoisie. He would have had to explain, too, that the Chinese bourgeoisie was not strong enough to lead the struggle for the overthrow of feudal survivals to a victorious conclusion, for which reason it could not fill the leading role in this revolutionary conflict, as did the European bourgeoisie in a similar situation, and that alone the revolutionary masses of workers and peasants, under the leadership of the Communist Party, could guarantee a victorious outcome to the struggle.

Further, an analysis of this kind would have provided him with the explanation why those writers or, more commonly, theoreticians, whose standpoint was that of the bourgeoisie and who were the disseminators of western bourgeois ideals in China, had no public following. Indeed, C. T. Hsia is himself obliged to confess (p. 23) that "the Anglo-American group found themselves, upon their return to China, already in a minority position, out of sympathy with the literary and ideological fashions firmly established by the Japanese-returned students." Only, of course, what was decisive was not the victory of this or that group of returned students, but the question of how to solve the general situation in China, to which bourgeois literature had no answer.

Such a statement of fact would have made a serious literary historian see the necessity for investigating the root causes of such a situation and not let him be content with the facile explanation that it was all due to Communist propaganda. Why did the most serious and profound thinkers of New China go the road of Marxism? There must have existed certain objective reasons why Chinese intellectuals saw no other solution of conditions in China than a social and socialist revolution.

We must consider it no less a shortcoming, too, that C. T. Hsia nowhere deals with the question of the significance of the literary revolution in the context of Chinese literary history. For him, the literary revolution can be reduced to the introduction of *pai-hua* into literature, which, in his view must mainly be accredited to Hu Shih, who also, as he claims, drew attention to the old literary traditions in *pai-hua*. Further, Hu Shih, according to C. T. Hsia formulated a certain nexus of social-reformist themes, which, in the eyes of our author, was already a dangerous narrowing down of literature. Chou Tso-jen then, he affirms, crowned this work by setting the new literature the aim of becoming "Humane Literature." Everything else was the work of radicals who were "downright irresponsible" (p. 9), who absolutely rejected the past, "would have no traffic with tradition," because "they were deeply ashamed of China's past" (p. 11), and so on.

C. T. Hsia passes over in silence the fact that Lu Hsün most certainly did more for spreading a knowledge of old literature than Hu Shih and that it was from the ranks of the leftist writers that the two greatest literary historians of New China came—Cheng Chen-to and A Ying 阿英 (his real name being Ch'ien Hsing-ts'un 錢杏邨). There was a world of difference, however, between evaluating the old culture as a rich national heritage, which must be known and studied, and fighting, in the name of the old traditions, against new ideas and social advance.

Had C. T. Hsia posed the question as to what tasks faced the Chinese literary revolution, he would have ascertained that Ch'en Tu-hsiu's formulation of 1917 could not be discarded as "a piece of fustian interweaving literary ignorance with critical irresponsibility" (p. 4), and that, on the contrary, Ch'en Tu-hsiu grasped the problems of the literary struggle then going on much more penetratingly than Hu Shih, who, according to C. T. Hsia, "in the main counsels avoidance of stale sentiments and themes and of outworn diction" (p. 4).

From the fact that the main social and political content of this time was the anti-feudal revolution, it followed that also in literature and in culture in general the whole complex of feudal culture and its traditions had to be abolished, for without such a spiritual revolution it was not possible to realize a social revolution. It was necessary to abolish the whole feudal cultural complex, for it was the codification and the most redoubtable stronghold of the old social order. This codex was a pet-rification of the undemocratic social hierarchy and bound the individual by endless rules and regulations. The jettisoning of this complex was also an essential prerequisite for the further development of spiritual and intellectual life in China. China had to effect in the span of a few years the process of the emancipation of thought from the medieval view of the world, a process which in Europe lasted from the Renaissance and the Reformation up to the French Revolution. If the problem is posed in this way, we see that the radical Chinese thinkers, such as Ch'ien Hsüan-t'ung, Lu Hsün, Li Ta-chao and others, were entirely in the right.

How inadequate was what Hu Shih recommended as the content of a literary reform is immediately obvious if we confront the new literature with the literature existing in China up to the 1911 Revolution and, indeed, up to the May Fourth Movement, even if we select for such comparison the relatively most advanced genre—the satirical novel of about 1900. Certainly, the novels of Wu Wo-yao, Li Po-yüan and Tseng P'u cannot be criticized for expressing "stale sentiments and themes." They are full of sincere indignation at the state of China, sharply attacking the old bureaucracy and containing likewise the social themes which Hu Shih recommends to new authors. As regards diction, it is not "outworn" in the sense in which C. T. Hsia uses the term, because he, following Hu Shih, judges the modernity of diction according to whether the author writes in *pai-hua* or in *wen-yen*, and, of course, these novels are written in *pai-hua*. And yet, these novels do not mark the beginning of a truly new phase in the development of Chinese literature, but are substantially a continuation of the old satirical-critical novel. The reason is that these authors, in spite of their critical attitude toward officials and sometimes toward the gentry as a class, still take their stand on the soil of traditional Confucian thought. They are, without exception, Confucians, who would try to graft certain European political concepts upon the old stock of traditional Confucianism. And so they are unable to enfranchise themselves from the old literary traditions and clichés, or to achieve a new vision of reality, with the result that they are also unable to find new forms of artistic expression. For the consummation of a revolution in Chinese literature, a completely new generation was necessary—one that had thrown off the shackles of the old way of thinking, rejecting Confucianism, taking its stand on new ideological positions and opening wide the door to all the achievements of modern world literature. The generation of Lu Hsün was the first to create a modern realistic literature in China. We can best measure the immense gulf between the old literature and the new if we contrast the passionate defense of Confucianism in the novel *Lao Ts'an yu-chi* by Liu O with the condemnation of Confucianism, as the morality of cannibals, in Lu Hsün's short story "The Diary of a Madman," two works separated in time by a mere twelve or thirteen years. The realization of a complete break with the old way of thinking and the old literature was the main content of the struggle then being waged in China, whence it follows that Ch'en Tu-hsiu was right in calling for "a plain, simple and express-ive literature of the people" and for "a fresh and sincere literature of realism," and not Hu Shih.

The main core of the struggle was not a question of establishing *pai-hua* and discarding *wen-yen*, for literature in *wen-yen* was dead even before the literary revolution, as admitted even by Hu Shih in his article, *Chien-she-ti wen-hsüe ko-ming lun* 建設的文學革命論 "On a Constructive Literary Revolution" (in *Hu Shih wen-ts'un* 胡適文存, Shanghai 1940, Vol. 1, pp. 77 et seq.). As we have already made clear, it was a matter of dislodging a whole complex of traditional culture, a part of which was not only literature written in *wen-yen*, but also old literature in *pai-hua*. This, too, was interlined with feudal habits of thought and its diction was outmoded. It was necessary to create an entirely new literary language, such as would meet all the exacting requirements of a new national literature.

A closer look at C. T. Hsia's picture of the development of Chinese literature in this revolutionary period reveals that the author is not capable of placing the literary phenomena of which he treats in the proper historical perspective, of showing their connection with the preceding development, or eventually bringing them into relation with world literature. Instead of employing a truly literary scientific method, C. T. Hsia is content to adopt the procedures of a literary critic—and of a very subjective critic at that. And though he frequently makes comparisons between Chinese authors and certain European writers, they are of an accidental character and not the result of a systematic investigation of such connections. In the whole book, we do not come across a single example which would show that C. T. Hsia has seriously considered the links binding the authors of whom he treats with the past, although in the case of a writer who is such a vehement opponent of the radical revolutionaries for their presumed rejection of the heritage of the past, the question of what in this heritage was still alive and what could still be made use of in the creation of a new literature should occupy a foremost place. And undoubtedly, among a large number of modern writers, we should find such links to be surprisingly numerous.

A systematic investigation of the relations of the new Chinese writers to various European authors is equally lacking. C. T. Hsia occasionally mentions points of resemblance between characters in the works of Mao Tun and characters "in the naturalistic fiction of Zola, Norris and Dreiser" (p. 157); he speaks of Lao She's predilection for English literature (p. 166), even noting that his novel *Niu T'ien-tz'u* is modeled on Fielding's *Tom Jones* (p. 180), and affirms that *Camel Hsiang-tz'u* reveals a close emotional affinity with Hardy's fiction, especially *The Mayor of Casterbridge* (p. 182). These, however, are nothing more than chance remarks, though a study of such affinities might have greatly assisted him in assessing the originality and maturity of the new literature.

This same lack of a systematic and scientific approach to the material explains why C. T. Hsia is unable to discover the relations between writers of this epoch and similarities in thier creative method, which would at least provide a basis for systematic grouping of writers. Such a procedure would certainly be preferable to a mechanical division, according to a writer's formal membership of this or that literary or political group.

This deficiency in the work of C. T. Hsia is caused, at least in part, by the author's inadequate knowledge and limited use of the existing special literature. His aim is to discover in the new Chinese literature another tradition than that pointed out by the Leftist Chinese critics and historians. He wishes, in fact, to make a reassessment of various writers. And that is undoubtedly his good right. But in order to do so, the author would need to give the views of other authors and critics, argue his own case and refute their opinions. His book is certainly large enough to give him ample scope for such a controversy. But the author rarely attempts anything of the kind. Of the European literature on the new Chinese literature he has a more thorough knowledge only of English and certain French works, which, however, he summarily rejects (these are the above-mentioned missionary works). But he is not acquainted with the literature in German—for instance, my comprehensive book on the literature of the Liberated Areas and a number of other studies and books, nor does he know any of the Russian literature, which includes a whole series of excellent monographs, such as those on Lu Hsün and other writers, as well as several comprehensive works. But, in general, he is not sufficiently familiar with Chinese pre-War literary criticism, of which van Boven, for example, made full use in his book. For a reassessment of the place occupied in pre-War literature by authors of the stature of Lu Hsün, Mao Tun, Ting Ling, Lao She, and others, an essential condition would be a confrontation with the criticism of that time, which presented, after all, a clearer picture of the general situation on the literary front.

An insufficient grasp and consideration of the basic social problems is apparent in all the general chapters of C. T. Hsia's book. As a result, he reduces all conflicts and discussions which took place on the Chinese literary front to the level of personal quarrels and struggles between individual coteries. Singled out by him as a particularly black sheep, who instigated campaigns against various Chinese writers, is the present Deputy-Minister of Culture and the well-known literary critic and theoretician, Chou Yang.

Thus, for instance, every social historian would at once grasp that the quarrel which broke out shortly before the beginning of the war with

Japan, as to whether the Leftist writers were to aim at the forming of a unified front of patriotic resistance in literature as well as in politics and cease hostilities against writers of a different political orientation, was far from being a mere "Battle of Slogans" and "a silly quarrel in itself" (p. 299), as C. T. Hsia affirms, but one of the most serious questions of Chinese politics at that time. It was this very struggle for the creation of a unified, all-national front, which the Chinese Communist Party carried through to a successful conclusion, even despite opposition from its own ranks, which is positive proof of how honestly the Communist Party put the interests of the whole nation first. On the other hand, it is an insinuation to attribute, as does C. T. Hsia, Lu Hsün's initially negative attitude to Party policy as due to personal vanity. The events of 1927 had shown Lu Hsün that it was difficult to trust the Kuomintang and right-wing elements and so he opposed what might seem to be a kind of capitulation. It is also probable that Lu Hsün was angered by attacks on his friends, for there can be no doubt that, among his opponents, there were frequent manifestations of petty bourgeois radicalism and dogmatism.

A completely distorted picture is given by C. T. Hsia of the ideological problems in the Liberated Areas during the War and of Mao Tse-tung's views, especially his "Talks at the Yenan Literary Conference" in 1942. C. T. Hsia does not see the absolutely urgent need to create a new literature and art for the broad masses, now politically and culturally awaking, the greater part of whom were still illiterate. Without a new and truly popular literature and art, such as would provide the people with entertainment and instruction, it was not possible to hold out through a protracted and terribly destructive war, to create new and deeply democratic forms of political life and to effect what can justly be called a cultural revolution in territories which till then had been the most backward in the whole of China.

Perhaps nowhere else and at no other time have the creative powers of the people been stimulated into growth on such a scale and produced such valuable fruit as in the Liberated Areas. Despite all C. T. Hsia's attempts to belittle its significance, the transformation which took place in all the domains of life in the Liberated Areas is perhaps the most glorious page in the whole history of the Chinese people. These things have been so often described by non-Communist visitors that it is unnecessary to speak of them here. All this could not have been achieved, however, without the energetic mobilization of all cultural workers, as is clear if we compare the development in the Liberated Areas with the part of China held by the Kuomintang.

2. Confrontation of Methods

After these general considerations let us take a closer look at the picture which C. T. Hsia gives of individual Chinese authors or groups of authors. In addition to occasional allusions to other authors, C. T. Hsia treats the following writers in greater detail: Lu Hsün, Yeh Shao-chün, Ping Hsin, Ling Shu-hua, Lo Hua-sheng, Yü Ta-fu, Mao Tun, Lao She, Shen Ts'ung-wen, Chang T'ien-i, Pa Chin, Chiang Kuang-tz'u, Ting Ling, Hsiao Chün, Wu Tsu-hsiang, Eileen Chang, Ch'ien Chung-shu, Chao Shu-li, besides several general chapters.

The first thing that strikes us in the disproportion in the space allotted to these authors: The largest number of pages, 43, is devoted to the woman writer Eileen Chang, whereas Lu Hsün is covered in 27 pages, Mao Tun in 25 and 10, Lao She in 24 and 10. The whole literature in the Liberated Areas and the whole post-War Chinese literature is disposed of in 28 pages, as compared with 29 pages devoted to a single novel by Ch'ien Chung-shu. These figures alone show a lack of balance in C. T. Hsia's work, and demonstrate that the author—as I pointed out above—was unable to approach his work with a proper measure of objectivity.

Still more are we amazed at the disparity of the judgments which the author pronounces: of left-wing writers he speaks with ridicule or at least very reservedly, whereas he does not stint in superlatives for anti-Communist writers or those who do not sympathize with the Leftist movement.

I think that the main shortcoming of the work lies in C. T. Hsia's inability accurately to characterize and differentiate the work of the various writers, and to bring out their main features. He has more to say about their persons and personal views than about their creative personality and artistic individuality. In treating of the works of writers, he confines himself, as a rule, in addition to a brief précis of the contents, to a few subjective remarks and judgments, without attempting to build up any systematic picture of their creative individuality. On the basis of his descriptions, we should find it difficult to see where lie the differences between the work of, say, Lu Hsün, Mao Tun, Chang T'ien-i or Lao She.

In order to illustrate the author's method, let us reproduce here, in detail, his description of the work of Lu Hsün.

Hsia stresses, in the first place, the importance of Lu Hsün's birthplace as his chief source of inspiration, noting that the three stories, "My Native Place," 'Benediction" and "In the Restaurant" are directly connected with a visit to his native town, and he seeks their genesis in the curious state of mind it engendered which, he affirms, is reminiscent of Joyce in his *Dubliners*.

Then he analyzes the story "The Diary of a Madman," characterizes its underlying intention, gives its contents and adds a few words of criticism. He deprecates the fact that, as he says, the author has not been able "to provide a realistic plot for the madman's fantasies" and, further, that "he fails to present his case in dramatic terms" (p. 33). Hsia notes that the title and form of the story "are indebted to a story by Gogol," and praises "a remarkable technical virtuosity as well as a good deal of irony."

The short story "K'ung I-chi" is described as "Lu Hsün's first story in the lyrical mode: a touching if sketchy portrait of a marginal member of the literati who has turned thief" (p. 33). He adds that the story "is told by the boy" and that it has "an economy and restraint characteristic of some of Hemingway's Nick Adams stories" (p. 34).

Though Lu Hsün himself liked best the story "K'ung I-chi," C. T. Hsia evaluates more highly the tale entitled "Medicine," of which he says that it is "a much more ambitious performance than either of its predecessors."

Hsia expresses the thought that "Lu Hsün has attempted in the story a complex structure of meanings." He draws attention to the names of the two young men, Hua 華 and Hsia 夏, and affirms that they "represent the hopeful and doomed mode of Chinese existence" (p. 34). He then elaborates this thought and stresses that the death of the revolutionary "indicates Lu Hsün's gloomy view of the revolutionary cause in China" (p. 35). In the same sense he also interprets the closing scene, where the mother calls to her son lying in his grave to give her a sign that he hears her, through a crow sitting on a nearby tree.

As regards the story "My Native Place" Hsia only speaks of the scene in which Lu Hsün meets a friend of his youth, Jun-t'u, now a farmer getting on in years, in Hsia's words, "a weather-beaten man burdened with family care" (p. 36.—Note this description, we shall come back to it later). Hsia then comments only on the closing passage, in which Lu Hsün poses the question as to "what was this so-called hope

of mine, if not also an idol fashioned by my own hands?" (p. 36). Hsia
comments: "In this passage Lu Hsün reveals a strain of honesty characteristic of his best stories. Much as he wishes to change the social
order, he also recognizes the naiveté of refashioning reality in order to
satisfy his didactic impulse."

In his judgment of "The True Story of Ah Q," the author allows
that it is "the only modern Chinese story to have attained an international reputation," but hastens to add that "as a work of art it has surely
been overpraised: it is mechanical in structure and facetious in tone" (p.
37). In addition to embodying the national failings, he considers Ah Q to
represent "the crude awakening to the need for better justice with which
modern Chinese literature has been vitally concerned" (p. 38).

Of Lu Hsün's second volume of short stories, published under the
title, *P'ang-huang,* for which Hsia gives the equivalent "Hesitation," he
says that it is, "on the whole, a finer volume" than "The Outcry," but
that "it has received less lavish praise because of its dominant mood of
despondency" (p. 38). Hsia then, on the contrary, values in this collection "the subdued presence of such personal passions as anger and
sorrow" (ib.), and ranks the four tales from the volume "Benediction"
(better known under the title "The New Year's Sacrifice"), "In the
Restaurant," "Soap" and "Divorce" "among the most profound studies of
Chinese society in fiction" (p. 39).

"The New Year's Sacrifice" is, according to Hsia, "the tragic tale of
Hsiang-lin Sao, a peasant woman hounded to death by feudalism and
superstition. Unlike most writers, however, Lu Hsün is not content
merely to illustrate the horrors of the two traditional evils; he defines,
first of all, the life of the heroine in the actuality of her ethos, which
prescribes conduct and a world view as explicitly as any religion or
philosophy of greater sophistication. The primitive peasant society to
which she belongs, therefore, emerges from the story no less strangely
and terrifyingly credible than the heroic society of Greek tragedy.
Instead of being derogatory terms in the arsenal of anti-traditional
propaganda, 'feudalism' and 'superstition' take on here 'flesh and body'"
(p. 39). Hsia also makes some mention of the religious world of the
heroine and adds that "personal touches," that is, the author's personal
participation in the tragic development of the story, "add a lyrical
warmth to the otherwise stark tragedy of feudal existence" (p. 40).

Speaking of the hero of the story "In the Restaurant," the author
states that "it was . . . Lu Hsün's explicit intention to depict his friend as

a wreck of a man who has lost his nerve and compromised with the old society" (p. 41). Hsia, however, affirms that the lesson of the story is, in effect, very different: "Yet as actually realized in the story, the kindness and piety of Lü Wei-fu . . . also demonstrate the positive strength of the traditional mode of life, toward which the author must have been nostalgically attracted in spite of his contrary intellectual conviction. For Lu Hsün, 'In the Restaurant' is a lyrical confession of his own uncertainty and hesitation" (p. 41).

Highest, in C. T. Hsia's estimation of Lu Hsün's short stories, stands the tale "Soap." In his view, it is "a brilliant satire which dispenses completely with nostalgia and doubt; it is also Lu Hsün's only successful story whose setting is Peking rather than Shao-hsing" (p. 42). In this story he also sees an underlying symbolism—"the beggar girl, in her dirty rags, as well as in her imagined state of freshly scrubbed nudity, stands at once for the shabby Confucianism which Ssu-ming ostensibly upholds and for the libidinous day-dream to which he actually yields" (p. 44).

The story "Divorce" is also positively assessed by our author. Its artistic success he attributes to the fact that "by dramatically presenting the quarrel and refraining from taking sides, Lu Hsün reveals the feudal system in all its moral turpitude" (p. 45).

The nine stories referred to above are considered by C. T. Hsia to be the best products of the first phase of the new Chinese prose. But to this weighing-up he adds various riders: "Though mainly descriptive of village and small-town life in a period of transition, they possess enough power and variety to command the interest of posterity. But even during this period of happy creativity, 1918–1926, Lu Hsün's taste is none too sure (stories like 'A Little Incident,' 'The Story of Hair,' 'The Happy Family,' 'The Solitary' and 'Remorse' show him very much at the mercy of a sentimental didacticism), and his incapacity to draw creative sustenance from other experiences than those rooted in his native town also indicates a real limiation" (p. 45).

C. T. Hsia still finds words of general praise for the book of prose poetry "Wild Grass" and for the volume of youthful reminiscences "Morning Flowers Picked in the Evening." Crushing, however, is the verdict he passes on the collection "Old Legends Retold," which, as he puts it, "combines topical satire with malicious caricature of ancient Chinese sages and mythological heroes. . . . In his fear of searching his own mind and disclosing thereby his pessimistic and somber view of

China at complete variance with his professed Communist faith, Lu Hsün could only repress his deep-seated personal emotions in the service of political satire. The resulting levity and chaos in 'Old Legends Retold' mark the sad degeneration of a distinguished if narrow talent for fiction" (p. 46).

Here we have reproduced nearly all that C. T. Hsia has to say about Lu Hsün's work, excluding only the contents. I think that this survey of the author's critical comments sufficiently confirms what I said above, namely, that C. T. Hsia is not able to give a systematic analysis of an author's work, that he is content to limit himself to purely subjective observations and that he misinterprets or, at best, obscures the true significance of Lu Hsün's literary production.

Let us now essay to show how very differently appears the general character of Lu Hsün's work and those of its features discussed by C. T. Hsia, and how different a picture and evaluation of his work we reach if we do not limit ourselves to accidentals, but submit his oeuvre to systematic analysis, seeing in its individual traits not isolated and chance singularities, but the components of a unified artistic whole, welded by the author's artistic personality. The order of importance of these individual elements is determined by the artist's intention, just as is the way in which he binds and makes use of all these elements for the realization of his creative conception. This intention—and also the artistic procedures employed for the realization of his conception— reflects the author's philosophical outlook, that is, his attitude toward the world, toward life and toward the society in which he lives, and then too, his relation with established artistic traditions, and so on. The special nature of all these attitudes is then determined by the author's ideological and artistic individuality; we see him as a member of a given human society and, at the same time, as an artist of specific qualities.

We shall begin our analysis of Lu Hsün's work with a question of basic importance, namely, whether this work shows evidence of a split in the author's attitude toward Chinese reality, such as C. T. Hsia re- peatedly suggests. According to C. T. Hsia, Lu Hsün rejected on the one hand the traditional forms of Chinese life, while being, on the other, continually attracted by them. This is for C. T. Hsia proof of the vacillating ideological orientation of Lu Hsün, which, as he would have us believe, went so far as to destroy, in the long run, his creative powers, for, after 1929, "he could no longer," as C. T. Hsia affirms, "summon the kind of honesty requisite for the writing of his best stories without also dragging to light the extreme superficiality of his new political allegiance" (p. 45). It is therefore necessary to establish whether there exists some tangible ideological difference between these best stories—in C. T. Hsia's estimate—and the works from the end of his life.

C. T. Hsia facilitates his argumentation by laying stress on certain things and suppressing or remaining silent on others, or by attributing a significance to them which they do not possess. Thus, at the very first, as we noted above, he compares Lu Hsün with Joyce and sees in his work a contradiction in the fact that, as it seems to him, "Lu Hsün repudiates his home town and, symbolically, the old Chinese way of life," and yet, on the other hand, "this town and these people remain the stuff and substance of his creation" (p. 32). That sounds very convincing, but this general formulation obscures the whole essence of Lu Hsün's work, for it says nothing of *whom* and *what* Lu Hsün rejected in Chinese life and why he chose, again and again, his native town as the theme of his stories. C. T. Hsia speaks in general terms of Lu Hsün's abhorrence of "the sloth, superstition, cruelty and hypocrisy of the *rural and town people*" (my italics—J.P.). The impression thus evoked is that Lu Hsün—like moralists in China for some thousands of years—struck out at common social evils, the fact being completely concealed that the aim and purpose of Lu Hsün's oeuvre was—as we shall show later—not only to lay bare the general insensibility and cruelty of Chinese society, but, above all, to point the finger at those who were responsible for this state of affairs. Later on C. T. Hsia is not content with such general statements, but formulates the thesis to which attention was paid above, namely, that Lu Hsün "must have been nostalgically attracted" to "the traditional mode of life, despite his intellectual conviction."

It is true that Lu Hsün could never throw off the memories of the past and that they were an important source of his creative inspiration, only in quite the opposite sense from that in which Hsia interprets it. In the preface to the volume *Na-han*, "Battle Cries," Lu Hsün expresses himself perfectly clearly: "I suffer, on the contrary, from not being able to forget everything, and part of what my mind is unable to get rid of, became the source on which I drew for my tales entitled 'Battle Cries.'" From this it is quite clear that for creative sustenance Lu Hsün drew not on a love for the "traditional mode of life," but on experiences so painful that he was unable to throw off their memory during his whole life. This persistence of memories is therefore the reason why he keeps returning to his native place for material for his writings.

Insofar then as Lu Hsün suffered from doubts and hesitations, it was not because he loved the old way of life, but because for long he was not certain whether China possessed the forces capable of destroying it. Of this, too, he writes in the preface to "Battle Cries." It was not till 1928 that he overcame his doubts.

But let us turn now to an analysis of the work, beginning with his aim and purpose, in order to answer the question formulated above.

Lu Hsün himself defines it in the well-known article, "How I Came to Write Stories," cited in all works relating to Lu Hsün. There he says: "So my themes were usually the unfortunates in this abnormal society. My aim was to expose the disease and draw attention to it so that it might be cured."[2]

I think that this quite unambiguously expresses Lu Hsün's ideological standpoint, which is altogether different from that imputed to him by C. T. Hsia. Lu Hsün has no sympathy for the society around him; he feels that it is a diseased society in need of cure and his work was aimed to help that cure.[3] It was this conviction that determined not only the orientation of his oeuvre, but also his artistic processes, all that gives his best work its specific and inimitable quality. La Hsün does not wish to describe some individual instance or fate, he wishes to depict a typical manifestation, and so he chooses themes on which he can demonstrate some general reality, some specific "disease." In order to realize his intention, he also creates completely new artistic methods, unknown hitherto in Chinese literature, so that Lu Hsün appears here as a bold and original artistic innovator. Very often it is the pushing of the actual story into the background, so that it forms only the backcloth against which the "disease" to which he wishes to direct his reader's attention comes out all the more starkly. I pointed out a number of examples

---

[2] *Lu Hsün ch'üan-chi*, Peking 1956, Vol. 4, p. 393. Compare *Selected Works of Lu Hsün*, Peking 1956, Vol. 3, p. 320.

[3] C. T. Hsia does, it is true, admit on p. 46 that Lu Hsün wished "to serve his country as a spiritual physician," but immediately adds that "in his best stories, however, he is content to probe the disease without prescribing the cure." As we shall show below, Lu Hsün in his stories points to those responsible for causing the disease and fights them with all the weapons in the writer's arsenal. And the fighting of disease-carriers must undoubtedly be considered as the first step toward cure. Lu Hsün then carried on his fight against disease in his essays and political activities. In other words, testing the validity of Hsia's judgment by the facts is sufficient for reaching the conclusion that Lu Hsün's work and development are completely of a piece, so that all Hsia's attacks on Lu Hsün's intellectual and artistic honesty are thereby rendered void.

illustrating this method in my study, "Quelques remarques sur la nouvelle littérature chinoise," to be published in the *Mélanges de l'Institut des Hautes Etudes chinoises* in Paris, and so it is unnecessary to repeat my conclusions here. I noted there, too, analogies with certain procedures of the European literary avant-garde, while stressing the very different motives which led to their employment.

As regards the stories dealt with by C. T. Hsia, examples of this method are "K'ung I-chi" and "Medicine." The aim of the first-mentioned, "K'ung I-chi," is not to give "a touching if sketchy" portrait of a member of the literati who has come down in the world, but to bring home to the reader the unfeeling cruelty of people who make fun of a poor human being and even laugh at him as he crawls through the mud of the streets on his broken stumps. Similarly, "Medicine" portrays a society for whom the blood of a revolutionary is only a physic for a consumptive darling son and which enthusiastically sanctions the torture and killing of a fellow-creature whose crime was that he wished to liberate them. The story of the revolutionary remains permanently in the background—we can piece it together only from disconnected remarks by visitors to a tearoom. This reduction of the subject is likewise a logical necessity in the story "The Diary of a Madman," if the tale was to become an indictment of Chinese society and not the portrayal of an individual case of madness. Herein lies also the basic difference between Lu Hsün's and Gogol's treatment, as has already repeatedly been pointed out by J. D. Chinnery, B. Krebsová and V. F. Sorokin. Thus Lu Hsün had no wish or intention "to provide a realistic plot for the madman's fantasies," or "to present his case in dramatic terms," for in doing so he would have given his story quite a different significance. From among all the possible manifestations of the man's madness, Lu Hsün limits himself to those best fitted to serve for the realization of his intention: he fixes on the birth of the madman's suspicion that the people among whom he lives wish to devour him; this suspicion then gradually passes over into the idea of the generally cannibalistic character of Chinese society. Lu Hsün, with the art of true genius, succeeds in giving the individual features of a specific phenomenon the stamp of universal validity, thereby creating a general picture expressing a universal truth. At the same time, however, Lu Hsün retains in his picture all the concreteness and realism of an individual portrait painted from life.

Lu Hsün's gift of creating general pictures summarizing the typical traits of whole social groups or even of a whole nation is excellently demonstrated in "The True Story of Ah Q," where Ah Q represents the whole nation, a certain social group and a specific individual, all in one person. Besides, the actual story of Ah Q is often no more than the canvas on which Lu Hsün depicts and exposes the character and behavior of the Chinese gentry.

The greatness and innovatory quality of Lu Hsün's art comes out very clearly if we compare his work with that of the social-critical literature which preceded it, i.e., with those satirical novels of the beginning of the twentieth century, whose authors were content with descriptions of individual phenomena, with isolated stories and sketches taken from reality, or with incidents of an anecdotal character. It remained for Lu Hsün to merge in a single whole, to embody in a single picture, the boundless multiplicity of living experience and, at the same time, to give a moral evaluation from the point of view of the progressive concepts of his day.

In these stories, a characteristic trait of Lu Hsün's art is already present which he fully develops in several of his poems in prose and especially in "Old Legends Retold." His pictures have, namely, a multiplicity of meanings, every moment relating to a number of layers of reality, their changing hues reminiscent of a winding scarf of rainbow colors. In this many-faceted iridescence lie the individuality and originality of Lu Hsün's artistic technique, which C. T. Hsia is unable to grasp and which is the reason for his condemnation of "Old Legends Retold."

In order to give his pictures general validity and, at the same time, evoke a maximum emotional reaction in the reader—for his aim was to rouse his conscience and induce him to take up the cudgels against the social disease they described—Lu Hsün had to delete from his pictures all that was of secondary importance, all details which would distract the attention from the main thing he wished to express. This is the reason for what Hsia characterizes in the story "K'ung I-chi" as "a sketchy portrait." If we keep in mind the aim of Lu Hsün's art, namely, to show the insensate cruelty of society, it is not difficult to see that a more detailed portrait of the principal hero or an account of his life would rather have weakened the effect of the story than strengthened it. And here I think we are at the root of Lu Hsün's special method which, in a large number of stories, departs from the method predominating in the realistic literature of nineteenth-century Europe. There the initiator and organizer of the story is an indeterminate "author's ego," all-present and all-knowing, able to present every detail of the action and of the setting and every thought and emotion of the characters concerned. With Lu Hsün, the narrator is often a definite person, either the author himself, as in the case of "New Year's Sacrifice" and some others, or some other specific person: the boy from the wine-tavern in "K'ung I-chi," the widower in "Remorse," and so on. The choice of a definite person as the narrator, who naturally knows only certain facts, enables the author to select from the multitude of individual phenomena at his disposal only a limited number—and those which are most characteristic of the manifestation he wishes to describe and, at the same time, most heavily charged with emotion.

Here, too, I see the main link between Lu Hsün's art and the Chinese artistic tradition, above all, with Chinese painting and poetry, where it is never the artist's intention to seize the whole of reality within the selected limits, but only to bring into prominence several characteristic and significant details, possessing a high emotive potential.

The emotional effect is then intensified by a certain atmosphere of mystery, which is the consequence of this special mode of narration. We learn only isolated facts; K'ung I-chi, for instance, is introduced to us crawling through the mud on his stumps, or we hear that the revolutionary has been maltreated by a brutal executioner, but we are obliged to fill in all the details of their sufferings for ourselves, which stimulates our imagination and makes us part-authors of the story.

This method of presentation is connected with and motivated by the consciously designed relegation of the main story to the background. It is interesting that even in those stories which are not presented as being told by a specific narrator, the same method is used, which shows how strong an attraction this compositional procedure had for Lu-Hsün. Thus the scene of the unsuccessful candidate's madness in "White Glow" is presented as if we were witnesses of it; that is, Lu Hsün employs here the descriptive method usual in the realistic works of the nineteenth century, as we pointed out above. But no sooner does the teacher leave his dwelling than the perspective changes. At the gate, we only *hear* (perhaps) his faint voice and then we only learn from hearsay that a corpse has been found floating naked on the waters of the lake, which is rumored to be that of the crazy candidate. His end is surrounded by mystery (suicide? murder? or mischance?), which heightens the tragedy of the whole incident and sharply illuminates the dull indifference of the milieu to a human fate: people are too lazy even to go and identify the corpse.

This method is applied with superlative effectiveness in the prose piece "New Year's Sacrifice," where the author presents the harrowing tragedy of the woman, Hsiang-lin, in the form of a short narration reconstructed from personal recollections and from what he had heard about her. We learn about the heroine only from what others have to tell of her and only twice do we make direct contact with her. The circumstance that we hear only indirectly how Hsiang-lin moves from one tragic event to another, without being able to follow her feelings and actions, imbues the whole description with a terrifying fatality and cruelty—the impression arises of the absolute helplessness of a human being dragged to destruction by obscure forces. Her life is reduced to several tragic episodes. Hsia is right when he says that the story reminds one of Greek tragedy, except that Lu Hsün clearly shows what forces hounded Hsiang-lin to her death, thus giving fate a very concrete human embodiment. So as to move the reader from the very start, he employs a device which is repeated in a number of his stories: he confronts the reader with the culmination of the tragedy. Hsiang-lin questions the author about an existence beyond the grave, and then, on a freezing New Year's night, she dies as a beggar, probably of hunger and exposure.

The strength of this story lies in the way Lu Hsün, within the limits of a quite short story, is able to express the terrible mode of existence of a Chinese woman in the old society: Hsiang-lin is not a chance, tragic instance, but a type, both in her human qualities and in her fate.

It was necessary to analyze the artistic method employed by Lu Hsün in order to show what an error of judgment is made by Hsia in ranking the collection of short stories *P'ang-huang* higher than that published under the title *Na-han*. It must be said, in all fairness, that in several stories Lu Hsün succeeds in giving admirable pictures of Chinese society, bringing out with remarkable plasticity its basic features, and kindling the conscience of the reader, whereas other stories, in spite of their technical perfection, do not differ greatly in character from the stories of his contemporaries. They lack that specific something which makes Lu Hsün Lu Hsün, namely, the art of sketching in a few telling strokes an unforgettable picture, summing up in an artistic shorthand some fundamental feature of Chinese society.

Among the stories which have not this specific quality is "Soap," so highly praised by C. T. Hsia. The story, depicting the hypocrisy of a member of the intelligentsia who had earlier made some pretence of being a progressive, is written in the normal descriptive method, without any sub-text, picturing an evening in his life. Certainly, the character-study of the man and the portrayal of his domestic milieu is extremely well done, and here Lu Hsün's irony is brilliantly effective, but it remains, after all, a story that is essentially anecdotal in character, without any of the generalizing power of the stories we have discussed above.

On the basis of this comparison we would indeed be justified in drawing the conclusion that the more sharply Lu Hsün expressed his standpoint, the more definite the position he took up in the social struggle, the more successful were his stories in every way.

We must completely reject the allegorical interpretation which Hsia seeks to work out in connection with this and other stories. Lu Hsün was able, as I showed above, to give his pictures multiple significance by relating them to various layers of phenomena, but for that very reason mere primitive allegory was utterly alien to his nature; as a deeply erudite student of Chinese literature, he knew very well to what sense- less toying with words and meanings the allegorical interpretation of the old novels was all too prone to lead, as in the case of the novel *Hung-lou meng*. And so we must completely reject an allegorical explanation of "Medicine." Insofar as the names of the two young men, Hsia and Hua, have any underlying significance, they simply underline the fact ex- pressed in the tale, that brother literally eats brother—another expres- sion of the idea of the cannibalistic character of the old society.

It is, however, typical that Hsia devotes so much space to these unfounded speculations, instead of trying clearly to formulate the ques- tion as to the meaning and purpose of Lu Hsün's creative production, and why he used such specific artistic means for the realization of his aims, as shown above. Here it is evidently not a matter of mere inability to grasp the character of Lu Hsün's oeuvre and to carry out a scientific analysis. Hsia, it is clear, consciously tries to obscure and even to distort the true significance of Lu Hsün's work, disregarding the facts and resorting to what are purely speculative interpretations. One of his theses is that Lu Hsün did not believe in the Revolution and he interprets in this sense the conclusion of the story "Medicine," although the text itself offers not the smallest grounds for it. Lu Hsün himself says in the Introduction to the collection *Na-han* that the flowers which the mother found on her son's grave were put into the story so that it might not end on too pessimistic a note. Earlier he speaks of his wish that, by means of this collection, he might "encourage those fighters who are galloping in loneliness so that they do not lose heart." That sounds very different from Hsia's interpretation ("symbolic questioning over the meaning and future of the revolution"). But Hsia is not content with allegorical constructions having no foundation in the text, but actually distorts the sense of the text. We quoted above his comment on the end of the story "My Native Place," in which he commends Lu Hsün's honesty, because, as he says, "he recognizes the naiveté of refashioning reality in order to satisfy his didactic impulse." The actual quotation as given by Hsia (p. 36) would, on the face of it, justify such an interpretation. Only, in Lu Hsün's text there follows a passage which shows that Lu Hsün wished to say the very opposite of what C. T. Hsia imputes to him. Lu Hsün, namely, ends the story with what is a reply to this mood of hopelessness: "I thought: hope cannot be said to exist nor can it be said not to exist. It is just like roads across the earth. For actually the earth had no roads to begin with, but when many men pass one way, a road is made." What can one say to such a distortion of a work on the part of a literary historian?

Only here still more is at stake. Indeed, it is a matter of the whole meaning of Lu Hsün's lifework. We have tried to show in our analysis that Lu Hsün's aim was "to expose the disease . . . so that it might be cured." It is evident that we can only cure a disease by removing the cause. And Lu Hsün was able not only to floodlight the terrible aspects of the Chinese disease, but also to point to those who were the cause of it. And this fact C. T. Hsia would carefully cover up, for then his whole interpretation of Lu Hsün's ideological and artistic development would fall to pieces. Up to 1928 Lu Hsün had still various doubts and fits of pessimism, but it never meant that he was reconciled for a moment to the existing order, or that he was ready to fold his hands in his lap. He had fought from his youth, as is irrefutably testified to by his essays, and this comes out very strikingly in the tendency of his short stories.

Let us now examine the stories from this point of view and seek an answer to the question as to whom Lu Hsün attributed the evil he saw in Chinese society. Let us go back, first of all, to the story "New Year's Sacrifice." Who bears the chief responsibility for the heroine's tragedy and death? C. T. Hsia speaks in general terms of feudalism and superstition, which (he affirms) hounded the heroine to death, but the subsequent stylization gives the reader the impression that the tragedy takes place in a purely peasant milieu and that implicitly this milieu is responsible for the heroine's death. Not a word does C. T. Hsia say about the main culprit of Hsiang-lin's sufferings, the one who exploited her, who made her a social outcast, who implanted in her the crazy idea of her guilt and drove her to madness, who deprived her of work and drove her into the streets, who let her die of hunger and cynically commented on her death—that was no "primitive present society," but the family of one of the gentry, the conservative upholder of Confucian morality, the honorable Mr. Lu.

In this tale especially Lu Hsün shows, in exemplary fashion, that the inhuman morality which can drive an innocent woman to madness and death is exclusively a product of the gentry and is then taken over from them by the other classes of society. Lu Hsün is, however, absolutely objective, and so he also shows the unfeeling brutality of the peasant milieu which out of greed treats the unhappy widow like a piece of cattle, kidnapping her and marrying her against her will, but with unrelenting sharpness he turns the edge of his satire against the representative of the gentry. This is true of practically all Lu Hsün's stories, as an analysis would easily show.

As a small example of how the need for a unifying idea and purpose influenced the whole of Lu Hsün's work, I may mention here an episode from "My Native Place," the close of which Hsia misconstrued as I have shown above. But it is not only a question of what Lu Hsün says in his conclusion; important is the whole manner of composition of the story. Lu Hsün's contemporaries stress the fact that there was no "Beancurd Beauty" in the vicinity of the author's dwelling. Why then did Lu Hsün create such a caricature of a figure and introduce it into a story based for the most part on actual recollections? An analysis of the story shows very clearly that Lu Hsün made use of that gossiping busybody, the grasping shopkeeper, so that by contrast the simple honesty of the farmer-friend of his youth might come out all the more strongly. It is obviously not possible to speak generally of Lu Hsün's abhorrence of the vices of "rural and town people," as does Hsia in the above-cited comment, for Lu Hsün differentiates very sharply between the various classes. It must be noted, too, that in his story Lu Hsün enumerates very precisely all the evils which had made a complete wreck of his friend—oppressive taxes, soldiery, children, Government offices, usurers, and not only "family care," as Hsia euphemistically puts it.

If, however, we keep in mind the clear orientation of Lu Hsün on the evils corroding China and his unrelenting fight against the gentry and the bourgeoisie, we must absolutely reject C. T. Hsia's basic thesis to which we drew attention above. According to this, the creative source for Lu Hsün's work lay in the contradiction between his rational repudiation of the old society and, on the other hand, the strong emotional attraction it had for him. We therefore also reject C. T. Hsia's conclusion, viz. that, in the question of the revolution, his attitude was vacillating. There can be no doubt that Lu Hsün, as a great humanist, had compassion for "the poor and despised" in the old society, of whom he wished to tell in his work, as he says in the above-mentioned quotation, but, at the same time, from his early youth, he stood irreconcilably opposed to the class he held to be the source of all China's misery, namely, the gentry. Here lies the key to his fundamental revolutionary attitude, which finally made of a petty bourgeois, revolutionarily inclined intellectual, a follower of Marxism. Nor is there ideologically the slightest contradiction between the early stories of Lu Hsün and his works written after 1929. On the contrary, a certain weakening is observable only in certain of the stories included in the collection *P'ang-huang*, which Hsia ranks highest; these stories have less of the fighting quality and also show less artistic individuality. In these the elsewhere firm hand of Lu Hsün trembled.

It is necessary to repudiate entirely all that C. T. Hsia has to say about the reasons why Lu Hsün, after his departure from Peking, did not continue to write short stories, about the decline of his creative powers, about the sacrifice of his art to politics, and other suppositions in the same vein. C. T. Hsia considers all sorts of causes, but has a blind spot for the most obvious: It was the murder of students by the reactionary regime of Tuan Ch'i-jui, on March 28, 1926, which drove Lu Hsün out of Peking, and it was the bloody *putsch* of Chiang Chieh-shih, in April 1927, which obliged him to leave Canton.

These two events are undoubtedly what convinced Lu Hsün of the necessity of devoting all his energies to the fight against reaction, and from that time Lu Hsün became an uncompromising fighter. That this struggle and the necessity, at the same time, to earn enough in small fees to keep his family, left him little time for calm creative work is obvious. But his essays from this period testify to exceptional intellectual strength and certainly far outstrip the essays written prior to 1925, which often deal with matters of small significance.

The whole presentation of Lu Hsün's life from the time of his activities in Canton to his death in 1936, as it comes from C. T. Hsia's pen, is a mixture of half-truths and distortions of fact. For every reader it would be highly instructive to compare C. T. Hsia's description with the altogether objective book by Dr. Huang Sung-k'ang, *Lu Hsün and the New Culture Movement of Modern China* (Amsterdam 1957).

3. Individual Portraits

Let us turn our attention now to what C. T. Hsia has to say about two authors toward whom he is not so prejudiced as against Lu Hsün, namely, Mao Tun and Lao She. We can bracket the two, as our author himself compares them. On p. 165, he writes: "Lao She and Mao Tun . . . offer in many ways an interesting contrast. Mao Tun uses an ornate literary vocabulary; Lao She at his best writes a pure Peking vernacular. Using the time-honoured test of Northern and Southern literary sensibilities, we may say that Lao She represents the North, individualist, forthright, humorous, and Mao Tun, the more feminine South, romantic, sensuous, melancholic. Mao Tun is distinguished for his gallery of heroines; Lao She's protagonists are nearly always men; whenever possible, he eschews romantic subject matter. Mao Tun records the passive feminine response to the chaotic events of contemporary Chinese history; more concerned with individual destinies than social forces, Lao She shows his heroes in action," etc.

I think this passage gives us a very good idea of the purely subjective approach of C. T. Hsia to literary questions. It has been proved innumerable times, in philosophy, literature and painting, that the differentiation, on the basis of innate qualities or natural disposition, between northerners and southerners, in Chinese culture, is completely invalid.

But let us seek to ascertain in what measure the true qualities of the authors are described, at least as real differences between them. First of all in the matter of style, C. T. Hsia states that Mao Tun "uses an ornate literary vocabulary," whereas Lao She writes "a pure Peking vernacular." It would take us too far to investigate the correctness of this assertion and, mainly, in which cases it applies and in which not. As regards Mao Tun, he undoubtedly consistently uses a "literary vocabulary," but only in parts of certain works do elaborate descriptions occur, his predominating style being that of simple epic narration; for instance, the greater part of his best short stories is written in a simple epic style. It is, therefore, necessary to pose the question as to the reason for this difference in the use of linguistic means between the two authors under comparison. It is clearly a question that every literary historian should feel obliged to solve.

In ascertaining the differences in the use of linguistic material, the literary historian, as I have shown in the case of Lu Hsün, would need to take into consideration the whole body of a writer's work and, step by step, discover what function the individual components fill in this work. He would then undoubtedly find that Mao Tun consistently uses the method of European classical realism and in this way erases in his stories every trace of the narrator. He presents his material in such a way as to give the reader the impression that he himself is a direct observer of the action described and not that somebody is describing it for him. It stands to reason that such an impersonal description, in which the author allots to himself the role of a photographic lens registering the action, requires a neutral language, that is, the established literary language. In certain cases, Mao Tun then lays the main stress on the suggestive power of the scene he pictures and then he employs what seems to C. T. Hsia to be "an ornate style."

Lao She, on the contrary, underlines the function of the narrator. In his first novels, the author-narrator is very much in the foreground and this calls for a strongly individualized language. This tendency comes out very clearly in Lao She's short tales,[4] which are very often in the form of lively narration by a specific narrator; hence, here the individualization of the language is still more striking.

Naturally, this difference in the use of linguistic material has deeper reasons, determined by the differing aims of the artistic production of the two authors. Here C. T. Hsia guessed the right reason, for Lao She is, indeed, "more concerned with individual destinies than social forces." Lao She aims above all at writing an interesting story, wishing to tell it in his individualized style, skilfully exploiting the liveliness and colorfulness of the language of everyday speech. This style and the complexity of the plots of his novels are reminiscent, on the one hand, of the art of the old Chinese story-teller and, on the other, of his favorite model— Dickens. His literary intention is the description of an unusual individual fate or psychological disposition, so that his works are often studies of queer human "characters." His interest in social problems is, in comparison, of quite secondary importance and, indeed, we may say that

---

[4]For my descriptions of Lao She's short stories I have drawn on the excellent anthology compiled and edited by my pupil, Z. Slupski.

often he does not understand these very correctly. Wherever he departs from stories of individuals and puts social problems in the foreground, the result is an artistic failure, an instance in point being his novel *City of Cats*. Incontestibly, in the choice of his characters and in the description of the often curious and never dull vicissitudes of their lives, there is considerable romanticism, and undoubtedly more than in Mao Tun. Let us recall only the ups and downs of fortune which mark the life-story of the boy Camel Hsiang-tzu, or the wide variety of portraits in his gallery of brigands and adventurers in his short stories. Nothing more is necessary to repudiate the theory of differences between the romantic South and the unromantic North as applied to these two authors.

The main difference between Mao Tun and Lao She must be sought elsewhere. Mao Tun aims to pinpoint the social problems of China at a specific moment in time, the singular fate of individuals being of interest to him only insofar as it serves to illustrate the problem in question. In order the more incisively to show the operation of these social forces, Mao Tun often decribes the fate of a human being crushed by these forces, which he vainly seeks to oppose. Thus, in the case of Mao Tun, it is not a matter of "passive feminine response to the chaotic events of contemporary Chinese history" (Hsia, p. 165), but of a carefully thought out procedure—we could (in the case of the novel *Twilight* for instance) speak in fact of a scientific method—for a correct and convincing description of Chinese social problems. As his intention is also to show the intolerable character of this social situation—for Mao Tun considers literature to be an important weapon in the political arsenal—he chooses women as the main characters in his novels, for their fate was, in the given social situation, as a rule more cruel than that of men. It must be said, too, that Mao Tun's heroes are not in any way less active than Lao She's heroes; they battle even more stubbornly against their fate—but the outcome, in conformity with their social standing in the relevant historical context, was usually tragic. Thus the whole theory put forward by Hsia of "a feminine, romantic, sensuous, melancholic South," as represented by Mao Tun's work, has no foundation in fact.

Thus we could continue to substitute a correct and systematic interpretation for the confused agglomeration of chance epithets which C. T. Hsia employs in his comment on the two authors.

I only wish to remark, in the case of Lao She, how the latter's outstanding achievements in the domain of the short story have evidently escaped C. T. Hsia, and that his selection of samples from Mao Tun is not much more judicious. To illustrate the work of Mao Tun he chooses the trilogy *Shih* (The Eclipse) and the novels *Hung* (The Rainbow) and *Tzu-yeh* (The Twilight). We can only say that the unfinished novel *Rainbow* is not particularly typical of Mao Tun, as follows from what we said above. In this novel Mao Tun aims to combine the analysis of a social situation with the story of an individual, and this attempt to combine two purposes is not altogether successful. As regards *The Eclipse*, it should have been explained that it was written under the impression of a despairing mood, evoked by the betrayal of Chiang Chieh-shih and the collapse of the revolution of 1928, instead of which C. T. Hsia awards the author marks for "honesty," to the disparagement of other fellow writers, such as Wang T'ung-chao, Chang Tzu-p'ing and Chiang Kuang-tz'u (p. 141). Beyond a passable reproduction of the content of these works, C. T. Hsia has not a single comment of importance from the point of view of the literary historian, who would certainly be impressed by the exceptional activization of the characters in the very first part of the trilogy (the impressions and feelings of the characters become the carriers of the narration), by the concentration of the narrative in internal monologues, a procedure which links Mao Tun with the most modern authors of the period following the first World War. Similarly, of interest for every literary historian would be the author's attempt to give a picture of a specific social situation in the second part of the trilogy by means of a large number of single episodes, illuminating it from different angles, a method allied to that used by John Dos Passos and elaborated by Mao Tun in his subsequent works.

We cannot refute all the unjust criticisms which C. T. Hsia directs against the novel "Eclipse," in which he characterizes Mao Tun's pen-portraits of various types of the Shanghai bourgeoisie and petty bourgeoisie as caricatures dictated by his Communist view of the world and wanting in "the accent of passion or conviction" (p. 157). At the same time he is silent on the fact that Mao Tun, in his striving after absolute objectivity, presents in this novel what is on the whole a negative picture of Communist Party functionaries and, with the same objectivity, describes various groups of women workers in Wu Sun-fu's factory. Possibly Mao Tun sees the world about him in too dark colors, but it is a grave injustice to reproach him for lack of "passion, convic-tion" or of "self-tormenting honesty" (p. 157). On the contrary, it is this self-tormenting honesty which is the main driving power in the creative make-up of this writer.

The short stories of Mao Tun, no less than those of Lao She, are treated by C. T. Hsia in a very stepmotherly fashion. He does not reproduce correctly the sense of the first highly ironical tale by Mao Tun, *Ch'uang-tsao* (Creation). It certainly is not true that "the heroine of 'Creation' feels compelled to leave her husband and mentor because she has advanced beyond his noncommittal intellectual dilettantism to a positive socialist position" (p. 161). The parting words of the wife are far too ambiguous to admit such a straightforward interpretation, nor can we say that she worked her way to any "socialist position," but only that she became used to thinking and acting independently and to taking an interest in politics, the latter of very indefinite orientation. The husband, however, then regrets that it was he who set her on this road to freedom, which is far from his liking. All his earlier preaching about emancipation was nothing more than a silly game. Mao Tun's art here reveals itself in a plot kept within moderate undramatic limits, in the description of fine nuances of feeling in the chief characters of husband and wife, and in the ironical confrontation of theoretical views and the reality of their being put in practice.

No less distorted is the picture C. T. Hsia gives of the medium-length story *Ch'un-tsan* (Spring Silkworms), which he rates the highest of all Mao Tun's stories. Certainly Mao Tun cannot be said to "invest the family," which he describes in this tale, "with the kind of unquestioned piety habitual with Chinese peasants" . . . "and unfaltering trust in a beneficent Heaven" (p. 163). In fact, Mao Tun describes with extreme irony and deprecation the superstition of the old peasant, T'ung-pao, who believed in the Bodhisattva; only his Bodhisattva was the god of wealth, *ts'ai-shen* 財神. His family did not share his belief and Mao Tun's portrait of this family is not at all a touching and "loving portrayal of good peasants," as C. T. Hsia would have us believe. Mao Tun proceeds to show the disintegration of this family under the pressure of cruel poverty and, in the end, old T'ung-pao must admit that his youngest son is right who already grasps that not senseless drudgery, but only the decision to fight for their rights can free the peasantry.

Despite the greater objectivity of the picture presented of the work of Yeh Shao-chün, as compared with the descriptions of the work of unequivocally Leftist writers, C. T. Hsia touches only very lightly on the basic problem which comes up in connection with Yeh Shao-chün, as well as with a number of writers of this period, namely, the problem of subjectivism, the close interlinking of the work of art with the personal experiences, feelings and views of the author. Very often the author does not seek to seize and hold fast objective reality, but records his own private experiences and describes his own inner states. And even where the author tries to give a more objective picture of the world, he does so by the objectivization of his inner world, by the generalization of his own experiences, expunging from these all that has merely individual validity. It would certainly be rewarding to devote some thought to this attitude of Chinese writers and seek to explain it. C. T. Hsia is aware of this problem, but devotes only occasional remarks to it, as, for instance, on p. 65: ". . . the sympathetic bond between author and hero is too personally close to generate the kind of ironic objectivity which distinguishes Yeh Shao-chün's better short stories." It is not merely a matter of irony; what is important is the measure of success with which the author is able to place himself outside his individual experience, which is always singular and isolated, and create a picture that is general and typical, a procedure we spoke of in connection with Lu Hsün.

An example of a writer who was able at least in certain of his works to recast his individual experiences and raise them to the level of general pictures is, undoubtedly, Yü Ta-fu, the only writer of the considerable group associated in the Creation Society of whose work C. T. Hsia gives a critical assessment. But C. T. Hsia's selection from his works is not particularly happy. True, our author does analyze one of the best of Yü Ta-fu's short stories, "Intoxicating Spring Nights," but leaves uncommented the story which shows most clearly that tendency to grasp and render the world through the projection of a personal experience, the tale *Po-tien* 薄奠 (A Humble Sacrifice). In this story of the tragic fate of a rickshaw-man whom he met by chance, the author concentrates the whole terrible fate of the Chinese proletariat. Similarly, C. T. Hsia overlooks the tale in which the author's personal tragedy is narrated with such power that it becomes the expression of human suffering in general. The story in question is called *I-ko jen tsai t'u shang* (A Lonely Man on a Journey), and it describes the death of the author's little son. Especially in these stories, Yü Ta-fu shows himself to be a master of style and composition so that it is not possible to censor him, as does C. T. Hsia (p. 109), for "a sentimental and careless style which blemishes all his stories."

If it was not right to ignore the problem of the close integration of the work of art with the author's life in the case of Yeh Shao-chün, it is all the less possible to do so when speaking of work of such marked subjectivism as that of Yü Ta-fu. Here an allusion to "a Rousseauist confession" (p. 105) is not sufficient. It would be necessary to investigate the connection of the whole trend with European romanticism, Japanese *watakushi shōsetsu* (*Ich-Erzählung*) and, mainly, with the native Chinese tradition. Without such research, it is, for instance, quite impossible to discover the roots of some of Yü Ta-fu's best sketches. In my view, C. T. Hsia does not fully appreciate the significance of this subjectivist literature, either in the social context of its time or in the literary context. C. T. Hsia makes this observation: ". . . the subjective hero is not without social significance, however: he is the impotent patriot, the harassed family man, the artist alienated from society" (p. 105). This is true, so far as it goes, but above all these frequently overwrought outbursts of Yü Ta-fu and Kuo Mo-jo are the cries of protest of an individual straining to break at last the fetters of a feudal society. It was necessary to show what man looks like, with all his faults and even vices, in order to be able to build up a new morality, founded on man's truly human qualities. And as regards the literary context, it was necessary to explore the complex labyrinth of human psychology, completely unknown to the older writers. In these respects, it would be essential to supplement C. T. Hsia's analysis.

The worst treatment of all C. T. Hsia metes out to the literature of the Liberated Areas and the literature of the period subsequent to the Liberation, in 1949, for it is literature serving the fight for freedom and the building of a socialist society, which is enough to prompt C. T. Hsia to pronounce the following sweeping judgment: "At their best, the recent novelists have rendered a superficial documentary realism, which is a fake realism because the deep-seated feelings and thoughts of the people have been systematically distorted to allow for the joyous note of the optimistic formula" (p. 481). C. T. Hsia cites several names, but not even such works, full of true feeling and describing in a splendid way regions hitherto completely neglected in Chinese literature, such as Ou-yang Shan's 歐陽山 *Kao Ch'ien-ta* 高乾大, or Chou Li-po's 周立波 *Pao-feng tsou-yü* 暴風驟雨 —"Hurricane," which are certainly worth the trouble of a short analysis, being incomparably richer in the facts and experiences of life than the works he so extols. Not a word of mention has C. T. Hsia for the output of exquisite short stories from the Liberated Areas, though those of Wei Chün-i 韋君宜, Wang Lin 王林, K'ang Cho 康濯, and the reportages of Hua Shan 華山 and Lin Pai-yü 劉白羽, maintain the high level attained by the Chinese short story before the War.

C. T. Hsia deals in detail only with the work of Chao Shu-li and

Ting Ling. As regards the former, C. T. Hsia is quite unable to grasp the special charm of these stories, in which the traditions of folk story-telling are skilfully turned to account. And so the first of Chao Shu-li's stories "The Marriage of Hsiao Er-hei" and "The Verses of Li Yu-ts'ai" (which have the same attraction of fresh folk inspiration as the New Year pictures dating from the same time), are dismissed with expressions of the greatest contempt (p. 482): They are, so he says, "two of the feeblest stories ever to have been thrust upon public attention . . . Chao Shu-li's clumsy and clownish style is utterly incompetent to serve the purposes of narration," etc. C. T. Hsia simply ignores the need to create a literature for the broad masses of the country people and, at the same time, a literature enabling them to find their bearings in the process of social change going on about them. This necessity Chao Shu-li grasped even prior to Mao Tse-tung's speech in Yenan, and to it he consistently subordinated his literary production. If we disregard the aim which the writer had in view, we cannot do justice to his work.

C. T. Hsia accords a higher rating only to Chao Shu-li's novel *The Changes in Li Village* or, at least, to its first part. For his latest work, *San-li Wan*, he has only words of ridicule. Undeniably, in this last work Chao Shu-li came up against the difficult problem of how to give his work dramatic tension, when its main task was to describe quiet development and to underline the positive aspects of the characters portrayed. He was faced here with a problem which is engaging at the present time the attention of many writers who are adherents to the principles of socialist realism.

As regards the work of Ting Ling, we were obliged above to protest against the offensive tone in which C. T. Hsia speaks of this writer. And so, too, from her whole extensive pre-War output, testifying to the exceptional range of her literary gifts and to the maturity of her view of life and of Chinese society at that time—Ting Ling was the first of the young writers to realize the harmfulness of a superficial and sentimental approach to reality—, C. T. Hsia discusses in greater detail only the novel *Water*, taking certain parts and treating them out of their context, greatly distorting the character of the work as a whole. Already in this piece of prose, Ting Ling succeeds in evoking in a highly suggestive manner the atmosphere of a Chinese village over which hangs the threat of a terrible natural catastrophe. On the other hand, it was a problem of considerable complexity to describe the life-story, not of individuals, but of a whole collective, and from this point of view, too, *Water* is a notable attempt to render artistically one of the most significant realities of pre-War China.

Of Ting Ling's equally large production of the War and post-War years, our author gives a short summary of the contents of the novel *Sun over the Sangkan River* and reproduces the description of the scene in which the people punish the landowner, Ch'ien Wen-kuei, again exploiting this passage for attacks on the Communist Party.

Of the art of Ting Ling, whose immense number of detail shots build up to an exceptionally lively and truthful mosaic of life in a Chinese village in the period of revolutionary change, C. T. Hsia says practically nothing. Her striving after the objective documenting of this complex and often painful process of social regeneration serves our author only as a pretext for seeking in the writer's work signs of "a latent hostility toward the Communist régime" (p. 488).

Naturally we have not such strong critical reservations toward all the chapters of C. T. Hsia's compendious volume as we have toward the passages to which we have given special attention above. But the very considerable material which the author has brought together on the new literature could certainly have been put to much better use if the author had moderated his political animosities and concentrated in greater measure on trying to grasp the great literary process which is going on in China today. Thus the value of his book is greatly depreciated, for practically none of it can be used without critical examination and reassessment. In many places, too, the book sinks to the level of malicious propaganda.

As an appendix to C. T. Hsia's book there is a study of literature on Taiwan by his brother Tsi-an Hsia. This survey, written with much more balanced judgment than C. T. Hsia's volume, can serve to point the moral of what happens to a literature that turns its back on the main social problems and, in accordance with the advice of C. T. Hsia, sets out on the path of "disinterested moral exploration." An escape literature of negligible significance arises, so that Tsi-an Hsia cannot, for the whole period of Kuomintang domination of Taiwan, cite a single writer of importance. This situation then actually awakes a longing for the socially engaged and vitally alive literature of pre-War China. Tsi-an Hsia asserts, it is true, that leftist literature in the Chinese People's Republic is as dead as on Taiwan, which of course is not true, but he adds a very interesting rider (p. 511): "Swinging to the other extreme of the political pendulum, the Taiwan writers today, especially the writers of fiction, are content with being mere day-dreamers. I do not know of a single novel published on Taiwan in the last ten years that deals, seriously or humorously, with the life of peasants, workers, or the petty-bourgeois class of teachers and government clerks to which the writers themselves, with few exceptions, belong. It is easy now to laugh at the naiveté and wishful thinking of the leftist writers and their unobservant distortion of social reality, but having surfeited myself with a steady diet of vaporous writings, I do sometimes miss the hardness, the harshness, the fiery concern with social justice that we find in the best works of the leftist school."

The judgment implicit in the above sentences is, in substance, a condemnation of all those views and theories, in the name of which C. T. Hsia goes into action against the main stream of Chinese literature since 1918. Had Chinese writers gone the way so highly commended by C. T. Hsia, they would not only have betrayed their historical mission, but also doomed their own work to insignificance. In this connection, it is worth pointing out how very different is the approach of the Taiwan author to the personality and work of Lu Hsün, as compared with the treatment meted out to him by C. T. Hsia: "the early stories and essays [of Lu Hsün] seem to me to have spoken best for the conscience of China during a period of agonizing transition . . ." (p. 509). I think that this confrontation of the view of the Taiwan literary critic and the assessment made of Lu Hsün by C. T. Hsia is the most conclusive proof of how completely C. T. Hsia has distorted the picture of the great Chinese writer. We must, in general, qualify C. T. Hsia's book as a lost opportunity. Considering the lamentable insufficiency of serious books on the new Chinese literature in western languages, we should welcome every work designed, even from a critical standpoint, to help the European reader to gain some idea of the immense cultural rebirth which China has undergone since the beginning of this century, and especially its reflection in literature. But the preliminary requirement for the author of such a work would have to be, at the very least, an honest endeavor to grasp this whole complex process and to present it in an objective and unbiased fashion. As it is, every future scholar returning to this theme will have to deal anew with the large body of material assembled here.

The fact that C. T. Hsia has done a considerable piece of work from the point of view of literary research is shown by the bibliographies, tables and indexes at the end of the book, which, although objection may be taken to their arrangement, present a considerable amount of useful data.

Appendix One
On the "Scientific" Study of Modern Chinese Literature— A Reply to Professor Průšek

by C. T. Hsia

I. Basic Problems

In his long review of by book[1] Jaroslav Průšek has in effect outlined a program for the "scientific" study of modern Chinese literature; he has defined the historical character and function of that literature and recommended objective methods for its analysis and evaluation. Since, in his view, my book had practically ignored all the premises and methods that should have guided an objective historian of modern Chinese literature, I appear to him the prime example of a subjective critic, and a subjective critic with ill-founded political prejudices at that. I am naturally disappointed that a distinguished sinologist should have found my work so unacceptable, though I am quite unconvinced that, however inadequate as a literary historian, I could have so fatally misconceived my task. Indeed I remain completely skeptical whether, beyond the recording of simple incontrovertible facts, the study of literature could assume the rigor and precision of "science" and whether, in the study of

Published in *T'oung Pao* (1963), pp. 428–474.

[1] J. Průšek, "Basic Problems of the History of Modern Chinese Literature and C. T. Hsia, *A History of Modern Chinese Fiction*," *T'oung Pao*, XLIX, Nos. 4–5 (Leiden, 1961), pp. 357–404.

It may not seem improper to introduce a personal note here. During Professor Průšek's visit to the United States in the spring of 1963, it was my good fortune to meet him and converse with him on many topics of traditional and modern Chinese literature. Needless to say, I was most impressed by his personal cordiality and his profound erudition. But since Professor Průšek had already submitted his article before making my acquaintance, necessity has forced upon me the unpleasant task of arguing with him in public. I trust he will find that throughout my article I have discussed only points of substance and refrained from unseemly polemics.

any literary period, an inflexible methodology could be formulated once for all. In this rejoinder, therefore, I am principally moved to protest the advisability of a rigid and indeed dogmatic scientific approach to literary problems: Průšek may have erred in judging my book with the utmost severity precisely because he has been misled by his untested major assumptions about the modern period in China and its literature.

Let me say first of all that there are certain tasks properly belonging to the literary historian which I could have undertaken were I not mainly concerned with what seems to me the basic task—a critical examination of the major and the representative writers of the period along with a succinct survey of that period designed to make their achievement and failure historically comprehensible. Thus I have not systematically studied the relations between modern experiments in fiction and the native literary tradition. Thus, though I have ventured many remarks concerning the impact of Western literature upon modern Chinese fiction, I have made no systematic study of that impact. I have indeed cited many Western works in a comparative fashion, but primarily as an aid to define more precisely a work under examination and not as an attempt to establish lineage and influence. Since, as Průšek admits, even "professional sinologists" are largely ignorant of modern Chinese literature and since my book is also designed for readers "who know little about modern China but are curious about its literature" (p. vii), such comparisons, however arbitrary, serve a legitimate function in my study. I also have not attempted a broad comparative study of the narrative techniques employed by Chinese writers of fiction, though such studies, as proven by Průšek's review-article and his other recent papers, can be of definite value in assisting the task of evaluation.

To ascertain influence and indebtedness, to compare the techniques of authors in a neutral and objective fashion—these are surely important tasks, as Průšek rightly believes. But for a pioneer survey of modern Chinese fiction, the primary task is, I repeat, discrimination and evaluation: until we have elicited some order and pattern from the immense body of work available for examination, until we have distinguished the possibly great from the good writers, and the good from the poor, we cannot begin the study of influence and technique, however temptingly scientific the latter kinds of study may be. In dealing with earlier periods, a literary historian may assume the key importance of certain writers, writers whose greatness has been attested to by generations of readers. But even the verdict of the ages may not be always infallible so that no literary historian or critic should slavishly rely upon the work of his predecessors. In dealing with the modern period in China, because so many of the native critics, aside from the question of their dubious training in their craft, were too much involved in the making of this modern literature to be unpartisan, the need to start from scratch appeared especially imperative. Yet Průšek berates me precisely for my "intrepidity" in having dared to make a new beginning, to exercise my independent judgment in apparent disregard of the authoritative critics of mainland China, and of a few European sinologists who have largely echoed these authorities.

As an instructive example of objectivity, Průšek recommends Dr. Huang Sung-k'ang's *Lu Hsün and the New Culture Movement of Modern China* (Amsterdam, 1957). Although Průšek has earlier criticized the book for its ineptitude as literary criticism,[2] yet in comparison with mine, Huang's book is "altogether objective," presumably because the author has shown no independent judgment, has not deviated to any appreciable extent from the Chinese sources she has consulted, both in regard to her estimate of Lu Hsün as a writer and thinker and to her interpretation of the new culture movement. "Objectivity," therefore, appears to mean uncritical compliance with the reigning opinion; to depart from it is to incur the risk of "subjectivity." Not only that, it is to betray one's sheer arrogance and "dogmatic intolerance." But I am afraid it is Průšek himself who may be guilty of "dogmatic intolerance" insofar as he appears incapable of even theoretically entertaining any other view of modern Chinese literature than the official Communist one.

In Section 1 of his review, Průšek drops many hints as to the kinds of ulterior motives that may have led me to uphold a position of "dogmatic intolerance." In one place, he thinks I must be the kind of liberal Chinese intellectual loyal to the memory of Hu Shih and to Lin Yutang. But he immediately concedes that I am critical of Hu Shih for "his narrow view of literature as an instrument of social criticism" (p. 9). But Lin Yutang he insists on regarding as a "favorite author" of mine and cites as evidence my description of his wartime role in America as "a best-selling author purveying the charms of old China and reporting on the heroism of the new" (p. 314). If Průšek has retained my earlier criticism of Lin Yutang's cult of "personalism, which eschews high

---

[2] See J. Průšek, "Lu Hsün the Revolutionary and the Artist," *Orientalistische Literaturezeitung*, Nos. 5–6 (1960), pp. 229–236.

seriousness" (p. 133), and other related faults, he could not have missed my ironic phrasing of his new role: certainly, the expressions "best-selling author" and "purveying the charms" are not meant to be complimentary. Then Průšek starts off on another track and aligns me with the traitors and collaborators under the Japanese occupation. Have I not warmly endorsed the early intellectual phase of Chou Tso-jen, who later became a collaborator, and have I not written appreciatively and at great length on the works of Eileen Chang and Ch'ien Chung-shu, who were living in occupied Shanghai during the greater part of the war period? Moreover, my summary dismissal of the bulk of wartime literature produced in the Nationalist interior and the Communist areas "points to an individual lack of those feelings and sentiments which seem natural in the citizen of any country." Průšek's own enthusiasm for China's heroic resistance against Japan and her subsequent "liberation" by the Communists, on the other hand, has led him to make the following assertion: "The transformation which took place in all the domains of life in the Liberated Areas is perhaps the most glorious page in the whole history of the Chinese people." I wonder how many sinologists of Průšek's eminence and objectivity would endorse this judgment.

Průšek simply cannot believe my statement, "In my survey of modern Chinese fiction, I have been principally guided by considerations of literary significance" (p. 498). So he quotes a sentence immediately following to prove that I subordinate literary considerations to political: "The writers toward whom I have shown critical approval or enthusiasm share by and large the same set of techniques, attitudes, and fantasies with the other writers of their period, but by virtue of their talent and integrity, they have resisted and in some notable cases transformed the crude reformist and propagandist energies to arrive at a tradition that represents a different literary physiognomy from the tradition composed principally of leftist and Communist writers." The test given here is whether writers have been able .o resist or transform "the crude reformist and propagandist energies," a literary rather than a political test. It is my conviction that with the majority of Chinese writers (and that would include Kuomintang propagandists), their preoccupation with social reform and political propaganda has incapacitated them from rendering the truth of things in all its complexity. Among leftist and Communist authors, I have singled out Mao Tun, Chang T'ien-i, and Wu Tsu-hsiang for praise precisely because their best works give evidence of that literary "integrity" which has enabled them to rise above the mere reformist and propagandist passion. In other words, I deplore literature which, to use Keats' phrase, has "a palpable design" upon us insofar as that design is incompatible with the full-bodied presentation of reality. Hence I prefer "disinterested moral exploration," a phrase singled out by Průšek for contemptuous disapprobation, to the less strenuous kind of literary endeavor which is ulteriorly motivated and which is merely content to illustrate some ready-made truth rather than explore it. Průšek is quite mistaken, therefore, when he maintains that "C. T. Hsia repeatedly reproaches Chinese writers for devoting too much attention to social problems and being unable to create a literature unshackled by these problems and unburdened by the struggle for social justice." Surely, in accordance with my emphasis on "disinterested moral exploration," the more problems a work of literature explores, not merely social problems but also political and metaphysical; the more it is concerned with justice, not merely social justice but the ultimate justice of man's fate — the greater it is, provided in tackling these problems, the author is not merely applying ready-made solutions in the spirit of didactic simplification. Surely, the modern Chinese novels to which I accord the highest praise, such as Mao Tun's *The Eclipse*, Pa Chin's *Cold Nights*, and Eileen Chang's *The Rice-Sprout Song*, are the very reverse of "escapist literature";[3] they are all ambitious works of passion and insight, exploring a wide range of social and philosophical problems touching on man's fate.

But the problems have to be concretely embodied. For this reason I quote in my concluding chapter a maxim of D. H. Lawrence, "Lose no time with ideals; serve the Holy Ghost; never serve mankind" and apply it to modern Chinese fiction by saying that its generally mediocre level is "surely due to its preoccupation with ideals, its distracting and overinsistent concern with mankind" (p. 499). Literature — imaginative literature — cannot deal with mankind in the abstract without forfeiting its specific character as literature; it can only deal with individuals. It should not merely adorn or affirm ideals, it tests them in the actuality of

---

[3] Průšek quite arbitrarily equates the literature of "disinterested moral exploration" with the kind of escapist literature fashionable in Taiwan, deplored by my brother in the appendix on Taiwan to my book, p. 511. Průšek also arbitrarily assumes that my brother has a much higher opinion of Lu Hsün than I by reference to his remark, "The early stories and essays (of Lu Hsün) seem to me to have spoken best for the conscience of China during a period of agonizing transition." But nothing in my chapter on Lu Hsün contradicts this statement.

the concrete human situation. Hence I contrast the concrete, the realistic, the individually human in literary representation with the abstract, the idealistic, the stereotyped. Professor Harry Levin of Harvard is surely right when he designates socialist realism as "more precisely, an uncritical idealism—or, as they [the Soviet critics] would put it in candid moments, a revolutionary romanticism."[4] Compared with the uncritical idealism of most socialist-realist and romantic-revolutionary fiction, the kind of critical realism, however unambitious, as exemplified by Lu Hsün and the good writers succeeding him appeared to me so praiseworthy that I have not hesitated to value it as the only tradition in modern Chinese fiction worthy of serious comment.

If, after stating my critical principles, I still appear dogmatically intolerant, at least my intolerance of bad writing will be seen to have been a consequence of my commitment to literary standards and not a consequence of my political prejudices. My only "dogma" would appear to be that the same standards of criticism should apply to all literature, irrespective of nation, period, and ideology. A literary historian, of course, should possess the necessary linguistic competence and the necessary biographical and historical knowledge for the proper appreciation of any writer, any period, but this historical scholarship cannot excuse him from the ultimate responsibility of literary judgment. Professor René Wellek has with his usual compelling judiciousness contradistinguished literary study from historical study:

> Literary study differs from historical study in having to deal not with documents but with monuments. A historian has to reconstruct a long-past event on the basis of eye-witness accounts; the literary student, on the other hand, has direct access to his object: the work of art . . . He can examine his object, the work itself; he must understand, interpret, and evaluate it; he must, in short, be a critic in order to be a historian . . . Many attempts have been made to escape the inevitable consequence of this insight, to avoid the necessity not only of selection but of judgment, but all have failed and must, I think, fail unless we want to reduce literary study to a mere listing of books, to annals or a chronicle. There is nothing which can obviate the necessity of critical judgment, the need of aesthetic standards, just as there is nothing which can obviate the need of ethical and logical standards.[5]

[4]Harry Levin, "Apogee and Aftermath of the Novel," *Daedalus* (Spring, 1963), p. 216.
[5]René Wellek, *Concepts of Criticism* (New Haven, 1963), p. 15.

Průšek, on the contrary, believes that, as a literary historian, I should have acquired a sufficient degree of historical sympathy so as to absolve me from the "necessity of critical judgment." Hence his second general charge about my "disregard for human dignity." Průšek is well aware, of course, that my book has repeatedly emphasized the need of compassion and respect for the individual. Thus I wrote, "Most contemporary Chinese writers reserve their sympathies for the poor and downtrodden; the idea that any person, irrespective of class and position, is a fit object for compassionate understanding is alien to them" (p. 91). Even if one agrees with Průšek and the Marxist historians that "the chief enemies of progress" in modern China were "landowners, usurers, speculators and the compradore bourgeoisie," it does not follow that the literary task is therefore to depict these groups in the blackest color possible and divest them of their humanity. To indulge in melodramatic distortion is ultimately to cheapen human life and to debase the humane profession of letters.

Yet in Průšek's view, I have disregarded human dignity nevertheless, because it is his impression that I have belittled so many writers for their mediocre performance. He actually shows little disposition to disagree entirely with me on these poor works, but he thinks it is the critic's duty to exercise his forbearance and take into sympathetic account the authors' intentions. "If we disregard the aim which the writer had in view," he chides me, "we cannot do justice to his work." Thus in defense of Chao Shu-li's early tales, he says querulously, "C. T. Hsia simply ignores the need to create a literature for the broad masses." Průšek agrees that Chao Shu-li's novel, *San-li Wan*, is a failure, but then he explains, "Undeniably, in this last work Chao Shu-li came up against the difficult problem of how to give his work dramatic tension, when its main task was to describe quiet development and to underline the positive aspects of the characters portrayed." Similarly, Průšek concedes that Ting Ling's *Water* is at least a partial failure, but the critic should nevertheless condone her lack of success because for her "it was a problem of considerable complexity to describe the life-history, not of individuals, but of a whole collective." Průšek applies this principle of forgiveness not only to works of fiction but to theoretical works as well. Thus he refuses to argue with me over the merits of Mao Tse-tung's *Talks at the Yenan Literary Conference*, simply dismissing my "completely distorted" appraisal with an angry remark, "C. T. Hsia does not see the absolutely urgent need to create a new literature and art for the broad masses, now politically and culturally awaking, the greater part of whom were still illiterate."

For Průšek's kind of critical approach, two distinguished literary theorists, W. K. Wimsatt, Jr., and Monroe Beardsley, have a phrase, "the Intentional Fallacy," which has met with almost universal acceptance in American and British academic circles. According to Wimsatt and Beardsley, "the Intentional Fallacy is a confusion between the poem [i.e., the work of literature] and its origins, a special case of what is known to philosophers as the Genetic Fallacy. It begins by trying to derive the standard of criticism from the psychological *causes* ᵥf the poem and ends in biography and relativism."[6] The intention of an author is not to be erected as "a standard for judging the success of a work of literary art,"[7] whatever valuable light it may throw on that work. As literary historians and critics, we cannot therefore evaluate a work by referring to its supposed intention at the neglect of its objective content, as has been Průšek's practice throughout his review, and certainly we cannot condone a poor work simply because we feel the author's intentions have been laudable. As I said in my concluding chapter, "A literature is to be judged not by its intentions but by its actual performance: its intelligence and wisdom, its sensibility and style" (p. 506). The same goes for works of theory and criticism. One cannot presuppose "the absolutely urgent need to create a new literature and art" from reading Mao's *Talks;* to analyze that document itself, on the other hand, is to provide us with clues why in 1942 Mao had called a halt to the petty-bourgeois trends of the earlier leftist literature and proclaimed a new era of propagandist literature.

The literary historian should ideally pass over bad works in silence. But when the said works have been praised as masterpieces to a credulous public, it is surely his duty to analyze them in some detail and expose their faults. However sympathetic toward such persecuted writers as Hsiao Chün and Ting Ling, I have therefore tried to exercise scrupulous objectivity in my unflattering appraisal of their works. In retrospect, I believe I have been unfair to Ting Ling not because my estimates of her particular works, *Water* and *Sun over the Sangkan River,* are mistaken, but because they are not her most characteristic works. If I

---

[6]W. K. Wimsatt, Jr., *The Verbal Icon* (New York, Noonday Paperbound Edition, 1960), p. 21.

[7]*Ibid.*, p. 3.

had focused attention on her early stories and Yenan stories, a different picture of her achievement would have resulted.[8] But as a modern woman who had intended to make her life an experiment in freedom, Ting Ling certainly would not have minded my few brief references to her love life: it is the systematic and malicious distortion of that life by her Communist persecutors during the 1957 trials that was truly frightening.

It is Průšek's intentionalist approach to the study of literature that has prompted his bitter complaint about my "disregard for human dignity"; it is also his intentionalist approach that characterizes his understanding of modern Chinese literature as a whole. To his mind, literature is but the handmaiden of history. Since he agrees with the "Marxist theoreticians" that modern Chinese history is nothing but a record of the Chinese people's self-conscious struggle, under the leadership of the Communist Party, against "the survivals of feudalism" and "foreign imperialism" toward their full liberation, little wonder that he reserves his highest praise for works that seem to have given the fullest embodiment to that historical struggle and that he assigns no weight to works that seem to have nothing to do with that struggle, whatever their other claims to human truth and artistic excellence. Hence he speaks repeatedly of the "mission of literature," an otherwise inexplicable phrase from a scholar passionately concerned with scientific objectivity. Thus preoccupied, Průšek is apparently unaware of the danger of using the literary record merely as a record of history, as a testament to the spirit of the age. I believe, on the contrary, that the literary historian should go about his task empirically: he should not allow preconceived notions of history to determine his quest for excellence, and he should form his own opinion about the vitality and culture of an age precisely on the strength of the literary record he has examined. To him, a lonely genius working in supposed defiance of the Zeitgeist may ultimately sum up that age much more meaningfully than a host of minor writers walking fully in step with the times. Thus, whatever historians and reporters may say of China since 1949, if one finds the literature produced since that date to be infinitely dreary, then this cultural fact should be taken into careful account in one's objective evaluation of the period. This

---

[8]I have indicated my changed view of her importance in my recent article, "Residual Femininity: Women in Chinese Communist Fiction," *The China Quarterly* (January–March 1963), pp. 175–176.

inductive method seems to me far more scientific than the contrary method, the deductive method adopted by Průšek of first broadly defining the historical image of a period and then of finding literature to fit that image.

One is not surprised that, preoccupied with the historical mission and social function of literature, Průšek appears a particularly didactic critic, a critic who supposes that all that really matters in literature is the correct message, the fighting spirit, the zeal and optimism. Thus even of Lu Hsün, whose best works all predate the Communist ascendancy in China and indicate an unregimented individualist contemplating the fate of China with a hope akin to despair, Průšek has the "intrepidity," if I may use his word, to make the following critical estimate: "We would indeed be justified in drawing the conclusion that the more sharply Lu Hsün expressed his standpoint, the more definite the position he took up in the social struggle, the more successful were his stories in every way."

Nothing else, apparently, matters: artistic success is "in every way" assured once a writer manages to express his standpoint sharply and take up a definite position in the social struggle. Even if Průšek assumes here Lu Hsün's customary stylistic excellence, he implicitly ignores all the attendant personal, emotional, and even physiological circumstances that normally play a part in determining whether the work now being contemplated or composed will result in an artistic success. Průšek apparently mistrusts the role of the unconscious—and with good reason. How can one maintain a sharply expressed viewpoint and a definite position in the social struggle if one opens the gates of the unconscious and lets one's dark and invariably subversive dreams, desires, and fears impede the full articulation of one's conscious, enlightened will? The inevitable corollary, therefore, is that the less emotionally charged a work is, the less exposed to the full exercise of the imagination, the more successful it will be in the business of maintaining a correct standpoint and positive position. Little wonder, then, that Průšek regards the wartime literature of the Liberated Areas as indicative of the most glorious age in the whole history of the Chinese people. Fully committed to the propagandist task of arousing the broad masses, the writers had no personal demon to wrestle with, no petty-bourgeois artistic conscience to hinder the full and glorious expression of their correct standpoint and position. Yet, by the same token, one wonders why Průšek still so highly values Lu Hsün, who, according to him, "up to 1928 had still various doubts and fits of pessimism," when the writers of the Liberated Areas were manifestly more dedicated to the task of the social struggle? Indeed, for clarity of standpoint, for definiteness of position, and for ease of comprehension (since Průšek is also vitally concerned with the broad masses), why should he not prefer slogans to the simple stories, poems, and plays of the Yenan period? Why, indeed, bother about literature? When one thinks of *Hamlet*, one shudders at its author's pronounced "doubts" and "pessimism" that disfigure every page of the play.

II. Lu Hsün

As a demonstration of his objective reading, Průšek devotes twenty pages of his 47-page review to Lu Hsün. Though the Lu Hsün chapter occupies only 27 pages in the 507 pages of my main text, apparently upon the test case of Lu Hsün rests the burden of proof that my entire picture of modern Chinese fiction is willfully distorted.

The reader should be reminded that I have not at all "debunked" Lu Hsün. Primarily concerned with his status as a short-story writer, I have examined nine of his stories—and three of them, "Medicine," "The New Year's Sacrifice," "Soap," in greater detail—and come to the conclusion that these nine "constitute the finest body of fiction for the first period [1917–27] and place their author in the forefront as a story-writer" (p. 45). I maintain at the same time that his talent is "distinguished if narrow" and that many of his stories are quite disappointing. On the evidence of two small collections, *Na-han* and *P'ang-huang*, one cannot in fairness say more: to assign him a greater importance is to be unjust to the more resourceful and dedicated fiction writers who came after him. Not to mention the novelists Mao Tun and Lao She, would it be fair to story-writers like Chang T'ien-i and Shen Ts'ung-wen, who in sheer creative fecundity far surpass Lu Hsün? In the face of the dozen or so distinguished volumes of short stories published by Chang T'ien-i in the thirties, how could one persist in believing Lu Hsün to be the greatest or most important story-writer of modern China? It is true that, because Lu Hsün came upon the modern scene first, some of his characters like Ah Q and K'ung I-chi have made an indelible impression upon the Chinese mind, whereas none of Chang T'ien-i's memorable characters seem to have possessed the same symbolic and representative importance. Partly, it is the accident of history that the initiators of a genre seem far more interesting and significant than its more mature practitioners; but princi-

pally, it is due to the unconscionable neglect by the Chinese critics that
Chang T'ien-i, a writer well within the mainstream of leftist fiction,
should have never been given a small fraction of that attention lavished
upon his senior.

By calling his section on Lu Hsün "Confrontation of Methods,"
Průšek indicates his intention to demonstrate that, whereas my "subjective" approach consistently "misinterprets or, at best, obscures the true
significance of Lu Hsün's literary production," his own objective method
has enabled him to "grasp the character of Lu Hsün's oeuvre and to carry
out a scientific analysis." My principal and inexcusable crime, according
to Průšek is that I have attributed to Lu Hsün a love for old China,
which colors my interpretation of his life and work. Průšek bases his
charge upon two passages in my text. The first compares Lu Hsün to
James Joyce (p. 32):

> One may indeed compare the best stories of Lu Hsün to *Dubliners*.
> Shaken by the sloth, superstition, cruelty, and hypocrisy of the rural
> and town people, whom new ideas could not change, Lu Hsün
> repudiates his home town and, symbolically, the old Chinese way of
> life; yet, as in the case of Joyce, this town and these people remain the
> stuff and substance of his creation.

The second comments on the hero of the story, "In the Restaurant"
(p. 41):

> Yet, as actually realized in the story, the kindness and piety of Lü
> Wei-fu, however pathetic, also demonstrates the positive strength of
> the traditional mode of life, toward which the author must have been
> nostalgically attracted in spite of his contrary intellectual conviction.

In both passages, I have been careful to maintain the distinction
between Lu Hsün's intellectual repudiation of the old Chinese way of life
and his emotional or nostalgic attachment to this way of life "in spite of
his contrary intellectual conviction." An artist does not live by the
intellect alone, and he cannot help the accidents of his birth and early
environment. The symbol of his ideological hatred, the home town
remains for Lu Hsün nevertheless "the principal source of his inspiration" (p. 31). Throughout my treatment of Lu Hsün never have I once
suggested that he was intellectually attracted or ideologically committed
to the traditional mode of life. On the contrary, I maintain that, as a
tsa-wen writer, he castigates "all manner of Chinese vices," needles

"popular assumptions of national superiority," and attacks "all lovers of traditional Chinese art and culture."

Průšek is completely mistaken, therefore, when he maintains against all evidence to the contrary that "according to C. T. Hsia, Lu Hsün rejected on the one hand the traditional forms of Chinese life, while being, on the other, continually attracted by them. This is for C. T. Hsia proof of the vacillating ideological orientation of Lu Hsün, which, as he would have believe, went so far as to destroy, in the long run, his creative powers." Never once did I suggest the slightest likelihood of the kind of "vacillating ideological orientation" formulated here. I believe, on the contrary, that his complex involvement with the home town—the traditional life—, far from being a sign of "vacillating ideological orientation," provided the necessary artistic impetus toward the creation of his finest work—not only his best stories, but also the prose poems in *Wild Grass* and the childhood sketches in *Morning Flowers Picked in Evening*. His eventual ideological vacillation, as I see it, is something quite different. It has to do with a crucial crisis in his personal and creative life in the years 1928–29 when, under the pressure of criticism and the dictates of fashion, he largely forsook his deep-seated, somber, individualist faith in modern enlightenment, which had been nourished since his early youth upon his reading in nineteenth-century European literature and thought, in favor of a superficial adherence to a Communist program of collective action. It is my belief that this new allegiance never took root in the soil of his emotional being, so that the voluminous and repetitive *tsa-wen* of his later years, frequently petty and strident in tone, betray the loss of his creative powers and the impairment of his personal integrity. It is in terms of this emotional sterility and ideological reorientation that I analyzed the failure of his last creative effort, *Old Legends Retold:* "In his fear of searching his own mind and disclosing thereby his pessimistic and somber view of China at complete variance with his professed Communist faith, Lu Hsün could only repress his deep-seated personal emotions in the service of political satire" (p. 46). His intellectual repudiation of old China is not in question here.

Committed to his scientific hypothesis of Lu Hsün's unwavering intellectual development as a revolutionary fighter, Průšek, typically, refuses to see any political re-orientation in his emergence as a nominal leader of Communist writers in the year 1930 following a period of painful ideological vacillation. He therefore misreads my account of this crisis as simply a matter of his being alternately repelled and attracted by "the traditional forms of Chinese life." Characteristically, he refuses to debate with me about the later phase of Lu Hsün's life and work, simply repudiating my account as "a mixture of half-truths and distortions of fact" and recommending the reader to Huang Sung-k'ang's "objective" study.

As regards Průšek's critique of my appraisal of individual stories, may I acknowledge first of all the justice of his complaint about my inadequate appreciation of "The Diary of a Madman." As a result of further reading and teaching, I have now come to the conclusion that it is one of Lu Hsün's most assured successes. The irony and the technical virtuosity, which I have commented on, now seem to me to go hand in hand with a subtle exposition of the theme, largely in imagistic and symbolic terms, so that it was quite wrong of me to expect the author to "provide a realistic plot" and present the madman's case in "dramatic terms." I am grateful to Průšek for having called public attention to my inadequate reading of this story.

But in general, when pinpointing my faults, Průšek writes as if he had expected from me a monograph on Lu Hsün rather than a comprehensive survey of modern Chinese fiction: he complains repeatedly of my confinement to "purely subjective observations" and inability to carry out a much more detailed scientific analysis. Moreover, these subjective observations are as a rule cunningly phrased so as to disguise and obscure the resolute, fighting charater of Lu Hsün's fiction. Thus, in discussing the story "My Native Place," he takes strong exception to my description of Jun-t'u as "a weather-beaten man burdened with family care" and points to the phrase "family care" as a misleading euphemism intended to cover up for "all the evils which had made a complete wreck" of this man. Průšek gives the list as follows: "oppressive taxes, soldiery, children, Government offices, usurers." The text, however, arranges it in a different order: "Many children, famines [sic], taxes, soldiers, bandits, officials, and landed gentry."[9] With his scientific objectivity and his scrupulous regard for an author's intentions, I wonder why Průšek has rearranged the list to unwarrantably emphasize man-made afflictions ("oppressive taxes, soldiery") whereas Lu Hsün gives greater emphasis to natural misfortunes (too many mouths to feed and frequent famine) to account for Jun-t'u's present misery.

My formulation, "burdened with family care," in contrast, does

---

[9] *Selected Works of Lu Hsün* (Peking, Foreign Languages Press, 1956), Vol. I, p. 72.

greater justice to this aspect of the peasant's plight duly stressed in the tale. When Jun-t'u first visits the author to pay his respects, he brings along his fifth child, a boy about eleven or twelve *sui* old.[10] In the ensuing conversation, a sixth child is mentioned—since he is able to help on the farm, he must be between ten and eight. During a subsequent visit, Jun-t'u brings along a five-*sui*-old girl, presumably his seventh or eighth child. And since he himself is only forty-one or forty-two, there could be one or two or three children who were born after her. The pathos of the situation is that, though Jun-t'u is able to correlate his misery with bad harvests and unjust financial exactions, he is incapable of the further reflection that his large brood is a bane rather than a blessing. A typical Chinese peasant, he complains with incomprehension, "Even my sixth can do a little work, but still we haven't enough to eat,"[11] because he looks upon his children primarily as producers and not as consumers. But to the author, since poor crops, taxes, soldiers, bandits, and gentry are endured alike by the peasants of the district, it is precisely the size of his family that defines Jun-t'u's peculiar misfortune, which has transformed a boy of exuberant spirits into a weather-beaten man of dashed hopes, clutching at his gods.

Průšek then accuses me of deliberate misrepresentation when I quoted a passage from the story to stress Lu Hsün's honesty in equating his own ill-founded hope for the younger generation with Jun-t'u's superstitious concern with his own welfare. According to Průšek, I should have cited instead a briefer passage at the end, which indicates that hope is like a road: there was no road to begin with, "but when many men pass one way, a road is made." I may first of all remind Průšek that a story, like a poem, is not paraphrasable: the only fair way to present "My Native Place" is to translate the text without comment, but even then, the translation, because it is cast in a different language, will also have distorted the meaning. In a one-page review, one could

---

[10]According to the story, Lu Hsün first met Jun-t'u when the latter was "a boy of eleven or twelve" and "that was thirty years ago" (*Ibid.*, p. 65). Until the author's visit home after an absence of "over twenty years" (*Ibid.*, p. 63), they "never saw each other again" (*Ibid.*, p. 68). It is therefore extremely odd to read later on that Jun-t'u's fifth child strikes Lu Hsün as "just the Jun-t'u of twenty years before, only a little paler and thinner" (*Ibid.*, p. 71). The phrase "twenty years before" should be corrected to read "thirty years before." However, with their hagiographical attitude toward Lu Hsün, no scholars on the mainland have to my knowledge ventured to point out or correct this obvious mistake, even though many editions of Lu Hsün's works have appeared in recent years.

[11]*Ibid.*, p. 72.

only point to the highlights. In the story, the author's reflections on the delusiveness of hope enjoy the position of a climax to a dramatic incident—Jun-t'u's asking for the censer and candlesticks to worship his idols with—and therefore should receive proper emphasis, whereas the oft-quoted passage at the end represents to me an afterthought, quite detached from the main body of the story. It is as typical of Lu Hsün as the wistful ending of "The Diary of a Madman": "Perhaps there are still some children who have not yet become cannibalistic? Save these children . . ." In both instances, Lu Hsün tries to convince himself that some ground for hope must be indicated even though the stories themselves provide no hope.[12]

Since Průšek cites the concluding passage from "My Native Place" to remind me that in *Na-han* at least, Lu Hsün is much more hopeful and optimistic than I have made him out to be, we may turn to the Preface to that collection to see how the author himself characterizes his mental condition in the writing of these stories. Indeed, with his high regard for the writer's intentions, Průšek himself quotes twice briefly from that document to prove Lu Hsün's resolute bravery, though both times he neglects to provide the necessary contexts to make the passages yield their full meaning. According to the preface, the title *Na-han* is part of an elaborate military metaphor by which the author views himself as a mere foot soldier in the battle against the tradition. The leaders of the new culture movement—the editors of *New Youth*—are viewed as lonely commanders on horseback charging into the enemy ranks. As in old-style military romances, the commanders are here given all the credit for the actual fighting, while the foot soldiers merely yell (the term *na-han* comes from such stock phrases as "wave the banners and yell"摇 旗 吶 喊 and "beat the drums and yell"擂 鼓 吶 喊) to boost the morale and provide the proper encouragement. As a reluctant conscript (earlier in the preface, he tells us how he has been pressed into service by Ch'ien Hsüan-t'ung, an editor of *New Youth*), however, Lu Hsün doesn't care whether his decorative yell is "brave or sad, repellent or ridiculous." "However, since it is a call to arms," he continues, "I must naturally obey my commanders' orders. This is why I feel no compunction in resorting to innuendoes, as when I made a wreath appear from nowhere

---

[12]I have discussed Lu Hsün's hopeful attitude toward the younger generation in *A History of Modern Chinese Fiction*, pp. 52–54. There I cited quotations from the story "The Solitary" and an open letter dated April 10, 1928, included in *San-hsien chi* 三 閑 集.

at the son's grave in "Medicine," while in "Tomorrow" I did not say that Fourth Shan's Wife had no dreams of her little boy. For our commanders then were against pessimism. And I, for my part, did not want to infect with the loneliness I had found so bitter those young people who were still dreaming pleasant dreams, just as I had done when young."[13]

The last sentence reverts to an earlier parable in the preface which states that many people—the Chinese nation—are sound asleep in an indestructible iron house without windows. Lu Hsün thinks it would be cruel to wake these people up because, once awake, they would only face the agony of suffocation and death without the hope of relief. His interrogator, Ch'ien Hsüan-t'ung, argues, however, that if enough numbers are aroused, there might be a chance of destroying that house. Lu Hsün agrees; even though he still sticks to his conviction that the house cannot be destroyed, he feels at the same time, "I could not blot out hope, for hope lies in the future."[14]

In these two carefully worked out metaphors, does the author see himself as a brave fighter rushing to the forefront to combat feudalism? (Mao Tse-tung's subsequent assertion that Lu Hsün was "the greatest and bravest standard-bearer of the new cultural army" and "the commander of the cultural revolution" [p. 29] appears to contradict completely the author's self-portrayal as an insignificant foot soldier yelling to the tune of his commanders and not knowing whether his cry denotes bravery or sadness.) Yes, he provides a hopeful note here and there, because it will be against the orders of the commanders to indulge in pessimism. More poignantly, he provides some hope because it would be too cruel to awaken these young people dreaming their pleasant dreams in an iron house. As a fully awakened person, he himself is faced with bitter loneliness and also saddled with the "conviction" that the house cannot be destroyed. Despite the reconstructed "scientific" facts in support of Lu Hsün's brave optimism, it would seem that my interpretation of "My Native Place" and other stories in the same collection is far more in accord with the author's appraisal of his intention as given in the preface, even though I set far less store by intentional statements and actually analyzed the stories without making specific references to these statements.

Průšek, however, would assign greater weight to a later document,

---

"How I Came to Write Stories," as an expression of the author's
intention. This article was written to order in the year 1933, when Lu
Hsün, as a prominent member of the Left-wing League, had to sustain
his image as a resolute fighter of the reaction. But, characteristically, in
this essay as in the slightly earlier preface to *Tzu-hsüan chi* (自選集), he
maintains scrupulous honesty in reporting on his earlier career and does
not at all repudiate the account of himself given in the preface to *Na-han*.
Indeed, he calls "How I Came to Write Stories" a "complement" to that
preface. He recalls the intellectual and literary climate of the May Fourth
period and says that he wrote "in the hope of enlightening my people,
for humanity, and of the need to better it . . . So my themes were
usually the unfortunates in this abnormal society. My aim was to expose
the disease and draw attention to it so that it might be cured."[15] The last
sentence is much less emphatic in the original; it reads, "My aim was to
expose the disease so as to draw attention to its cure."[16] Though Lu
Hsün assumes here a firmer tone as befits his new cultural role in the
thirties, his statement of aim does not contradict my account: "It must be
remembered that Lu Hsün's primary ambition as a writer was to serve
his country as a spiritual physician. In his best stories, however, he is
content to probe the disease without prescribing a cure: he has too high a
respect for the art of fiction to present other than the unadorned truth"
(p. 46). In his *tsa-wen* essays, he is emphatically didactic. In his best
stories he exposes the disease and draws attention to its cure, but he does
not prescribe a cure.

From this digression on intentions, we return now to an examination
of some of the other stories. According to Průšek, "Medicine" is another
tale I have misread because I am not appreciative of its hopeful note. He
believes my account of the story implies that "Lu Hsün did not believe
in the Revolution [the anti-Manchu revolution, by the way, and not the
Communist revolution]," whereas all I said in this connection is that "the
death of Hsia indicates Lu Hsün's gloomy view of the revolutionary
cause in China" (p. 35). Lu Hsün's personal belief or disbelief is
immaterial here, but the unjust and unavenged execution of the hero
assuredly places the revolutionary cause in a pessimistic light. (In section
3 of the story, the small citizens gathered at the teahouse, the would-be
benefactors of the revolution, gossip about the martyr in tones of

---

[15]*Selected Works of Lu Hsün*, Vol. 3, p. 230.
[16]Lu Hsün, *Nan-ch'iang pei-tiao chi* 南腔北調集 (Hong Kong, 1958), p. 83.

malicious contempt.) But I immediately qualified my earlier statement by saying that, in spite of the author's pessimism, "he lodges a memorable protest over Hsia's unjust execution" (p. 35) by placing upon his grave a Western-style wreath. But perhaps even the word "protest" is too strong, since the officials responsible for his death would not visit the cemetery for the poor on a festival day like the Ch'ing Ming, and even if they did, they would be, like Hsia's mother, completely baffled by the anachronistic significance of the wreath. If Lu Hsün had really wanted to be militantly hopeful, he could have conceived the story in an entirely different fashion. Hsia could have escaped from the prison, with or without the assistance of his comrades; he could also have saved the life of Hua by sending him to a Western-style hospital in Shanghai (alas, there were then no socialist hospitals with free service for the poor). He could, furthermore, have given Hua's parents a lecture about the inhumanity of their superstitious practices. If the new plot sounds too much like a present-day Communist story where the hero is invincible, the poor are getting the best of care, and everybody in the end is enlightened and happy, my intended parody shows how wrong it is for Průšek to read into the story a firmer message of hope than the text warrants.

Průšek appears thoroughly irritated by my symbolic reading of the story. He objects particularly to my linking the names of the two youths to read *Hua-hsia* (華夏), China. It is his belief that, as a "deeply erudite student of Chinese literature," Lu Hsün knew only too well what a senseless game it is to toy with words and meanings. The stories supply the contrary evidence, however, that precisely because of his literary erudition, Lu Hsün chose the names of his characters with particular care, investing them often with symbolic and/or comic connotations. A simple example is Kao Erh-ch'u 高爾礎, the ridiculous hero of "Professor Kao," who styles himself after Gorky 高爾基. A particularly happy example of the author's ingenuity is the name Ah Q. As Chou Tso-jen has aptly observed,[17] Q stands as a pictograph of a man's head with the dangling end of his queue showing. And since "Q" is an exact homophon for the word "queue" and since the queue is a shameful badge of feudalism, one is not surprised that the queue plays a highly symbolic and comic role in the satiric story of Ah Q. According to Chou Tso-jen, the real-life counterpart of K'ung I-chi was surnamed Meng and

---

[17]Chou Hsia-shou 周遐壽, *Lu Hsün hsiao-shuo-li ti jen-wu* 魯迅小說裡的人物 (Shanghai, 1954), pp. 64–65.

nicknamed Master Meng 孟夫子.[18] Since Lu Hsün regards this character as a marginal member of the Confucian scholar-official class, he changed his name to the even more symbolic K'ung.

In like fashion, as critics have long pointed out, Lu Hsün chose the name Hsia Yü 夏瑜 for the martyr in "Medicine" to commemorate the woman revolutionary Ch'iu Chin 秋瑾. Ch'iu (Autumn) parallels Hsia (Summer), and the synonyms *chin* and *yü* share the same *jade* radical and go together as a phrase. (Thus among the famous personages of the Three Kingdoms period, Chou Yü 周瑜 is styled 公瑾 and Chu-ko Chin 諸葛瑾 is styled 子瑜.) Once Lu Hsün hit upon the surname Hsia, it was only natural that he should assign the other victim of feudal ignorance the surname Hua, to enhance the symbolic or allegoric meaning of the story. As Hua is not a common family name, if Lu Hsün had not intended the additional dimension of meaning which the two names in conjunction would immediately suggest, he could have used any number of commoner names, like Wang or Li. As for Průšek's alternative suggestion that the two names "underline the fact expressed in the tale, that brother eats brother," it simply doesn't make sense. Both Hua and Hsia are victims of the old society, one ravaged by a wasting disease and the other murdered for his revolutionary crime. It is the executioner, the officialdom standing solidly behind him, the indifferent and malicious gossipers at the teahouse, who represent the "cannibalistic character of the old society."

Průšek strongly disapproves of the kind of cannibalistic society as portrayed in "Medicine" in that it "enthusiastically sanctions the torture and killing of a fellow-creature whose crime was that he wished to liberate them." In his discussion of "K'ung I-chi," "White Glow," and "The New Year's Sacrifice," he also comments repeatedly on the "insensate cruelty of society" and "the dull indifference of the milieu." Inexplicably, however, at the same time he takes strong exception to my inclusion of "the sloth, superstition, cruelty, and hypocrisy of the rural and town people" as an inherent part of Lu Hsün's fictional world. According to Průšek, this description completely conceals the fact that "the aim and purpose of Lu Hsün's oeuvre was . . . not only to lay bare the general insensibility and cruelty of Chinese society, but, above all, to point the finger at those who were responsible for this state of affairs." To prove his point, he asserts that the principal villain in "The New

---

[18]*Ibid.*, pp. 14–15.

Year's Sacrifice" is the heroine's employer, "the conservative upholder of Confucian morality, the honorable Mr. Lu." A few pages earlier, however, he has spoken of Hsiang-lin Sao's tragedy in terms of "a terrifying fatality and cruelty," of "the absolute helplessness of a human being dragged to destruction by obscure forces." These obscure forces, it turns out, are now incarnated in the very visible person of the detestable Mr. Lu.

In order to ascertain Mr. Lu's crime, we have to review the story at some length. The main event which unhinges Hsiang-lin Sao's mind, as every reader of the story will agree, is the death of her young son. Upon her second return to Lu-chen, she continually talks about this tragic incident, to the eventual disgust and contempt of the townspeople and her fellow servants. Though her second husband and her son have died within a short time of each other, she never refers to the former, and yet there is nothing in the text to indicate that their conjugal relationship had been unsatisfactory. Hsiang-lin Sao, nevertheless, is obsessed with the death of her son because it is through her negligence that a wolf has devoured him. Thus her set speech begins, "I was really stupid, really. I only knew that when it snows the wild beasts . . . may come to the villages; I didn't know that in spring they could come too."[19] If it were indeed Lu Hsün's aim to point his accusing finger at the gentry, why should he have made a hungry beast the agent of the son's death? And for that matter, why should her second husband die of typhoid, when he could have easily died as a victim of gentry oppression? "The New Year's Sacrifice" could have become a precursor of, say, *The White-haired Girl*, but apparently Lu Hsün had no intention of coveting this dubious honor.

The wolf is not even part of the human world of feudalism. Hence I speak with justice of the "primitive peasant society" to which Hsiang-lin Sao belongs. It is only in that society that wolves are permitted to roam at large in daytime and snatch infants, that mothers-in-law can forcibly sell their daughters-in-law so that their younger sons may marry, that a convalescent typhoid patient can gobble down a bowl of cold rice to bring about a relapse and hasten his death. (This last detail, usually unmentioned in discussions of the story, indicates how, as a one-time medical student, Lu Hsün was very much concerned with the peasants' carelessness about their welfare and health: Jun-t'u's large family is

---

[19]*Selected Works of Lu Hsün*, Vol. 1, p. 165.

another instance.) And it is not inappropriate that the wolf should play a crucial part in that world; for like Hsiang-lin Sao's mercenary and cruel mother-in-law, it too stands for that relentless struggle for existence in a forever hungry world of predators and helpless preys. And when one remembers the many references to the wolf in Lu Hsün's other stories and also his prose poems, the symbolic dimension becomes unmistakable.

After the townspeople, through their indifference and contempt, have caused Hsiang-lin Sao to repress her sorrow and guilt over her son's death, the maidservant Liu Ma, described as "a devout woman who abstained from meat,"[20] turns her attention to another of her supposed crimes that calls for expiation. Liu Ma reminds her that she should have remained chaste to the memory of her first husband and should have killed herself when being forced to marry the second time. Hsiang-lin Sao hasn't thought of this before, but now frightened, she decides to save enough money to donate a doorsill to a temple. In the process she works hard and doesn't mind much the continual teasing by the townspeople about the scar on her forehead, the shameful badge of her crime.

The final crushing blow, of course, is delivered by her mistress, Fourth Aunt Lu, who intercepts her in the act of fetching utensils to be used in the ancestral sacrifice. Hsiang-lin Sao thought her crime has been expiated with her purchase of a doorsill, but apparently she is still regarded as an unlucky woman. From then on, she steadily deteriorates. Because Fourth Aunt Lu and her husband can be seen in this respect as the final link in the chain of events leading to her death, Průšek wants us to believe that Mr. Lu is alone responsible for her tragedy.

According to Průšek, it is Mr. Lu who "exploited her, who made her a social outcast, who implanted in her the crazy idea of her guilt and drove her to madness, who deprived her of work and drove her into the streets, who let her die of hunger and cynically commented on her death." Průšek makes here no mention of the many events in Hsiang-lin Sao's life we have just reviewed; he ignores completely the more important agents of her tragedy but magnifies the villainy of Mr. Lu out of all proportion to his minor role in the story. First of all, one cannot speak of her "exploitation" by the Lus in the sense that, given the conditions of feudal China, the widow Hsiang-lin Sao could not aspire to better employment than being retained by a genteel family. In her initial term of service, she actually regains her spirits and finds a new purpose in life

---

[20]*Ibid.*, p. 169.

so that, if her mother-in-law has not forcibly abducted her, she will remain a quite contented person. In the context of the Communist revolution, perhaps her lot will still be considered a miserable one, but since Lu Hsün does not write from the Communist viewpoint, one cannot make this anachronistic accusation. She works hard, of course; "nevertheless, she, on her side, was satisfied; gradually the trace of a smile appeared at the corner of her mouth, and her fact became whiter and plumper."[21] The Lus' willingness to employ her for the second time is even more a case of benevolence, since most families would not hire a woman who has been twice a widow and shows visible signs of emotional disturbance. On her part, Hsiang-lin Sao feels now she is unwanted not because the Lus treat her harshly (as a matter of fact, they tolerate her inefficiency and frequent spells of absent-mindedness), but because they forbid her to give any menial help in connection with ancestral sacrifices. In this respect, both she and her masters are seen as victims of feudalistic supersition. If either side can take the matter of religious worship less seriously, she will not have felt being rejected.

In my chapter on Lu Hsün I have praised the story for its "flesh and body" representation of feudalism and supersition. With the exception of the first-person narrator (but even he respects the consolatory power of feudal religion so that he doesn't know how to answer Hsiang-lin Sao's despairing questions), everyone in the story is in the grip of the superstitious fear of the gods and hell, be he a peasant or a member of the gentry. Lu Hsün makes it clear that Mrs. Lu is quite benevolent, judging by traditional standards, though her husband is more suspicious of and ill-disposed toward people. But the fact of primary importance is that they are both superstitious, and initially, Mr. Lu more than his wife, because he respects more the taboo against hiring a widow. The author's attitude toward him is satiric not because he is depicted as cruel but because, given his Confucian education, he at least should rise above folk superstition. Cunningly, in the introductory section of the story, the author calls Fourth Uncle Lu a Neo-Confucianist, mentions some of his favorite books by title (one is an annotated edition of the *Chin-ssu lu* 近思錄), recalls his having been exposed to such Neo-Confucian assertions as "Ghosts and spirits are properties of Nature,"[22] to underscore his possible freedom from superstitious fears by virtue of his rationalist educa-

---

[21]*Ibid.*, p. 158–159.
[22]*Ibid.*, p. 156. This is a loose translation of a statement by Chang Tsai 張載 ,鬼神者二氣之良能也.

tion. Yet, to the author's disenchantment and disbelief, he is the one who seems most zealous about preparing the New Year's Sacrifice and he is the one who makes that unfeeling remark about Hsiang-lin Sao's death. Průšek thinks his remark is "cynical," but on the face of things, he is too superstitious to be cynical. He is actually highly incensed that the beggar should have died not earlier nor later, but exactly on the eve of the New Year festival when his family needs all the luck in the world and can ill afford the interference of an inauspicious accident. Fourth Uncle is certainly not charitable, but with ironic objectivity, Lu Hsün shows us at the same time that a temporary servant in the employ of the Lus, a man surely of plebeian origins, regards the event also with distasteful contempt.

Despite the long catalogue of villainies attributed to him by Průšek, in the subsequent retelling of Hsiang-lin Sao's past history, Fourth Uncle is only assigned a subsidiary role. He complains and grumbles several times, mostly over her unlucky widowhood, and following the climactic scene, after the horror-struck Fourth Aunt has asked Hsiang-lin Sao to desist from helping at the sacrificial table, he orders her to leave the room. Subsequently, of course, the Lus dismiss her after her worsened condition has incapacitated her from domestic service. But since no other family gives her employment, the whole town is in agreement about her undesirability. In dismissing her, Mrs. Lu has not suddenly become cruel; she has become finally convinced that Hsiang-lin Sao is indeed an unlucky person. Like Philoctetes stranded on an island with his incurable wound, like the blinded Oedipus sent to exile, what gods hate, man cannot help—hence my reference to the ethos of "the heroic society of Greek tragedy" (p. 39). And in the term "man" is included every person in Lu-chen who has long jeered at her misfortune. Because of his enlightened education, the author-narrator alone feels keen commiseration and regret over her death. To him, the whole town in its festive gaiety, too preoccupied with the ritual of soliciting "boundless good fortune" for the next year to spare a thought for the unlucky dead, is implicated in her death. But an unwelcome visitor himself, he certainly cannot change its ways of pitiful and largely unself-conscious cruelty; he plans to leave tomorrow.

It is also by reference to Průšek's presuppositions about the aim and purpose of Lu Hsün's fiction that we can understand his otherwise tales, Lu Hsün has not singled out the gentry as the primary object of his hatred but has contemplated with sorrow and restrained anger, with compassion and ironic objectivity, the superstition and heartlessness of all "the rural and town people" living under the blighting influence of elementary hunger, disease, and feudalism. It would seem that Průšek has read the story in a very biased way precisely because he feels so certain about "the aim and purpose of Lu Hsün's oeuvre." He has read the story primarily to vindicate the thesis that Lu Hsün always points his accusing finger at the evil gentry.

It is also by reference to Průšek's presuppositions about the aim and purpose of Lu Hsün's fiction that we can understand his otherwise puzzling disagreement with me about the importance of the story "Soap." He concedes that "the character-study of the man and the portrayal of his domestic milieu is [*sic*] extremely well done" and that the "irony is brilliantly effective"; yet he begrudges it a high place among the author's tales. Lu Hsün himself thought of it very highly: along with only three other stories of his, "The Diary of a Madman," "Medicine," and "Divorce," he placed it in a volume of stories bearing the general title, *A Comprehensive Anthology of Modern Chinese Literature*.[23] Průšek nevertheless thinks that "Soap" lacks "that specific something" uniquely Lu Hsün and does not sum up and "generalize" about "some fundamental feature of Chinese society." What he means, I suppose, is that the story does not chastise feudal society too harshly but holds it up for seemingly inconsequential ridicule. He seems to believe on principle that the impersonal comic style is incompatible with the serious aim of Lu Hsün's fiction.

It remains for me to say a few words about *Old Legends Retold*, now that I have answered in detail Průšek's specific charges against my misinterpretations of stories from *Na-han* and *P'ang-huang*. Průšek regards the later collection very highly and speaks of my inability to grasp the "individuality and originality of Lu Hsün's artistic technique" to be discerned in that volume. In its defense, however, he resorts rather uncharacteristically to the poetic vocabulary of impressionistic criticism and speaks of the "many-faceted iridescence" of Lu Hsün's art. I wish he had analyzed at least one episode from any one of the stories in this collection to demonstrate how it conveys "a multiplicity of meanings, every moment relating to a number of layers of reality, their changing hues reminiscent of a winding scarf of rainbow colors." In the absence of

---

[23]Lu Hsün, ed., *Hsiao-shuo erh-chi* 小說二集, Vol. 4 of Chao Chia-pi 趙家璧, ed., Chung-kuo hsin-wen hsëh ta-hsi (Shanghai, 1935–36).

this demonstration, I could only say that Lu Hsün, whose opinion Průšek usually respects, is none too proud of these creations. In the preface to *Old Legends Retold* and elsewhere, he dwells upon his personal dissatisfaction with his first story in the style of satiric fantasy, "Mending Heaven," and the faults of that story—a levity of tone and the intrusive note of personal peevishness and ephemeral satire—are largely present in most of the other tales. I would allow that "Pacifying the Flood" and "Picking Ferns" are better than the rest: in the first story, the satiric sketch of the intellectuals on the Culture Mountain, to borrow a phrase from Průšek, sums up a "fundamental feature of Chinese society" and in the second, the hapless heroes, Po-i and Shu-ch'i, in spite of the author's open mockery, are somewhat reminiscent of the many weakling characters in his non-historical fiction. But the remainder of the volume, in its levity and chaos, marks what I have called "the sad degeneration of a distinguished if narrow talent for fiction" (p. 46).

III. Other Writers

Průšek devotes twenty pages to Lu Hsün; the rest of the writers receiving individual attention in my book, however, are treated together in a third section called "Individual Portraits," which has only twelve-odd pages. There his attention is mainly focused upon Mao Tun and Lao She (their pre-war works), Yeh Shao-chün, Yü Ta-fu, Ting Ling, and Chao Shu-li. Even such well-known authors as Chang T'ien-i, Shen Ts'ung-wen, and Pa Chin are barely mentioned. I have taken pains to demonstrate the literary importance of Eileen Chang and Ch'ien Chung-shu, but Průšek dismisses them as merely authors "congenial" to my taste. For a scholar insisting upon scientific objectivity, is it fair that he should so dismiss them? Is it not rather his duty as a reviewer to examine their works and then decide whether they deserve the high praise I have given them? It also seems to me that Průšek has skirted around the long chapter on "Conformity, Defiance, and Achievement," which treats in detail the continuing ideological struggle among leftist and Communist writers from 1936 to 1957. He touches upon some of the earlier debates, but the major events of the fifties, such as the anti-Hu Feng campaign and the persecution of rightist and revisionist authors, are passed over in silence.

Of the writers discussed in this third section, Průšek shows on the whole less sharp disagreement with my interpretations. (Even on the works of Ting Ling and Chao Shu-li, as has been earlier shown, he admits that I am partially or in the main right, though I have not grasped their intentions.) He seems, however, much more concerned with the problem of omission, noting, for instance, that I failed to discuss any of Lao She's short stories. Writing a comprehensive history, I had to observe the requirements of proportion and economy. Since I believe that Lao She's distinctive contribution to modern Chinese literature is as a novelist rather than as a short-story writer, I discussed all his novels, with the exception of the negligible *City of Cats*, in Chapters 7 and 14. If my interpretation of Lao She is indeed faulty, why couldn't Průšek pinpoint the mistakes in my accounts of the novels, instead of deploring my neglect of the much less important stories?[24]

In the five-odd pages devoted to Mao Tun and Lao She, Průšek focuses his attention principally on the opening paragraph of Chapter 7, where a general comparison of the two authors is attempted. I have already covered the pre-war career of Mao Tun, and now I proceed to Lao She by way of a transitional passage. It is the penalty one has to pay for writing a book also intended for the general reader that such passages, which would have served no purpose for the specialist, are sometimes necessary. In the said passage, I had to be content with generalities, making no provision for the kind of qualifying statements that would have to be made if I were attempting an exact, detailed comparison: the reader knows that a much longer critique of Lao She will follow. Průšek, on the contrary, lingers over this designedly transitional passage, while paying no attention to the rest of the chapter. Particularly, he exhibits the sentence, "Using the time-honored test of Northern and Southern literary sensibilities, we may say that Lao She represents the North, individualist, forthright, humorous, and Mao Tun, the more feminine South, romantic, sensuous, melancholic" (p. 165), as

---

[24]Most of Lao She's short stories strike me as disappointing. In Chapter 8 of *Lao-niu p'o-ch'e* 老牛破車 (Shanghai, 1937), Lao She tells of the difficulties and frustrations he had encountered in writing short stories. The only group of stories he spoke of with some pride are the longer tales which are actually condensations of novels he had intended to write but didn't have the time. Among these, "Yüeh-ya erh 月牙兒," because of its proletarian subject-matter, has received the highest praise in Communist criticism. But a complementary story in the same style about a rich girl, "Yang-kuang 陽光," first collected in *Ying-hai chi* 櫻海集 (Shanghai, 1935), is decidedly much superior. Since both tales should be regarded as novelettes rather than short stories, the inescapable conclusion is that Lao She has little aptitude for the short story.

an example of my "purely subjective approach" to "literary questions."
Any objective reader will see that I set little store by that expression,
"the time-honored test of Northern and Southern literary sensibilities,"
since I refer to this test only once and not again. And even in this single
instance of adoption, I use the weak auxiliary verb "may" to indicate the
conditional or concessional nature of my statement: "If we use this test,
we may say that . . ." Moreover, it surely does no harm to my readers,
most of whom are non-specialists, to be informed of this concept of
geographical differentiation in traditional Chinese literary and art criticism, even if, according to Průšek this concept is "completely invalid."
In the same captious vein, Průšek goes on to take exception to this and
that formulation in my paragraph, without once reminding the reader
that I have indeed taken care of these exceptions in my detailed critiques
of the two authors.[25]

When Průšek finally passes on to a discussion of Mao Tun's individual works, he again reminds me that, as is the case with Lu Hsün, I have
not grasped the aim and purpose of his oeuvre and subjected it to a
scientific analysis. According to him, Mao Tun "considers literature to be
an important weapon in the political arsenal," and presumably all his
own works should be evaluated primarily with reference to that political
objective. This, indeed, has been the standard procedure of the Communist critics in China ever since they greeted his first masterpiece, *The
Eclipse*, with a barrage of vituperative criticism. With his undoubted
Communist sympathies, they could not understand why he should have
cared far more for an honest representation of the revolutionary situation
during the Northern Expedition than for the long-term interests of the

---

[25]Thus because I referred to Mao Tun's "ornate literary vocabulary," Průšek infers
that I am incapable of discriminating between the several kinds of style in Mao Tun's work.
Actually I was referring to his vocabulary rather than to his style: the large number of
words and phrases taken from classical literature that does give his novels and many of his
short stories an "ornate" quality. Similarly, because I contrasted the "individualist" Lao
She with the "romantic" Mao Tun in that transitional passage, Průšek believes that I have
failed to see the considerable amount of romanticism in Lao She's fiction. Actually, in
Chapter 7 I refer to his romantic heroes—the "romantic Ma Wei" (p. 174) and Lao Li with
"his romantic dream of a world with poetry and meaning" (p. 178)—and properly stress
the strong note of individual heroism and chivalry in his work. Unfortunately, "romantic"
being one of the most imprecise words in the English language, I applied it to Mao Tun
primarily to suggest the erotic character of his fiction: hence the word is used in
conjunction with two other adjectives, "sensuous" and "melancholic." Lao She, of course,
has as much right to that epithet if we intend it to denote the world of individualism,
heroism and chivalry.

Party. This political emphasis still obtains in Communist appraisals of Mao Tun today, so that his first two great works, *The Eclipse* and *Rainbow*, are always assigned a lesser importance, while a later and coarser work, *The Twilight*, because of its political orthodoxy, is invariably given the highest praise. I am sorry to see that, with his far greater literary sensitivity and erudition, Průšek nevertheless endorses this critical approach. Thus he apologizes for the fact that *The Eclipse* was "written under the impression of a despairing mood," whereas it was precisely this despairing mood, as I have demonstrated in my book, that had contributed so immensely to its human truth and emotional power. Again Průšek apologizes that *Rainbow* is "not particularly typical of Mao Tun," even though Part I of that work shows the novelist at the peak of his form. I may remark that, though he enjoys universal fame as Communist China's greatest novelist, on the mainland only two of his novels and a handful of his stories have received unqualified praise. Even monographs devoted to a survey of his writing career hardly discuss such later works as the novel *Maple Leaves as Red as February Flowers* and the fine stories collected under the title *Grievances*.[26] His oeuvre has suffered drastic amputation on the Procrustean bed of Communist criticism.

I rank *The Twilight* "among major contemporary Chinese novels," though I deem it a big failure in terms of what the author could have done with his material if he had followed the lines of development indicated in *The Eclipse* and *Rainbow*. Lifting phrases from my book, Průšek accuses me on the contrary of having failed to notice "the accent of passion or conviction" and the signs of a "self-tormenting honesty," though I have taken pain to explain why "the self-tormenting honesty of *The Eclipse* and *Rainbow*" (p. 157) is missing from the later work. As a proof of the author's "self-tormenting honesty," he cites the "on the whole negative picture of Communist Party functionaries" and of women factory workers presented in the book. Now the novel takes place in 1930, when the Communist activists in Shanghai were all perforce following the Li Li-san line. Mao Tun composed it in 1931–32, at a time when the then Communist leadership had harshly repudiated that line. Writing from hindsight, he had no choice but to present a "negative picture" of such misdirected Communists as K'e Tso-fu and Ts'ai Chen.

---

[26]Cf. Yeh Tzu-ming 葉子銘, *Lun Mao Tun ssu-shih-nien ti wen-hsüeh tao-lu* 論茅盾四十年的文學道路, 1959), and Shao Po-chou 邵伯周 *Mao Tun ti wen-hsüeh tao-lu* 茅盾的文學道路, 1959).

To give a more flattering portrait, on the contrary, would have called for the exercise of personal courage and "self-tormenting honesty." For a succinct presentation of the political content of *The Twilight*, the reader is recommended to T. A. Hsia, *Enigma of the Five Martyrs* (Berkeley, 1962), an engrossing study of the intricate connections between Communist literary workers and party leaders in 1930.

Because in the chapter on Mao Tun I direct my attention primarily to the novels, Průšek accuses me of treating his short stories in "a very stepmotherly fashion." Again, as with Lu Hsün, he expects me to have written a much longer chapter, if not a monograph on the author. In support of his charge, he cites my supposed misunderstanding of two stories, "Creation" and "Spring Silkworms." In regard to the former, I have written only a one-sentence summary, which goes, "The heroine of 'Creation' feels compelled to leave her husband and mentor because she had advanced beyond his noncommittal intellectual dilettantism to a positive socialist position" (p. 161). Průšek believes, on the other hand, that the heroine has reached only a "very indefinite" political position, and proceeds to give his own interpretation of the story, in more words. Of course, neither my brief summary nor his longer commentary could have done adequate justice to a story of over thirty pages. I could say of Průšek's account, for example, that he has completely ignored the conspicuous erotic element in the story: in his early fiction (as I have shown in my discussion of *The Eclipse* and *Rainbow* and my briefer comment on *The Wild Roses*), Mao Tun's distinctive forte lies in his passionate dual concern with the ideological and the erotic.

As for Průšek's objection to my phrase, "positive socialist position," I believe that its mention in my summary is justified by the text so long as I do not specify the political party, whether Communist or anarchist, to which the heroine is drawn. Her husband is a great reader of political philosophy, including "Kropotkin, Marx, Lenin," though his political views remain strictly non-subversive. He has encouraged his wife to read about politics, but the unexpected result is that she shows so much interest and concern that she has lately joined an "unsound and illegal (= subversive) political movement."[27] She takes to another mentor, a Miss Li, who completely upsets her husband's program of education for her. (In stories of this type, highly popular in the late twenties and early thirties, the mysterious stranger to whom the hero or heroine turns for

---

[27]*Mao Tun wen-chi* 茅盾文集 (Peking 1958), Vol. 7, p. 27.

guidance is usually a Communist, though to bypass the censor, his political identity is frequently not disclosed.) So the husband laments his ruined creation: "He had destroyed Hsien-hsien's easygoing nonchalance, but materialism had replaced it; he had destroyed her affectation of an old-style scholar's distaste for politics, but radical and extremist political thought had usurped its place, not to be dislodged."[28] Taking into consideration the censorship requirements of the times, one should think that such words and expressions as "unsound and illegal political movement," "materialism," "radical and extremist political thought," along with the specific mention of the names of Kropotkin, Marx, and Lenin, are not at all ambiguous in indicating Hsien-hsien's commitment to a socialist, if not Communist, position. And Průšek to the contrary, her parting message to her husband, relayed by a servant, removes all possible doubt as to what the author is driving at: "She's gone. She has asked me to tell you: she's now going ahead first, and may you catch up with her . . . And she added, if you don't intend to catch up with her, she's not going to wait for you either."[29]

Průšek berates me for distorting the meaning of "Spring Silkworms," a story I praised highly, perhaps too highly. Prior to offering my own interpretation, however, I gave the reader the standard reading: "As a Communist commentary on the Chinese scene, 'Spring Silkworms' shows the bankruptcy of the peasantry under the dual pressure of imperialist aggression and traditional usury, and as such the story is usually praised" (p. 163). I suppose if I had continued in this vein, Průšek would for once have praised me for my objectivity. But I found this didactic reading quite inadequate and so I traced the story's "strength and appeal" to the author's ritualistic attention to the minute details of silkworm-raising and to his largely sympathetic portrayal of the old farmer T'ung-pao and his loyal family working beside him. I was well aware, of course, that Mao Tun does not approve of "their unsparing diligence and unfaltering trust in a beneficent Heaven" and that it is his "articulate intention to discredit this kind of feudal mentality" (p. 163). But I insisted nevertheless that "almost in spite of himself, one feels that Mao Tun is celebrating in his tale the dignity of labor." The youngest son, To-to-t'ou, of course, is his principal instrument for discrediting feudal mentality, but he plays only a minor role and he

---

[28]*Ibid.*, p. 29.
[29]*Ibid.*, p. 34.

remains an artificial character. His undisguised superiority actually confirms our sympathy for his father and the other less enlightened members of his family. Their unremitting labor, of course, only brings them nearer ruin, but this failure, due to external causes beyond their control, does not deprive them of their impressive dignity.

Průšek is therefore positively wrong when he maintains, "In fact, Mao Tun describes with extreme irony and deprecation the superstition of the old peasant, T'ung-pao, who believed in the Bodhisattva; only his Bodhisattva was the god of wealth, *ts'ai-shen*." Průšek has here confused "Spring Silkworms" with its sequel, "Autumn Harvest." In that story, T'ung-pao is made into a pathetically ridiculous fool who acknowledges on his deathbed the rightness of his young son's expedient ways. To prepare for this change in characterization, early in the story (the third paragraph) Mao Tun gives us this piece of belated information that it has been the old man's life long habit to repair to a shrine outside the village to worship the god of wealth. During the entire season of silkworm-raising, not once is he seen worshipping at that shrine: he is too busy caring for the silkworms and cocoons. Moreover, in the earlier story, he is depicted as the soul of honesty and rectitude. He is so much of a stubborn and proud Chinese peasant that he hates anything foreign and refuses to yield to the counsels of expediency. He would raise Chinese silkworms and expect a smaller profit rather than raise the foreign kind. And one of the best scenes in the story registers his hatred toward a passing foreign-style steam boat:

> A small oil-burning river boat came puffing up pompously from beyond the silk filature, tugging three larger craft in its wake. Immediately the peaceful water was agitated with waves rolling towards the banks on both sides of the canal . . . The peaceful green countryside was filled with the chugging of the boat engine and the stink of its exhaust. Hatred burned in Old Tung Pao's eyes.[30]

The author appears here in complete sympathy with T'ung-pao's point of view. But in "Autumn Harvest," this sympathy has been completely withheld. Though the two stories, along with a third, "Winter Ruin," are today commonly referred to as *The Rural Trilogy*, Průšek should not have been misled into thinking that the characterization of T'ung-pao in the first two stories is consistently the same.

---

[30]Mao Tun, *Spring Silkworms and Other Stories* (Peking, 1956), p. 13.

Most of Průšek's comments on Lao She, Yeh Shao-chün, and Yü Ta-fu are in the nature of supplementary or independent remarks having little to do with my text. Thus he discourses typically on the intentions and narrative techniques of these authors, with frequent digressions on the problem of subjectivism, of "the close interlinking of the work of art with the personal experiences, feelings and views of the author"—a problem with which Průšek has been much concerned in recent years. Some of these remarks betray his intolerance of non-Marxist ideas: thus Lao She is criticized because he "often does not understand these [social problems] very correctly." The implication is that there is only one correct, scientific way to understand social problems, and Lao She is so much the poorer as a writer for his failure to follow it. Not to contradict his present high reputation in China, however, Průšek charitably adds that his concern with social problems is "of quite secondary importance," though the truth is that all his best pre-war novels are vitally concerned with social problems.

In his comments on Yü Ta-fu, however, Průšek does make the specific complaint that I failed to include for discussion two of the author's best stories: "A Humble Sacrifice" and "A Lonely Man on a Journey." The latter, by the way, is not even a story: it is a confessional essay written in memory of his deceased young son Lung-erh, and belongs with the series of diaries, confessions, and thinly disguised fictions about his relationship with his disapproving mother, miserably neglected wife, and sickly son. In my chapter on Yü Ta-fu, I devoted some attention to this theme and referred to three specific titles: the diary "A Trip Home" and the two autobiographical stories, "Smoke Silhouettes" and "In the Cold Wind." Since these three works are comparable to "A Lonely Man on a Journey" in emotional intensity and stem from the same domestic inspiration, I do not see any absolute reason why I must single out that confessional essay for special attention.

But judging from the fact that Průšek links this essay not with the other domestic pieces but with two stories with a proletarian setting, "A Humble Sacrifice" and "One Intoxicating Spring Evening," it is obvious that he is not so much concerned with Yü Ta-fu's obsession with remorse and guilt—his dominant emotions since his first story, "Sinking," and they are especially poignantly rendered in his domestic pieces—as with the fact that in this naked account of his son's death, the author is finally seen sharing the same kind of "human suffering" with his proletarian brothers and sisters. Yü Ta-fu's reputation would be surely improved if we could ignore his decadence and regard him primarily as an humanitarian author preoccupied with "the whole terrible fate of the Chinese proletariat"! But unfortunately, even in his proletarian stories, Yü Ta-fu always regards himself as a bohemian. His camaraderie with tramps, coolies, and factory workers is largely an extension of his self-pity; there is nothing revolutionary about it. In "A Humble Sacrifice," as in most of his stories, the author sees himself as a poor person; yet in terms of leisure and means, he lives in a completely different world from the ricksha man whom he befriends. Once he witnesses a quarrel over money between the ricksha man and his wife and he stealthily leaves them a silver watch of his. After a siege of illness that lasts two weeks, he visits them once again only to find a distraught family crying over the news of the ricksha man's death. (He is accidentally drowned, but the widow entertains the doubt that he may have deliberately thrown himself into the water.) The author consoles her, buys for her a papier-maché ricksha, and later joins her and the two orphans in the funeral procession.

The author's sympathy is unmistakable in the telling of the story, but still it is never quite separable from his commiseration over his own fate. At first, he even envies the ricksha man because, however poor, he at least enjoys his family and his night's sleep, whereas he himself "hadn't enjoyed a whole night's sleep for two years"[31] and has been away from his wife and son for so long. After the death of the ricksha man, the sight of the disconsolate widow and her younger son first of all "reminded me of my pitiful woman, of my Lung-erh, who would be now about the same height as the crying child crawling on the floor."[32] Even the final outburst of rage against the gaily dressed pedestrians in the street expresses as much indignation at their indifference to the plight of the ricksha man's family as his habitual disgust with the respectable bourgeoisie. Despite the elaborate pathos at the end, the story is nevertheless in the author's usual autobiographical-sentimental mode, so that it is misleading to say with Průšek that in this story "the author concentrates the whole terrible fate of the Chinese proletariat."

Since Průšek cites this story to refute my charge that Yü Ta-fu's style is "sentimental and careless," I may quote a passage for detailed examination. The author is speaking of his poverty and bohemian life:

---

[31]Yü Ta-fu, *Han-hui chi* (Shanghai, 1931): "Po tien" 薄奠, p. 6. Each item in that volume has its own separate pagination.

[32]*Ibid.*, Po-tien," p. 17.

When bored to death, if I didn't betake myself from the north-western section of the city to the southern section, to mingle with my own kind of merry people at the theaters, teahouses, brothels, and restaurants, to forget my own existence and to learn from them how to forget both life and death in a drunken stupor, then I would go alone outside the P'ing-tse Gate to enjoy its local scenes. It wasn't that I didn't feel the compelling attraction of the serene quietness of the Jade Spring Mountain or the recessed calm of the Temple of the Great Awakening, but I a man in need of money three hundred fifty-nine days of the year, absolutely could not have the surplus cash to enjoy their sublime beauty.[33]

Well read in classical Chinese literature and foreign literature, Yü Ta-fu, of course, was never illiterate or ungrammatical as some writers of the May Fourth period were. Though his periods (as the first sentence in our specimen) are sometimes too complex and Europeanized to read well, and though he often uses Southern colloquial expressions and records them in characters of his own choice that may not prove readily intelligible to readers ignorant of the Wu dialect, his style appears on the whole candid, wordily eloquent and remarkably adapted to the require-ments of autobiographical and psychological fiction. But if one examines the style closely, one finds that even his best stories are blemished by touches of sentimentality and compositional carelessness. To emphasize his self-pity and occasionally to suggest the effect of overwhelming sexual stimulation, Yü Ta-fu resorts to exaggeration, and this exaggera-tion would often bring about inconsistencies in the text resulting from one sentimental excess canceling out another. In the first sentence of our specimen, the author makes himself out to be a bohemian decadent bored with bourgeois life; so if he is not visiting the haunts of pleasure, he is strolling outside the city wall, enjoying his solitude. In the second sentence, he employs ironic exaggeration to indicate his actual distaste for the scenic resorts frequented by the middle class by saying that he cannot afford visiting these places of sublime beauty. Writing in a hurry, he does not realize that he would need a great deal more money to be a regular frequenter of brothels, theaters, and restaurants than to make occasional trips to the nearby resorts. To emphasize his poverty, moreover, he does not say that he is short of cash nine days out of ten; he has to invent the cumbersome locution that he is in need of cash 359 days out of a year. Depending thus upon whether he counts by the traditional Chinese or the modern calendar, he is not in want only one day or six

---

[33]*Ibid.*, "Po-tien," p. 8.

days out of a year. Why he is suddenly not poor on that day or these six days we are not told. Of the early writers, Lu Hsün, Yeh Shao-chün, or Ping Hsin would never be capable of this type of careless exaggeration; only the members of the Creation Society, with their weakness for emotional display, could have committed such rhetorical excesses. The most brilliant and talented of the group, Yü Ta-fu is nevertheless also blameworthy in this respect.

In this section as in the earlier section on Lu Hsün, I have tried to re-examine those texts that, according to Průšek, I have misinterpreted or willfully ignored, thereby confirming in most instances my original judgments on these works and their authors. I cannot claim that I am naturally a better reader of these texts than Průšek: I would think it is precisely his dependence on a "scientific" theory of modern Chinese history and literature and his unvarying habit of judging every work by its supposed ideological intent that have frequently misled him into simplifying a text or misinterpreting its import whereas, with all my "subjectivity," I have at least tried to do justice to every author and every work without having first to accommodate my honest reactions to a predetermined theory of modern Chinese fiction. The concrete examples gathered from the works of Lu Hsün, Mao Tun, and Yü Ta-fu are therefore intended to support my general criticism of Průšek's principles and methods governing his study of modern Chinese literature. I am sure Průšek believes as strongly as I do that unlimited opportunity exists for Western scholars to make outstanding original contributions toward an understanding and assessment of this literature, though I wish he could also agree with me that this endeavor would seem to call for the exercise of the true critical or scientific spirit—a refusal to rest content with untested assumptions and conventional judgments and a willingness to conduct an open-minded inquiry, without fear of consequence and without political prepossessions.

Appendix Two
A Selected Bibliography of Průšek's Papers on Modern Chinese Literature

"Liu O et son roman, le *Pèlerinage du Vieux Boiteux* (Preface a la traduction tcheque du roman *Lao Ts'an yu-chi*)," *Archiv Orientální* 15 (June 1946), 352–385.

"Le president Mao Tse-tung et la nouvelle littérature chinoise," *Archiv Orientální* 22 (1954), 1–19.

Die Literatur des befreiten China and ihre Volkstraditionen. Prague: Artia, 1955.

"Subjectivism and Individualism in Modern Chinese Literature," *Archiv Orientální* 25, no. 2 (1957), 261–286.

"The Importance of Tradition in Chinese Literature," *Archiv Orientální* 26, no. 2 (1958), 212–223.

"La nouvelle littérature chinoise," *Archiv Orientální* 27 (1959), 76–95.

"Lu Hsün the Revolutionary and the Artist," *Orientalische Literaturzeitung* 55 (1960), 229–236.

"Einige Bermerkungen zur Chinesischen Literatur in dem Zeitraum 1919–1937," *Acta Orientalia Academiae Scientiarum Hungariae.* T.15, Fasciculi 1–3 (1962), 219–231.

"Basic Problems of the History of Modern Chinese Literature and C. T. Hsia, *A History of Modern Chinese Fiction*," *T'oung Pao* 49, livr. 4–5 (1962), 357–404.

"On the Question of Realism in the Literature and Art of China Today," *New Orient* 3 (Aug. 1962), 107–108.

"Literatura osobní angažovanosti" (Literature of personal commitment), *Světová literatura* (World Literature) 1964, 3, 139–152.

"A Confrontation of Traditional Oriental Literature with Modern European Literature in the Context of the Chinese Literary Revolution," *Archiv Orientální* 32, no. 3 (1964), 365–375.

"Reality and Art in Chinese Literature," *Archiv Orientální* 32, no. 4 (1964), 605–618.

Introduction, *Studien zur modernen Chinesischen Literatur* (Studies in modern Chinese literature). Berlin: Akademie-Verlag, 1964.

"Quelques remarques sur la nouvelle littérature chinoise," *Mélanges de sinologie offerts à Monsieur Paul Demiéville*. Vol. I, Paris: Presses Universitaires de France, 1966, 209–223.

"Outlines of Chinese Literature," *New Orient* 5 (Aug. 1966), 113–120; (Oct. 1966), 145–151, 156–158; (Dec. 1966), 169–176.

Three Sketches of Chinese Literature. Prague: Oriental Institute in Academia, 1969.

"Lu Hsün's 'Huai Chiu': A Precursor of Modern Chinese Literature," *Harvard Journal of Asiatic Studies* 29 (1969), 169–176.

"The Changing Role of the Narrator in Chinese Novels at the Beginning of the Twentieth Century," *Archiv Orientální* 38, no. 2 (1970), 169–178.

"Yeh Sheng-t'ao and Anton Chekhov, "*Archiv Orientální* 38, no. 4 (1970), 437–452.